MUHAMMAD ALI

CO

c

400405

CELEBRITIES
Series Editor: Anthony Elliott

Published

Ellis Cashmore, *Beckham*

Charles Lemert, *Muhammad Ali: Trickster in the Culture of Irony*

Forthcoming

Ellis Cashmore, *Mike Tyson*

Daphne Read, *Oprah Winfrey*

Chris Rojek, *Frank Sinatra*

Nick Stevenson, *David Bowie*

Jason Toynbee, *Bob Marley*

MUHAMMAD ALI

Trickster in the Culture of Irony

CHARLES LEMERT

polity

Copyright © Charles Lemert 2003

The right of Charles Lemert to be identified as Author of this Work has been asserted in accordance with the UK Copyright, Designs and Patents Act 1988.

First published in 2003 by Polity Press in association with Blackwell Publishing Ltd.

Editorial office:
Polity Press
65 Bridge Street
Cambridge CB2 1UR, UK

Marketing and production:
Blackwell Publishing Ltd
108 Cowley Road
Oxford OX4 1JF, UK

Distributed in the USA by
Blackwell Publishing Inc.
350 Main Street
Malden, MA 02148, USA

A catalogue record for this book is available from the British Library.

Library of Congress Cataloging-in-Publication Data

Lemert, Charles.
  Muhammad Ali : trickster in the culture of irony / Charles Lemert.
    p. cm.
Includes index.
  ISBN 0-7456-2870-2 (hardcover) – ISBN 0-7456-2871-0 (paperback)
1. Ali, Muhammad, 1942– 2. Boxers (Sports) – United States – Biography.
3. African American boxers – Biography. I. Title.

GV1132.A44 L46 2003
2003000074   796.83'092—dc21

Typeset in 11 on 13 pt Palatino
by Kolam Information Services Pvt. Ltd, Pondicherry, India
Printed and bound in Great Britain by MPG Books Ltd, Bodmin, Cornwall

For further information on Polity, visit our website:
www.polity.co.uk

Remembering Matthew,
Achilles trickster.
He was beautiful, noble, courageous,
and, when he could, he too laughed at death.

CONTENTS

FROM THE BEGINNINGS

GG is Gonna Whip Everybody

Glooscap the God & the Baby Trickster

The god Glooscap had vanquished all races known to him – the most powerful, the most cunning, and the most wicked of peoples. He felt there were no others he could conquer.

One woman to whom he bragged of his conquests was not impressed. She merely laughed and told him that she knew of one he could not overcome. His name was Wasis. Glooscap was astonished, but defiant, when the woman warned him that to challenge Wasis was to put his power at risk.

Glooscap must have been all the more amazed when he discovered that Wasis was but a baby who did as babies often do – sit about, sing little tunes, and enjoy sweets. Because he had never been married, Glooscap knew nothing of the ways of children. He set about to subjugate the baby Wasis to his powers.

First, he tried seduction. But Glooscap's smiles and entreaties were met with Wasis's self-certain smile of recognition. Otherwise the baby sucked on his candy and sang, indifferent to the god's presence. Even when Glooscap sang a beautiful birdsong, Wasis was unmoved. Soon enough Glooscap grew frustrated and angry. No one had ever treated him this way. He menaced the baby with loud shouts and threats. Wasis did no more than cry out with just enough force to drown out Glooscap's shouts.

Finally the god was at wit's end, whereupon he resorted to the powerful magic by which had subdued even the most clever and wicked. But as Glooscap struggled to conjure up an effective spell, Wasis remained as he had been, perhaps by now a trifle bored.

In the end Glooscap quit the scene in abject failure. He had met his match. The baby's only comment was a gentle chant, "Goo, Goo." Ever after, the people believed that when a baby sings "Goo" he is remembering the time he conquered the terrible Glooscap.

An Algonquin Creation Story[1]

We called Muhammad "GG" when he was born because – you know how babies jabber at the side of their crib – he used to say "gee, gee, gee, gee." And then, when he became a Golden Gloves champion, he told us, "You know what that meant? I was trying to say Golden Gloves." So we called him GG, and sometimes I still do.

Odessa Clay on her son Cassius

We who grew up in river towns, deep inland and far from the sea, grew up with weather in our bones, one weather deeper than all others. Depending on which river, where, the cool or cold months can rub the skin raw. The rainy seasons can soak the feet. But the winter skin will soften, and the wet feet will dry. Summer is the season we carry about on the inside. Even after you move away from the rivers of childhood, the heavy air is there, waiting.

I grew up in one such town on the Ohio River, the principal eastern tributary of the vast Mississippi valley system of rivers that, since Mark Twain's stories, has fed the American imagination as much as its waters help feed the world's middle belly. These days I seldom return to that river. But there are times when it returns to me. Still today, living in the mild climate of New England, I can feel the humid compress on my bones from the first return of tropical weather to the north. I can wake chilled by the cool of night. But the first step outside renews the soggy weight of childhood summers. Unlike any other atmosphere, a humid one hangs on you, then soaks through to the bone. Damp air, unlike rain, cannot be gotten away from. Even after air-conditioning came into the houses, you brought the sweat inside as a chill the freshest towel could not wipe away. When life itself gets heavy, you remember the soggily depressed summers long after you've forgotten the streets and playmates of childhood.

The Ohio River
© Tim Darling

Louisville, Kentucky, is another Ohio River town – a day's lazy float downstream on Huck Finn's raft from where I spent my childhood in the 1940s. A good half-century later, early in the twenty-first century, I visited Louisville on a muggy Friday in June. Even late in the afternoon, as the sun reclined westward toward the vast plains watered by the Mississippi, the streets were slow. Shoppers sauntered, reserving energy for the months yet worse to come. Kids coasted on their bikes, gathering false breeze. Flags hung limp. This still southern city comes alive for a few weeks in May when the horses run at Churchill Downs. Whatever stirs its citizens the rest of the year is unclear. Through the haze, a billboard left from Kentucky Derby week proclaimed Louisville's metonymic pride of place – River City.

———

I had come to River City in late June 2001 to look for what traces may remain of its long-gone, most famous native son, Muhammad Ali. His parents had died. His younger brother is said to have returned to town. But I had, more or less intentionally,

3

made no plans to find people from Ali's life there. This brief visit was to be a kind of archaeological dig. I wanted to learn what I could from the place itself. Among other things, I wanted to see what could be seen of the place where The Greatest found and made himself.

Already there are more films, essays, and books on and about Ali than may be required. Still, I dare to think, another is proper so long as it is not completely preoccupied with the icon – with, that is, the man himself, whose story is told nearly every night of the year beside children's beds or on the parental screens of cable channels devoted to sport. Of course the life of the man is the earthly surface on which the icon thrives. But there is a something more, beyond the details of what even his detractors agree has been, at the least, one of the truly remarkable athletic careers of all times. That something is the Ali phenomenon itself – fame so global and enduring as to defy even the conventions of celebrity and, thus, a cultural something that invites a rethinking of both celebrity and of culture, the field in which celebrity grows.

As with most of the many intrigued by Muhammad Ali, very little of my life has been like his. Perhaps this gap invites the electromotive energy of celebrity. The one celebrated is *so very* different, beyond the experience of the ordinary. At the same time, unlike many of the gods we invent or discover, mortal beings cannot enjoy the celebrity without supposing *some* common ground. Gods are meant to be *other*. Celebrities are simply *more* in some astonishing way. We are fascinated by the gods, but astonished by the celebrity. The one is beyond reach; the other can be touched, though just barely.

In my case, I imagine – and one can only imagine one's like-nesses to those who are so inconceivably different, even *more* – that Ali and I shared something of a boy's growing up in river towns with their terrible summers and peculiar effects on the young. In my mind, Cassius Clay became an exceptional being by taking, from the beginning, his own exception from the norm of his river town. How had he gotten through the summers that kept down so many of the white boys I knew from my childhood – just five years ahead of Ali, just 90 miles upriver?

In the dull white suburbs of the river town of my youth, we of bourgeois privilege seldom rose before noon. Breakfast was long on cereal and the sports page. By August, the lazy afternoons drifted one into the other. Occasionally, I'd amble flat-footed into a pick-up game. The fields were dusty. Not many boys my age wanted to be in the sun. Those willing said little, moved slowly. One summer I gave over to tennis, thinking I had a special talent for the game. If I did, I lost the rhyme of it all. Our sport was all too instrumental, devoid of poetry. Most summers, I was sent away to camp on the Maine coast, where we played and swam outside the blanket of heat. Without such fortune, who knows how those idle summers might have led me down or astray.

My visit during early summer of 2001 to Louisville was to learn, if I could, how it happened that a boy downriver where the heat bore deep as river heat does – a boy with no thought of camp at the seaside, but plenty of feeling about white boys like me – could have made so much of those summers, thus of his life. Even today, long after Ali fell ill and out of the light that shone upon his beautiful prowess, the Ali phenomenon has the power to evoke feelings of all kinds. Charisma, as Max Weber taught, usually has a very short shelf-life. Ali's seems to be slow to die. The phenomenon outraces the man. Such a mysterious social thing, like the man to whom it is attached, must have had its beginnings in Louisville.

———

From the first, before boxing ever occurred to him, Muhammad Ali was more than a boxer. Cassius Clay was a different kind of child. He was born to a modest, but not poor, home at 3302 Grand Avenue in Louisville's West End. The street of his birth runs west from the city center to its end at Chickasaw Park on the Ohio River, just where the Ohio takes another of its turns south and west toward confluence with the Mississippi at Cairo, Illinois. The neighborhood surrounding Cassius's childhood home was then, as now, safe for play. Trees of such a height as to have been there in his day shade the street on either side of Grand Avenue. The homes up and down are small, close to-gether, but nicely kept – many decorated with flowers and fresh paint. You can walk for blocks without seeing more than one or two in disrepair. The riverbanks were close enough for child's play. Whenever the prevailing breeze, such as it is, makes its way upriver from the Deep South and West, the heat comes upon the cooler waters down from the western hills of Pennsylvania upstream at Pittsburgh. The meeting stirs a soupy mix over the Clay home. Even in early summer the hot air catches enough river water to make out-of-doors a slow move.

On that Friday in June, in the early afternoon, I drove down Grand Avenue, then parked and walked. Those at home had had their lunches. The streets were nearly deserted. I came upon a postman many blocks east on Grand. He had only the vaguest recollection of Ali's native address. Just the same, he gave me a number – the wrong address by five blocks. You would think he'd have known right off. But then neither did the boys out for a desultory ride, going no place, weaving as boys do on aimless bikes. They slowed to my question. You would think they too might have known exactly where their neighborhood's most heroic man might have wasted a summer's moment on his bike. Not so. A girl of about 14 was out walking, overdressed for the weather with a jacket tight against a scowl. I hesitated before disturbing her mad. When I did, she was friendly enough but had nothing to say. At least I got the beginnings of a smile. An older boy, beyond teenage indolence, was mowing the lawn in the far back corner of a churchyard two blocks up from the park. I decided to leave the space to him.

Farther on, two women (mothers both, and sisters, I supposed) were sitting on a porch. Without thinking about it, I walked the walk I'd invented when as a boy I visited what people then called the colored neighborhoods. I can't quite say how it goes, but I can describe the talk, which is just a smidgen too earnest – a thinly veiled white guy's minstrel of familiarity. The women, no doubt, recognized the show before I did. They let it pass as had their mothers before them. They were friendly enough to discuss my question between themselves. I finally realized then that I was treading ground not my own and needed to keep my distance. A boy of about 12 appeared at the door. He took unnatural interest in my visit. We all three asked if he knew which had been Muhammad Ali's house. The boy was more familiar with this sort of transaction, somewhat in the manner of schoolchildren in far places who interpret tourist English for their parents.

I was the only white person to be seen on Grand Avenue that day. It occurred that the generous ignorance of the fact I had come to find may have drawn down from years of visits by strange white men of too apparent purpose, their cars too well polished, their questions all too innocent. Walking on, I followed another useless clue while thinking about the man himself. Today, Ali himself is said to want to return to Louisville, but he lives on a farm in Berrien Springs, Michigan. He is, it seems, generous to a fault. Strangers will think nothing of leaving the highways of their vacation trips to stop at his door. Word is that he never fails to greet them, invite them for a visit, thus to add to the list of cares his wife Lonnie must take on. Perhaps those who inherited his childhood street have been visited once too often. What the retired and crippled Ali may get from his fame, and give in return, is one thing. What the respectable citizens of Grand Avenue in Louisville get from it is exactly nothing.

What strikes one so about Louisville today is that in 2001, some 40 years after he made the city world famous, there was yet to be a permanent monument to him. The only nod in his direction was Muhammad Ali Boulevard, which stretches west from downtown to Shawnee Park, also on the river. The decision to honor Ali by changing the name of Walnut Street was passed grudgingly in 1978, by one vote in the city council. Muhammad Ali Boulevard is a good ten blocks north of Grand Avenue, closer to the point where the Ohio River abruptly turns south after its easy westerly flow around the city center. Today the Boulevard is the principal artery of the West End. So far as the superficial eye can tell, the whole of Louisville proper west from downtown is home to no more than a few white people. Other than several older whites on the streets about the once stately homes down by Shawnee Park, the West End would seem to be black. Louisville today is as segregated as any border city can be so long after the rules changed. The West is black. The East is white.

After so long a delay, finally there is material progress toward the construction of the Muhammad Ali Center in the center city along the river, adjacent to City Hall and the Kentucky Center for the Arts. A Ford Foundation grant of $5 million brought the total pledged to $26 million in 2001. More has been pledged since. Ground was broken in June, 2002. The Ali Center's purpose will be to celebrate the man's "deeply rooted values and world wide influence" by offering what seem to be serious education and action programs.[2] At last, the Muhammad Ali Center will be the long-deferred local monument to Louisville's most famous native son.

Still, until it comes to life, the fact is that it will have taken more than 40 years since Ali first became a global figure for Louisville to participate in a lasting monument to the man who, more than anyone, has put the city on the global map.

Local monument building is of course a strange but true symptom of local history, and nearly as interesting for its exclusions as its inclusions. Boston, with all its remarkable literary and political heroes, includes bronze statues of its most famous basketball coach, not to mention ducklings from a revered children's tale, among the notables of its history. Perhaps it includes too many. Slow cities, like Louisville, are slow to include. Paris, for example, did not dig up and rebury Alexandre Dumas until 2002, well more than a century after this death. Yet, Paris and Boston, however quirky their latter-day memorials, did not shrink, when the time came, from memorializing a long list of their proper heroes. Louisville, with its many statues to military heroes of the Confederacy, obviously excluded Ali because of the racial history of the American South. This was not an accident. Exclusions of this sort, whatever their causes, have their effects – ones that tell of forces that shaped Cassius Clay, the child, and of those whom he left behind.

Curiously, none of the 20 or so people I talked to in the West End mentioned the Ali Center downtown. Several, however, volunteered the location of an African-American cultural center seriously under construction in the near West End just off Muhammad Ali Boulevard. The confusion of the individual for the race by the identification of Ali with African-American culture itself seemed at once to affirm the importance of the man while pointing to River City's general lack of regard for him. *If he were honored here, we'd have to do it.* The most prominent among the Board of Directors of the Muhammad Ali Center are national figures like Larry King, Colin Powell, and sportscaster Bob Costas. On the Center's website, local names are listed among its active supporters, but it is clear that the driving force behind the project comes from those closest to Ali, most probably his wife Lonnie. Plans project a 2004 opening date for what will be a major tourist attraction in downtown Louisville, yet it remains unclear how many of the residents of Louisville, eastside or west, are among the movers of the project.[3] If even the most ambitious of tributes to the man must be moved from outside Louisville itself, then why should the people of Grand Avenue give information to still another white guy asking questions?

In any case, River City is black and white. By chance, after my visit to Louisville, I meet Ayana Blair, a black woman of professional parents who had grown up on the far East Side, long after Ali's school days. She knew little of Muhammad Ali, or of the cultural geography of his West End. She had gone to a magnet high school, but the one just east of downtown. Ali's Central High School at 1130 West Chestnut, three blocks south of Muhammad Ali Boulevard, is also a center city magnet school. Though only blocks apart, the two schools, like the city itself, are cultural miles distant from each other.

If today the city is divided along racial, if not strict class, lines, then all the more in Cassius Clay's day. Myth and legend have grown up around his acquaintance with racial segregation, notably the apocryphal story of his having thrown his 1960 Olympic gold medal into the river in disgust[4]. How could his hometown not have been, as Mike Marqusee suggests (after Paul Gilroy)[5], the home place where he learned the stories of the Black Atlantic, of his alien ties to those who, by suffering slavery, bind him to Africa? Why, then, would Ali have not made something else of his slave name, even if the color line cut less harshly on him than on others?

And why would not those who live on in a city so intently slow to celebrate its most famous son be properly cautious in the face of a strange white man asking questions? Such is the color line that I will never know – and could not, while there, have found – the answer. The mystery is good enough. Unanswered questions encourage the social imagination. It is possible, I suppose, that ignorance of the Cassius Clay home is a sincere contrivance to guard against the resentment of being twice left behind – by the great man, by the East Siders.

Anyhow, while still walking Grand Avenue late of a June afternoon, I met one older woman who bore no evident traces of resentment. She greeted me warmly, received my question generously, then described the house perfectly as it turned out to be, adding: "I don't remember the address, but I've been here since 1957. He lived in that one I'm sure." This was a woman who had seen it all. She'd moved in when Cassius Clay was still a boy learning to box. She must have seen him bike or run along Grand Avenue to the gym downtown. She'd also, I let myself believe, seen enough of black and white over the years not to give any mind to this stranger. She was, I guessed, about the generation of Cassius's mother, Odessa, and may have known her. I was so taken by the fact of the matter I'd come to look for that I hastened off without asking more questions. Only later did I realize that I'd neglected to offer her a ride. I supposed she'd have accepted. Even now, four decades after apartheid fell in the American South, even well-meaning white folk who know something of color don't know how to behave in black neighborhoods. That too must be part of the mix of social things upon which Muhammad Ali's celebrity plays on, and on.

Still, whatever Ali touches in the hearts of others, he was from the very beginning a boy out of the ordinary of his time and place. As a child he enjoyed the attentions of both parents. Not surprisingly, they tell the stories of their attentions differently, much as might be expected of bread-winning fathers and care-giving mothers of their generation.

Cassius Clay, Sr, spoke of his oldest boy as do proud fathers of limited means. He provided as best he could, and that best was far from nothing. He cared, it seems, as much about values as about material things. The two may have come down from his desire to be thought of as an artist, for which he enjoyed a talent insufficient to earn more than the middling status of a sign painter. Failed aspirations are just the sort of experience that promotes a father's pride in providing, and especially so when the failures and the providing are constrained by social unfairness. Still Cassius, the father, took pride in his fathering:

> He [Cassius] was a good child and he grew up to be a good man, and he couldn't have been nothing else to be honest with you because of the way his mother raised him. Sunday school every Sunday. I dressed them [Cassius and his brother Rudolph] as good as I could afford, kept them in pretty good clothes. And they didn't come out of no ghetto. I raised them on the best street I could ... And I taught them values – always confront the things you fear, try to be the best at whatever you do. That's what my daddy taught me and those are things that have to be taught. You don't learn those things by accident.[6]

As fathers go, Cassius, Sr, did well, but not perfectly well. Eventually his womanizing led to separation from the home. When Cassius became the celebrated champion, the father claimed credit for the boy's success – to which the son replied (just as his father had taught him to do) that he, and he alone, was responsible for his success. When the son rejected the name he shared with his father, the father felt the Nation of Islam had stolen him away – to which the son responded over time by living a life of faith such that people would hope to raise a Muhammad Ali Center precisely to celebrate his "inner values" (again, as the father claimed he taught him).

On the other side, there is not a word of anything but good about Odessa, his mother, who (as truly good enough mothers do) gave the child all the credit for his difference. Odessa worked in domestic labor, cleaning the houses of white folks to supplement what her husband brought in from his sign business or left behind when he disappeared from time to time. They paid $4,500 for the house on Grand Avenue early in their marriage, before Cassius was born on January 17, 1942. Rudolph (later, Rahaman Ali) was born in 1944. Whatever

Ali with his mom, Odessa Clay
© The Courier-Journal

Odessa suffered from her husband's philandering, she took none of it out on the boys.

> We called Muhammad "GG" when he was born because – you know how babies jabber at the side of their crib – he used to say "gee, gee, gee, gee." And then, when he became a Golden Gloves champion, he told us, "You know what that meant? I was trying to say Golden Gloves." So we called him GG, and sometimes I still do. When he was a child, he never sat still. He walked and talked and did everything before his time. When he was two years old, he'd wake up in the middle of the night and throw everything from his dresser onto the floor. Most boys run around flat-footed or walk; GG went around on his tip-toes all the time.... Everything he did as a child was different.... His mind was like the March wind, blowing every which way. And whenever I thought I could predict what he'd do, he turned around

and proved me wrong.... I always felt like God made Muhammad special, but I don't know why God chose me to carry this
child.[7]

Where the father wanted to stake his own claim to the extraordinary boy, the mother thought of him as special in his own
right, as God's gift. One can respect without blindly trusting a
mother who, years after, tells the story of her boy as if she *always*
knew how special he would become.

Just as the child makes what he does of himself out of the stories
he hears in childhood, so the mother makes something of the
child out of the retelling of those stories. We all are who we are
by mysterious dint of the stories we imbibe, retell, and reinvent
over a lifetime. Sometime in his childhood Cassius Clay chose the
stories of his mother who let him be what he was over those of his
father who thought of himself as the teacher of values. At some
point on Grand Avenue, before the boy thought of fighting for a
career, he danced about on his toes, as he would in the ring of his
fame – and took something from Odessa, as well as from within,
that allowed him to think of himself as special, as one deserving
the distinctive Islamic name Elijah Muhammad bestowed upon
him.[8]

Many children are told they are special. Many take it seriously,
some too seriously. The difference made by Muhammad Ali
is that he did the hard work that needs to be done in order to *be*
special. More times than not, the celebrity appears, as Ali did
to his mother, as if he were endowed with supernatural grace. If
so, it is a grace that defies the Lutheran rule. No one gains the
saving power of popular acclaim without very many, precisely
calculated good and difficult works. Were the celebrity pure
grace, one need not bother with the details of the life. If,
by contrast, celebrity is at least as much work overcoming resistance, the place that provides the friction against the grace can be
interesting.

So this is why I went to Louisville to see what I could see of the
place where Muhammad Ali, the celebrity, had done the work
that led to such a grand and global life. What better way is there to

begin to take his measure than to examine what remains of his beginnings, or to get some sense of what gave him his start or what he had to overcome? The jazz musician and the rock star may seem to be naturals, but they too, like all celebrities, put in grueling hours late into the days or nights working up a sweat for their art. The same is true by half for professional athletes. Frank Sinatra like Louis Armstrong, Madonna like Gene Kelly, Michael Jordan like Babe Ruth, were famous or notorious because they made their art seem so easy, as if it came from nothing.

Of all the performance arts, save perhaps ballet or opera, none requires, as boxing does, such an extreme ratio of practice to performance, of painful preparation to the remote odds of pleasing conquest. A boxer must train for years with no assurance even of a chance to vie for a championship of any kind. It is said that boxing a three-minute round against a serious opponent is like no other demand upon the mind and body. If you doubt it, try it. I once did, without training, but as a boy of young and wiry body. After the first minute my arms fell to the side like cement, after the second I was gasping for air, at the end I literally collapsed. And this was a pick-up match between very well-conditioned boys at summer camp. I can't imagine anything more terrifying all at once to body, heart, and soul – and especially not when one faces someone out to kill you and able to do it.

Boxing grace comes along once in a great while. Before Ali, the master of this grace was Sugar Ray Robinson, of whom there are many copies in the lighter-weight divisions. But balletic grace is hard to come by among heavyweights. Archie Moore had a bit of it, but his was more cunning. Joe Louis was thought of as having had it. But his was bestowed by adoration for his metaphoric destruction of the Nazis in his second bout with Max Schmeling in 1938. Jack Johnson, so long ago as to be vaguely recollected, may have had some grace in the ring, but, through it all, his extraordinary gifts were likely a displacement of white confusion with his sexual and interracial life outside the ring.[9] Others among the great great heavyweight champions (four of whom Ali fought) – Rocky Marciano, Sonny Liston, the young George Foreman, Joe Frazier, even Larry Holmes (who all but ended Ali's career on October 2, 1980[10]) – were, like Louis, bombers more than dancers or even boxers.

Some fighters win their prizes on brute strength. Some add to it the touch of art. None does either, much less both, without years of pain. When even the very best try to get by in less than perfect physical condition, they lose – as Ali himself did to Ken Norton in 1973 and to Leon Spinks in 1978. He avenged both losses after particularly grueling preparation (the second at 36 years of age, ancient by boxing standards). Success in boxing begins not in a moment, but in years of hard work, one day at a time. No matter what the weather outside, the fighter must rise before the sun, or stay on the road after it has set. Otherwise, he risks injury more terrible than defeat.

The story of Ali's start in boxing is so often retold as to be the primordial of the legend. Its sources are his mother and his first trainer.[11] In 1954, when Cassius was a boy of 12 (not much younger than Emmett Till, who was lynched the following year), he rode his bike downtown to the Louisville Service Club near 4th and York. Boys would beg treats from the white businessmen who took refuge in the pretense service clubs of this kind organize. This was the fifties, when one hardly thought of locking up bikes, much less cars or even houses. Cassius's brand new bike was stolen while he played. He was so enraged that he went about threatening to whip the thief, whereupon Clay ran into Joe Martin, a policeman who trained boys to box at the Columbia gym in the basement of the Service Club. Martin embraced Cassius with the obvious questions: Did he know how to fight? Wouldn't that be a good idea before he challenged anyone?

Thus, and then, it all began. From then on Cassius Clay gave himself over to boxing, for which he had a talent not altogether evident at the beginning. Joe Martin remembered Cassius as at first special only in his determination:

> I guess I've taught a thousand boys to box, or at least tried to teach them. Cassius Clay, when he first began, looked no better or worse than the majority.... He was just ordinary, and I doubt whether any scout would have thought much of him in his first

year. About a year later, though, you could see that the little smart aleck – I mean, he's always been sassy – had a lot of potential. He stood out because, I guess, he had more determination than most boys, and he had the speed to get him someplace. He was a kid willing to make the sacrifices. . . . It was almost impossible to discourage him. He was easily the hardest working kid I ever taught.[12]

Like nearly every teacher of the very young, Martin did the hard work at the beginning only to give over his star pupil to Angelo Dundee after the 1960 Olympic championship. Perhaps anyone thus left behind might have understated Cassius Clay's talent to make room in the story for his own skills as a trainer. Surely, Clay's gifts were, if not given by the gods, quite extraordinary. But still, it may be that his determination was the greatest gift of all – beginning with the determination to whip the kid who stole his bike, then to become the greatest of all fighters by whipping very nearly everybody he faced over the next quarter century.[13]

———

The mystery of social things always turns on the *what-might-have-been?* What if Cassius had not gone downtown that day in 1954? What if his bike had not been stolen? What if Joe Martin had been away when Cassius stormed into the gym? No one can know what other series of virtual events, if any, might have led this boy to the life and celebrity he made for himself. But what is known is that the ride downtown was not a simple one, especially not in the hot river months of his training. Between the known and the unknown, one unknowable intrigues beyond all others.

What if, at the extreme of virtual possibilities, Cassius Marcellus Clay, Jr, had not been born in 1942 on Grand Avenue in Louisville? Would *we* have had to invent him out of some other determined little boy? Who such a "we," if one exists, would have had to invent would be not just any boy, but one like Cassius who lived with and understood the very special circumstances of being the child of generations of other-than-white, colonial subjects. Those who grant Muhammad Ali his celebrity (as distinct from his boxing prowess) grant that his importance is – as the planners of the Muhammad Ali Center say – global in sweep. For such a celebrity as Muhammad Ali to have come upon the global stage *when* he did, certain attributes were required. He could not have been white, or well off; nor, if American, could he have been of the North; nor, if from some other place, from a center of colonizing power. He, or she, need not have necessarily been of the African diaspora, though in 1960 he likely would have been. In 1960, also, he would still have been, almost certainly, not a she. And, he would have descended from the colonized at least by a familiarity with the injuries of racial hatred. His descent need not have been to Louisville, Kentucky. But, if some other locale, he would have had to be at least one who could fit the understandings of any or all of those who, at the time, were beginning to shake the foundations of the capitalist and white world system. The Ali phenomenon came fully into its own with his stunning upset of Sonny Liston early in 1964 – just when Rhodesia and Kenya were declaring independence, just when Malcolm X was beginning the last year of his life, just before Mobuto Sese Seko seized control of the Congo, just when Black Power was beginning to assert itself around the world. It was the dawn of global time. These were still and particularly the early days of the hitherto powerless, segregated, and colonized, if not quite yet of woman.

If someone other than Cassius Clay, then (and strikingly so) such a celebrity would have necessarily come from the more southern tier of the human globe – probably thereby from the banks of some or another river. If not the Ohio, then the Congo, where Patrice Lumumba led the revolt against the Belgians. If not the Congo, then the Yangtze, in which Mao had swum against the Nationalists; or the Mekong, from which Ho Chi Minh chased the French and the Americans; or even from the mountain streams of Oriente Province, down from which Fidel Castro led his revolution. If not these, perhaps even the Amazon, around which were based the native communities that Paolo Freire would eventually inspire to covert rebellion.

It would be foolish even to suggest that Muhammad Ali's celebrity was somehow of a kind with any of these leaders. Though his celebrity has had a political influence, he was not himself political. His racial politics drew from the most conservative and separatist of sources. Though his trickster act disturbed the status quo, he was not self-consciously a rebel. His signifyin' on white culture was in good humor, just shy of minstrelsy, and more indebted to Gorgeous George than to guerilla theatre. He renounced his brother Malcolm X, surely one of the purest revolutionary voices of that day, on the orders of Elijah Muhammad, surely one of the more compromised moral leaders imaginable. However much he sacrificed for principle, as he did by standing up to the American war in Vietnam, he was, as his detractors will tell you, more than willing to sacrifice the good name of opponents like Joe Frazier in order to raise a good purse for his fights. Cassius Clay delivered himself to the pure discipline of his art, by which he became the celebrity trickster, Muhammad Ali. But Ali, as wonderful as he is, is not pure. In fact, it may be that – unlike the single-minded politics that led Lumumba to death or Mao to the Cultural Revolution – Ali's global celebrity is the kind of fame that depends on notoriety. As he himself had to say, in the language of his culture, "I'm bad." He did what good he did by being pretty, yes, but also bad.

What Ali became had its beginnings in a river town of a most definite South. To get to Joe Martin's gym, he had to endure a swelter worse than what I encountered on my visit to Louisville, one just as bad as the summers of my childhood upstream. How long after his bike was stolen he got another, I do not know. Without it, he would have had to walk or ride nearly 40 blocks to the Columbia gym – about three miles each way. School days, the gym was close by Central High. After training in the winter, he would have had to get himself home in the dark, often after working odd jobs at Nazareth College (today's Spaulding University, across the street from the gym). Summers, Cassius would have had to make the six miles before and after exhausting days, against the oppressive river heat. The determination began in the overcoming of all the good reasons to stay put in the shade of Grand Avenue, just as all my pals in that day avoided the playing fields of our never-to-be triumphs.

After it all, he did his roadwork instead of homework. John Powell, Jr, who kept a shop in the Grand Avenue neighborhood, was just one of those amazed by the boy's discipline.

> He would leave his house on Grand and head for the river, then circle around Shawnee and come back. I'd still be in the store at night closing up, cleaning up, and he come through. He would tap on the window, make sure I'd see him. He was always moving his arms, making sounds with his jaw. He was dedicated, totally. I know that. He came through one night and said, "I'm going to box Charley Baker on the 'Tomorrow's Champions' show." Well, I told him, "You're crazy if you get in the ring with him." See, Charley Baker was the bully of the West End. I mean people wouldn't even talk too loud around Charley Baker. He was huge and muscular. But Cassius said, "I'm gonna whip him," and he did whip him. And after that, I said, "Man, you are the *baddest* dude I know, now."[14]

At Central High, he was known as the one who drank water with garlic to build his health, and the one to fear, even though he always played on the fear associated with his discipline, his growing local fame, and his enormous size even in youth. He was bad. But he always tapped on somebody's window to let them know he was there.

Today, as then, Louisville is just yards across the Ohio River from the North, but it is a town marked by the remains of the Old South. In the finer neighborhoods there are stately mansions, many in antebellum style with great pillars at the front, imposing center staircases within, verandas for sitting through the evenings, gardens in bloom. Depending on which route he followed from home, Ali probably did not often come upon the mansions one block east from the Columbia gym at Fourth Street. But surely he knew of them.

If Lexington is horse country, Louisville is liquor and tobacco country. More than half the world's bourbon is distilled in Louisville. There is wealth, to be sure – and from it came the local sponsoring group for Cassius Clay's early professional career. The ten wealthy patrons of the young black athlete were white. Their investment was more a lark than a cash calculation. The odds against any single boy rising to a world championship are beyond calculation. In that day, it was certain that those, like Sonny Liston, who did, were likely to have been sponsored by the mob that controlled the fight world by fixing the outcomes in favor of their bets. For Clay to have been sponsored by an independent, and apparently legitimate, group was itself a difference; but not one that transcended the racial segregation that held the city in its grip.

The cities of the American South and borders were never racist for emotional reasons alone. The racism followed from the original feudal economy, one that demanded enforced labor to grow the cotton, hops, and tobacco on which the American South relied for what it was and for which reason it was unable to industrialize as did the more northern centers of the European diaspora. These are the economic conditions that gave life to the culture of the Black Atlantic. Clay never saw the Atlantic Ocean until his 1960 trip to Rome for the Olympic Games. But this does not mean that a black boy growing up way inland did not know the Black Atlantic.

The name "Cassius Marcellus Clay" came down on his father's side of course – from a plantation owner in western Kentucky who was said to have been an abolitionist. He had been prominent enough to have been the subject of one of President Lincoln's letters to his wife on Kentucky politics.[15] But, if an abolitionist, he remained a slave owner, even after Emancipation. If a sympathetic owner, he was not beyond enjoying sexual congress with those he owned.

On his mother's side, as on his father's, Cassius Clay the boxer came from the rich farmland south and west of Louisville in the corner formed by the descending Ohio and Mississippi rivers and Kentucky's border with Tennessee. His great great grandfather on his mother's side was Tom Morehead, who was half-white, a freedman, and once owner of a large parcel of productive land. Eventually, the land was bought out by whites. The Morehead line joined with the Bibbs family, both lines racially mixed. Both racial sides had fought in the Revolutionary War.[16]

Where whites will pass over their mixed racial backgrounds, blacks pass less often. Those who do are more aware of what they are doing than whites, who simply forget over the years. No one of African descent who must learn in the first grades to spell a name so Romanesque and white as "Cassius Marcellus Clay" could possibly fail to attend to the stories passed down at family picnics and church suppers. Before his conversion to the Nation of Islam sometime in or about 1962,[17] Cassius took a certain pride in the name. After, he rejected it as the slave name it was. Even the rejection of one's past in the name of an insistent new set of beliefs is itself a passing down – not a passing over – of the experience of Black Atlantic. The stories of Cassius Marcellus, the original, and of Tom Morehead, the freedman, are also found in the stories of Elijah Muhammad, who told what he had heard from Wallace Fard to Malcolm X and other of the Nation's ministers who brought Ali into his second name and new life.

Social scientists know so little about how what they call *culture* really works. How does it happen that simple stories told here and there at knee or table become over time the source of a person's idea of who she is? How do these stories, always simple in the telling, often told late at night as the children doze off, become the bearers of so massive a social thing as culture – whether that of the "the American way of life" or of "Western civilization," or those of the Middle Passage of Black Atlantis? The sociologist of culture will tell you how he thinks culture works, and he may be right. The young man finding himself in a strange new world will, if he is lucky or determined, take on the culture that suits his new social experience. By becoming Muhammad Ali, by the teachings of a much-feared religious sect, Cassius Clay laid upon himself another laminate of story telling – one that suited perfectly his personal discipline, one that – however shocking to some – gave him a story and a name of global proportions. The determination alone could not have made him what he became, anymore than did his divine beauty and physical gifts. He is of interest today because, beyond being the greatest boxer ever, he became Muhammad Ali – and thus gave a new meaning to an ancient, much-revered Islamic name.

———

For the longest while after his rise to global celebrity in 1964, when Ali first became the world heavyweight champion, his face was easily the most conspicuous on the planet.[18] At the dawn of the twenty-first century, 20 years after retiring from boxing, Ali very probably is still as famous as any alive, just as he was at the zenith of his crossing beyond the Western skies.

Muhammad Ali's celebrity endures for many and complex reasons. More than a few sources named him the athlete of the twentieth century. The case for this nomination is a good one, arguable only to the legions of sports talk-radio fans with too many worries to bother with anything serious. What is beyond argument is that Ali's celebrity far exceeds his already remarkable athletic gifts. Even today, his speech slowed to a whisper, *Sports Illustrated* found that people will pay $100,000 for a "speaking" appearance – more than for any other retired athlete.[19] What is arguable is why the celebrity endures beyond the ring where he left (as sportswriters are beginning to say) his "body of work."

Why is Ali's name almost always on everybody's short list? For example, *Time* magazine (the media pioneer of name making) early in the new millennium published a special collection of stories on the theme "America's Legends – Our Nation's Most Fascinating Heroes, Icons, and Leaders."[20] Of the hundred, only four faces were chosen for the magazine's cover, a parody of Mt Rushmore – Franklin Delano Roosevelt, Marilyn Monroe, Ronald Reagan, and Muhammad Ali, whose visage was fixed second in line, just slightly lower than FDR's. If, as I believe, the standard for celebrity is not so much the amount of public good done as the degree of public enchantment inspired, then this is a fair, if troubling, list. Save for FDR, anyone could be left off according to taste. The question is why, of all those who could be on it, was Ali on this very short list.

In fact, Muhammad Ali's celebrity drives some people to distraction. One notable example is Mark Kram, a sportswriter who for many years covered Ali's boxing career for *Sports Illustrated*. Kram's *Ghosts of Manila* (2001) begins inauspiciously with the remark that his book "is intended to be a corrective to the years of stenography that have produced the Ali legend."[21] Kram sneers at writers who praise Ali too unqualifiedly as mere "stenographers," taking down the legend, hence also uncritical hagiographers. Many people feel this way about Ali. Kram wrote for them, and he may have a point.

Ali is a celebrity, and it is the nature of celebrity to overwhelm the fan such that critical reasoning is all but obliterated. What it means, and how it happens, are different questions. There will always be those who hate the celebrity because they fear his hold over others. Ali has always had to contend with those put off by his comedic but magical ways. There is a long tradition of writers on the boxing beat, who simply will not grant that there could be any moral substance to the man behind the celebration. From the first, just after Ali doubly confirmed his place as a global figure in 1964 – first by crushing Sonny Liston to become, against all odds, boxing's champion and then by coming out as a member of the Nation of Islam – Ali was greeted with a chorus of denunciation. Jimmy Cannon (late of the *New York Post*) was in those days chief among the writers who denounced him doubly – first by refusing to use his chosen name, then by saying: "I pity Clay and abhor what he represents" (meaning, of course, black separatism).[22] Nearly four decades later, Kram continued the tradition. Though he granted Ali's genius as a fighter, he attacked his character. Like a few others, Kram believed that the uncritical adulation of Ali ignores the evidence that he was, at times, at least uncaring, sometimes cruel, to those about him. Though many are mentioned, Joe Frazier is held up as the chief victim of Ali's alleged abuses. This is a convenient choice because Frazier himself is one of the few who holds on to his grudge. Long after Sonny Liston, Floyd Patterson, and George Foreman forgave him his pre-fight antics, Frazier continues to hate Ali for having called him an ignorant gorilla, among other taunts.[23]

Any attempt to "correct a legend" is too much like pissing in the wind. Celebrity legends, at least, ride along on the wave of their appeal to the adoring masses. George Foreman, for example, who had been humiliated every bit as much as Joe Frazier, responded differently. Though Ali's three epic battles with Joe Frazier may well be the ultimate and most dramatic rivalry in the sport, his 1974 fight with George Foreman in Kinshasa, Zaire (now, again, Congo) had more the makings of legend. During the excruciating wait in Africa (due to a six-week postponement caused by a training injury to Foreman), Ali seized many an occasion to torment the world champion, notably by calling him "ignorant." In those days Foreman was a young and terrifying man. He had already destroyed both Frazier and Ken Norton, while Ali had lost to each and was unable to knock out either in winning the return matches. Foreman was, in a word, ferocious. Yet, Ali, ever the genius, worked a certain kind of boxing magic – first by beginning with right-hand leads in the first round, then by absorbing Foreman's punches by relaxing into the ropes. When Foreman had spent himself, Ali knocked him out in the eighth round. The photograph of the moment is one of the iconic images in all of sports. Ali towers above the fallen Foreman, fist cocked, holding back the final punch that in being withheld asserted Ali's reserve of prowess and, one must add, aesthetic taste[24]. It took George Foreman the better part of two years to begin to overcome the humiliation.

Yet, years later, after George Foreman had transformed himself into one of America's most genial public figures, he was able to say, "I'm proud of Muhammad. I'd rate him deep down inside as the strongest individual in my lifetime. . . . Ali is still the greatest show on earth."[25] Any man – and I mean *man* – who has been humiliated by word and fist, yet who can transcend the masculine ego (particularly pronounced among fighters) to come to love Ali, as Foreman has, is himself exceptional. Foreman has been drawn in by something real, something beyond the ordinary. Or it might be better to say that such a man as George Foreman may have had the extraordinary *within* drawn out by the extraordinary *without*, the celebrity of his interior attentions. In any case, it is clear that when people are drawn to someone like Ali, something real is at work.

The question is *what* is the reality here? Among much else it is the way of the celebrity. People like Cannon and Kram who recoil at the legend may be right to do so – or at least, setting aside their own prejudices, they may speak for the rest of us who may fear the celebrity too little. My parents, had they lived to see him in action, would have adored Ronnie Reagan just as much as they despised FDR, and I would have fought with them over the difference in our celebratory tastes. Celebrity does indeed work a magical power that is not rational. Much of life is irrational. It is not wrong to worry about the celebrities we lift up beyond criticism. Still, a celebrity like Ali can work his magic to good or evil purposes. The question to be asked of him or any other, including Marilyn Monroe, should not be *Is he or she a celebrity?* But, *What kind of a celebrity? And to what effect?*

It is one thing for a white river boy like me to be intrigued by Ali, or for millions of others of this or another kind to celebrate the phenomenon the man has become. It is quite another for a professional peer – a man who has invented his own special and kindly charisma, a great boxer like George Foreman – to join in the fun. Foreman has also said, "I don't believe Muhammad Ali's conversion was a religious experience. I'll believe until the day I die that it was a social awakening. . . . It was something he needed at the time, something the whole country needed."[26] Could there be a better description of celebrity – *something he needed / something the whole country needed* – and, one might add, *something the world needed?*

Perhaps more even than gods, celebrities are unique. They play upon some unusual, timely, even miraculous, mutual feeding of personal and social needs. The celebrity cannot reinvent him or herself according to felt necessity without the renown only a social group of some scale can give. The social whole will not celebrate unless the magnificent one fills some shared lack in the *among* of social life. The contract is by its nature vulnerable to whim – which, among other reasons, is why this particular trickster is so very interesting.

two

CELEBRITY, TRICKS, AND CULTURE

Float like a Butterfly, Sting like a Bee

The Wonderful Tar-Baby Story

"Didn't the fox never catch the rabbit, Uncle Remus?" asked the little boy....

"He come might nigh it honey, sho's you bawn – Brer Fox did. One day ... Brer Fox went ter wuk en got 'im some tar, en mix it wid some turkentime, en fix up a contrapshun wat he call a Tar-Baby, en he tuck dish yer Tar-Baby en he sot 'er in the big road, en den he lay off in de bushes for ter see wat de news wuz gwinter be.... Brer Rabbit come pacin' 'long twel she spy de Tar-Baby, en den he fotch up on his behime legs like he wuz 'stonished....

"'Mawnin'!' sez Brer Rabbit," sezee – "nice wedder dis mawnin" ...

Tar-Baby ain't say' nuthin' en Brer Fox, he lay low....

"How you come on, den? Is you def?" sez Brer Rabbit ...

Brer Fox, he sorter chuckle in his stummuck, he did, but Tar-Baby ain't sayin' nuthin'.

"I'm gwineter larn you howter talk ter 'specttubble fokes ef hit's de las' ack," sez Brer Rabbit, sezee. "Ef you don't take off dat hat en tell me howdy, I'm gwineter bus' you wide open," sezee.

Brer Rabbit keep on axin' im, en de Tar-Baby, she keep on sayin' nuthin' twel present'ly Brer Rabbit draw back wid his fis', he did, en blip he tuck 'er side er de head.... His fis' stuck, en he can't pull loose. De tar hilt 'im....

"Ef you don't lemme loose, I'll knock you agin," sez Brer Rabbit, sezee, en wid dat he fotch 'er a wipe wid de 'udder han', en dat stuck. Tar-Baby, she ain't sayin' nuthin', en Brer Fox, he lay low. Den Brer Rabbit squall out dat ef de Tar-Baby don't tu'n 'im loose he butt 'er cranksided. En den he butted, en his head got stuck. Ben Brer Rox, he sa'ntered fort', lookin' des ez innercent ez wunner yo mammy's mockin'-birds.

"Howdy, Brer Rabbit," sez Brer Fox, sezee. "You look sorter stuck up dis mawnin'," sezee, en den he rolled on de groun', en laft en laft twel he couldn't laff' no mo'. "I speck you'll take dinner wid me dis time, Brer Rabbit. I done laid in some calamus root, en I ain't gwineter take no skuses," sez Brer Fox, sezee.

... [Here Uncle Remus interrupts and sends the little boy to whom he is telling the story on his way. The boy, enchanted by Brer Rabbit's dilemma, returns some days later when he finds Uncle Remus sitting by idly.] ...

"Uncle Remus," said the little boy ... "did the fox kill and eat the rabbit when he caught him with the Tar-Baby?" ...

"W'at I tell you w'en I fus' begin? I tole you Brer Rabbit wuz a monstus soon beas'; leas'ways dat's wa't I laid out fer ter tell you. Well, den, honey, don't you go en make no udder kalkalashuns, kaze in dem days Brer Rabbit en his fambly wuz at de head er de gang w'en enny racket wuz on han', de dar dey stayed. 'Fo' you begins fer ter wipe yo' eyes 'bout Brer Rabbit, you wait en see whar'bouts Brer Rabbit gwineter fetch up at. But dat's needer yer ner dar.

"W'en Brer Fox fine Brer Rabit mixt up wid de Tar-Baby, he feel mighty good, en he roll on de groun'' en laff. Bimeby he up'n say, sezee:

"Well, I speck I got you dis time, Brer Rabbit" sezee; "maybe I ain't, but I speck I is. You been runnin' roun' here sassin' atter me a might long time, but I speck you done come ter de een' er de row. You bin cuttin' up yo' capers en bouncin' 'roun' in dis naberhood ontwel you come ter b'leeve yo'se'f de boss er de whole gang. En den youer allers some'rs whar you got no bizness," sez Brer Fox sezee.... "You des tuck en jam yo'se'f on dat Tar-Baby widout waitin' fer enny invite," sez Brer Fox, sezee, "en dar you is, en dar you'll stay twel I fixes up a bresh-ile and fires her up, kaze I'm gwineter bobbycue you dis day, sho," sez Brer Fox, sezee.

Den Brer Rabbit talk mighty 'humble.

"I don't keer wa't you do wid me, Brer Fox," sez Brer Rabbit, sezee, "so you don't fling me in dat brier-patch. Roas' me Ffffox," sezee, "but don't fling me in dat brier-patch."

"Hit's so much trouble fer ter kindle a fier," sez Brer Rox, sezee, "dat I speck I'll hatter hang you," sezee.

"Hang me des ez high as you please, Brer Rox," sez Brer Rabbit, sezee, "But do fer de Lord's sake don't fling me in dat brier-patch," sezee.

"I ain't got no string," sez Brer Fox, sezee, "en now I speck I'll hatter drown you," sezee.

"Drown me des ez deep ez you please, Brer Fox," sez Brer Rabbit, sezee, "but do don't fling me in dat brier-patch," sezee he.

"Dey ain't no water nigh," sez Brer Fox, sezee, "en now I speck I'll hatter skin you," sezee.

"Skin me, Brer Fox," sez Brer Rabbit, sezee, "snatch out my eynballs, t'ar out my years by de roots, en cut off my legs," sezee, "but do please, Brer Rox, don't fling me in dat brier-patch," sezee.

"Co'se Brer Fox wanter hurt Brer Rabbit bad ez he kin, so he cotch 'im by de behime legs en slung 'im right in de middle er de brier-patch. Bar wuz a considerbul flutter whar Brer Rabbit' struck de bushes, en Brer Rox sorter hang 'roun' feer ter see w'at wuz gwineter happen. Bimbeby he hear somebody call 'im, en way up de hill he see Brer Rabbit settin' cross-legged on a chinkapin log koamin' de pitch outen his har wid a chip. Den Brer Fox known dat he bin swop off mighty bad. Brer Rabbit wuz bleedzed fer ter fling back some er his sass, en he holler out:

"Bred en bawn in a brier-patch, Brer Fox – bred en bawn in a Brier-patch!" en wid dat he skip out of des ez lively ez a bricket in de embers.

An African-American Folktale[1]

In the summer of 1962, early in graduate school days, I took a summer job in very rural New Hampshire. Though there is tourist money in the state's mountain district to the east, I was stationed in Croydon to the bleak west. Croydon is a town of one store, a one-room schoolhouse (with stove), a desultory town building (with library), and not much else but the worn homes (many of them trailers) scattered up in the hills. I worked out of the town library, which otherwise went unused. I found lodgings in the next town of some size – a room in the home of Mrs Helen Trow, who was well into her eighties.

Mrs Trow had a gentleman friend of about the same advanced age and comparable zest. I don't recall his name. He owned the local men's clothing store, which he still opened each morning at an early hour. At day's end, 5:30 exactly, he closed the shop, occasionally to walk the three, tree-lined blocks to Mrs Trow's on the north end of the town common. They would have a drink on the porch, then a dinner, after which some television until he left at ten for his place. Some evenings he came, others not. But Friday evenings he never failed to show.

All over America, in the most unlikely of places, Friday night was fight night in the early years of television. And Mrs Trow and her gentleman friend never failed to watch the fights. I was invited to join them only once; never again. They were polite, but my presence altered the delicate intimacy of a friendship that turned each week on the shared spectacle of near-naked men dancing, holding, hitting until one or the other was declared the victor. Even Mrs Trow, otherwise proper and conservative in a small town way, would occasionally yelp as did my mother back home in Cincinnati when her favorite fighter gained the upper hand.

That summer of 1962 was the second of Cassius Clay's career in professional boxing. He had won the gold in Rome in 1960. He wore his medal with such joy and his pride with such ebullience that he came to be known as the mayor of the Olympic Village. He fell into a kind of love with Wilma Rudolph, the women's sprint champion. He greeted any and all athletes with a comedic pleasure so off the charts that none could resist his charms. But that was 1960. He was 18, on the outer cusp of youth. Two years later, at 20, he was well on his way to the professional championship. On July 20, 1962, when I was in New Hampshire, Cassius Clay fought someone by the name of Alejandro Lavorante.

Young fighters are brought along slowly. Few strike it rich. Those who do, strike it very rich for themselves, their backers, and their hangers-on. Their first opponents are carefully chosen losers from the lower ranks. For a prospect to challenge for the big prize, he must establish a record as Clay was doing when he knocked out Lavorante in the fifth round. This was his

thirteenth knockout in fifteen professional bouts without a loss. His next fight would be in November with his one-time trainer, Archie Moore – a four-round knockout that would end Moore's distinguished career and begin Clay's march through the more challenging ranks that led to a date with the champion Sonny Liston two years later.

I do not know whether Mrs Trow and her man friend watched the fight late in July from Los Angeles, or even whether it was televised (though probably it was[2]). What I know, almost for certain, is that they had to have known about this strange and surprising kid from Kentucky. No one who followed the fight game could not have heard of him – not even a lady in her ninth decade of life in rural New England nor her gentleman caller. They were proper enough by the standards of the day and place that he always went home by ten, but improper enough to refuse to hide their love of boxing.

Or, were they proper in *all* ways? Why should one think of a spectacle that celebrates courage and athletic perfection, even at risk of personal injury, as somehow improper? Today, perhaps so – after ears have been bitten off, corruption exposed, and so many died or been put down by the beatings. But then, if less so today, courage and war were as much a part of the culture of the West as good manners and modest attire. And if things are changed, it is the manners and the modesty, not the regard for courage and fighting.

That summer of 1962 I had no idea just how much the fight world appealed to all manner of people. I had even forgotten that my own Midwest conservative parents loved the fights – wrestling first, but also boxing. My father the doctor could not have told you who Ewell Blackwell of the Cincinnati Reds baseball team was. But he could go on at length about Joe Louis and Billy Conn. Since Conn, whom Louis defeated for the second time in 1946, was then the great white hope,[3] it is possible that my father knew what he knew about boxing for all the wrong reasons. Perhaps so it was with Mrs Trow and her companion. Baseball is said to be the quintessential American game. This may once have been more true than it is today. But even baseball or cricket or the football Americans call soccer cannot compare to the vast volume of feeling and faith that can be condensed into the received persona of a man willing to strip all but naked before the world, to fight with his hands for gains more urgent and elusive than the evening's purse. In the early years of his career, Cassius Clay often took home less than $1,000 for the night's work.[4] But it was worth it. He was headed somewhere. And his unusual way of heading there, with all the boasting and fooling around, was at one and the same time both unheard of and within the rules of the game. From the beginnings of his public life, Cassius Clay was that most unusual of characters – one able somehow both to break and to reset the prevailing norms of work and play.

I AM the greatest, he would shout. Nothing like it had been heard before, at least not among prizefighters. Boxing as we know it today began as early as 1743,[5] when men of marginal circumstances, many of them black, performed for the pleasures of gentlemen of high standing. The sport, such as it became, began as a spectacle, but a show defined by precise rules of bourgeois masculinity. Boxing then, as today, drew out the feelings of those who came with their hatreds and hopes, disappointments and all the rest. Performances of this kind can be spectacular, but only when they incite those who watch and cheer or jeer to a riot of feelings not so easily expressed in the course of daily life. No one can possibly touch the deeper parts of so many if those touched do not at least secretly want the rules he breaks broken while hoping against hope not to lose their own protective cover. Boxing is far from the only spectator sport to cast celebrities across the public imagination. But it is, surely, among the better night skies for stars of the kind Cassius Clay was soon to become.

––––––––

It is hard to imagine how any social group would survive without celebrities. When we-the-people gather over time for the purpose of living mundane lives in our given locales, we need to see the terrain of our living as *other* – where possible, *better* – than it is. There are few situations where the collective *We* of all human persons is more surely drawn toward the wish for more than has been given. The human *We* may be otherwise

31

rent by the varieties of tastes in food (or music), by the gods worshipped (or rebuked), by the games played (or dreamt of), by the work engaged (or denied), . . . on without seeming end. But this otherwise non-existent *We* of humanity comes together in the wish for a world other and better than the daily round.

Our saints and shamans entreat us to enjoy each day for what it is – a fine and honorable ideal. But for the vast majority of folk the daily is a grind. The all-too-poor face a succession of terrible days on the streets, thirsty for any drink that will quench. The too-well-off face the countless channels of their boredom, thirsty for some potion to dull the pain. Those between, unlucky in their work, sit idly in the traffic of their limited prospects, filled with rage at the unfairness of it all. Only the saints, and a relative few of the ordinary, come to terms with the mundane lives they lead. Hence, the desire for something more – or, when that something is not reasonably within reach, for the dream of the better.

Celebrities are one, but only one, of the elixirs that quench the dry throat of the ordinary. There are others, to be sure. For the higher-minded, and well-disciplined, the local gods – even if they are the gods of hard work at unrewarding tasks – refresh the spiritual electrolytes. For others, leisure activities of varying degrees of merit – from the televisual to the less mediated forms of entertaining distraction – serve to calm the soul. For the tragically afflicted, drink and drug fill the always half-empty well of desire.

Celebrities may not bear close scrutiny, but when considered against the alternatives, they are far from the worst – and they may even be among the better antidotes to dampened aspirations. To celebrate the achievements, real or imagined, of some bigger-than-life member of the race may distract us from running on our own. But to celebrate is, at least, to rise off the couch of resignation, to stir the blood for something more that budges the celebrant from the slow death of a one-dimensional life.

So ubiquitous are these celebrities that it is not far wrong to say, in the spirit of George Foreman, that we invent them out of a shared need. To speak of *need* in this way is risky business. The slope from need to *desire* is slippery, and especially so in the more affluent of the global societies, where the modes of production depend on a commerce that trades a simple desire for the illusion of a necessity. Still, we may be in the presence of something real, if not absolutely necessary, when the desired object is so utterly magical as to blind us to its flaws and faults.

The celebrity is somewhat like a god. Both deal in transcendence of one kind or another. But the celebrity serves his or her social purpose by virtue of an unbreakable tie to ordinary humanity. Gods, in most places, are humanoid in their ways, but they serve precisely to the extent that their magic owes to an unbreakable bond to the extraordinary. Their paradises may be dreamt in earthly images, but their power comes from a heavenly above.

When, by contrast to the gods, we celebrate one of our own, we may behave at times as though we were celebrating the eucharist of a god. The external form of political rallies, rock concerts, or public hangings may often take on the appearance of divine sacrifice. But between the secular and the sacred there is an interior difference that cannot be abridged. To give oneself over to the worship of a god – even one who is said to have slept or supped with men – is to knowingly give flight to the possibility of passing beyond the boundedness of ordinary life. Religion is thus, and famously so, the experience of being bound – of accepting life's limitations, its finitude. Divine worship is the act of affirming the death that makes for some other life. To celebrate one breath after another, as the Buddhists do – or one crucifixion or exodus after another, as Christians and Jews do, or to bow day after day toward Mecca, as the Muslim does – is to celebrate the limits of the human. These are limits beyond which may lie something other – the non-self beyond self, a land flowing with milk and honey.

But to encourage celebrity is to pretend that the deadliness of ordinary life is not as it is. We invent celebrities because, as recompense for our gifts to them, they encourage us to escape for a time from what is and must be. It is not that celebrities are unable to serve a higher social good. Some do in fact transform the desire for something better into the necessity of social change. But not all. Most celebrities lose their magic in short course. Michael Jackson, Madonna, Pelé, Mao, Eva Peron, Ringo. Even as we continue to enjoy their magic, we know that their day will come. Only a few endure beyond a few years. Frank Sinatra, *Zapata*, *Dylan*, *Che*, *Nelson Mandela*, *John*. These perhaps inspire something deeper in the collective life – its longing for love, its humor, its rebelliousness, its heroic suffering.

Still another difference between divine beings and human celebrities is in the extent to which their celebrants are prepared to ignore faults. It goes without saying that a god cannot bestow the life beyond this life if her own death is final. Even the Buddha, who disdained the very idea of gods, transcends common celebrity by promising at least the nirvana where death does not matter. And even the most mundane of those gods and goddesses with whom Ulysses cohabited over the seas was understood to have inhabited a mountaintop higher by some than the plains to which the hero longed to return. The celebrity is like the god in this regard too, but again with an exception.

The celebrity's transcending brilliance must be willfully repaired and maintained. To believe in a god is, as I say, to give oneself away. To believe in a celebrity is to turn the other cheek to his or her failings. What in fact did Michael Jackson do with that child? Could Madonna really be that wicked? How corrupt were Sinatra's gangster pals? And JFK? Diana? It is very difficult to out a celebrity, if only because the celebrant works so hard at the self-deception. One works with such irrational energy only when the desire for the object of affection achieves the false status of a virtual need. Thus, while religious and secular celebrities may rise from the common ground of human ordinariness, the shared interior lives they nurture are quite different in tone and quality. The one reaches for the beyond of life itself. The other embraces the best that can be in the life at hand. Between aspiration and embrace the soul inclines differently – toward the heavens in the one case, toward the ground in the other. Neither the god nor the celebrity is as good, or as mundane, as some or another science might want to demonstrate. And neither is *necessarily* bad or good.

———

Then, from time to time, there comes along a celebrity who, unlike any god or man, seems to embody the bad and the good so perfectly well as to change the name of the game.

This is the trickster – the critter who prowls on the margins of a social group, often in the low hills on the night horizon.[6] The coyote descends to prey, retreats to howl, but seldom allows himself to be caught in the act. He is considered among the wisest of the beasts of prey for his occasional practice of entering the thick of the social group to change the game, to turn the tables, to reinvent the daily run of things. The trickster plays his tricks both on the settled town but also as a member of the mundane community. Or, better put, the trickster is a both-at-once creature. Usually in the form of an animal – rabbits, snakes, bees, ravens, very often coyotes, badgers, spiders, and any number of others – the trickster makes jest of the ordinary. The bad he does to the gathered ordinary is somehow part of the good in his surprise attacks. The trick is in the neither-good-nor-bad of it all. Peoples native to the plains take both comfort and terror from the trickster's nighttime calls. Unlike the carnival fool, the trickster offers more than mere and temporary relief from the common. He transforms – sometimes even to the extent of inspiring a new reality, even a new world, at least a new possibility.

The trickster therefore partakes of the same magical powers as do gods and celebrities. But he (more often than not he is a he[7]) partakes of them oddly. Surprise, if not quite irony, is the trickster's potion. By contrast, both the gods and your average celebrity are deadly serious. John Calvin's God may have been inscrutable, but this did not keep the Calvinists from figuring out their hard-working methods for petitioning him in this life. The sober joke of religious earnestness is that of aspiring to heaven by some sustained habit of this-worldly predictability. Similarly, even Michael Jackson's remakings of himself, or Madonna's labored sexual play, not to mention the wit and tease of the Beatles, are more serious by a good measure than the play of the trickster. The trickster, by trading on surprise and reversal, turns the trick that passes understanding. The serious believer eventually becomes all too sure of an unthinkable equation between his repetitive mumbling and the will of the gods. Likewise, those who love, say, the Beatles of *Yellow Submarine* know what is going down, as even the most uptight get the point of Madonna's show of gender trouble. The trickster might be said to be the god who shits on the gods, the celebrity who defies the celebration. The trickster seldom relishes his peculiar privilege in the order of social things.

True, the trickster is, if he must be any one thing, a special kind of celebrity. Certainly he is closer in kind, if he can be said to be close to anything, to the celebrity than to the god. His extraordinary powers are encouraged less by a shared faith in the Olympian Other than in the powers silenced by the drone of ordinary life. There is nothing wrong with thinking of the trickster as half-god, half-man – save for the fact that by taking the form of animal life the trickster reminds both the god and the man that between the beyond of life and death lies the forgotten power that everyone knows. The trickster thus plays his magic tricks as much to reveal the ordinary for what it is as to lift the downtrodden to higher hopes. A trickster, quite literally, tends to piss on the ground, thus to piss off the unnatural depression that settles on the mundane like dust from the ever-expanding African deserts.

Though, for the most part, the trickster does his work in what social theorists might call premodern or traditional societies, occasionally one arises in the thoroughly modern, even postmodern. When he does, the effect disturbs the peace.

The story is told of a visit Muhammad Ali paid to Fidel Castro in Cuba sometime in 1996.[8] Ali had been retired from boxing a good 15 years. He was 54. The Parkinson's syndrome inflicted on his nervous system by his last over-the-hill fights at the very end of the 1970s had silenced Ali to a whisper. Still, the Cuban leader, himself a boxer of sorts, wanted to meet Ali again.

The setting was a reception hall in the Place of the Revolution in Havana. It was evening. Castro was late, interminably late. There were no chairs, no refreshments. None of those waiting had eaten. Still, they waited. When Fidel arrived, he of course engaged Ali, as he did the others. But Ali, if not an idol, was clearly special. The chat was muted, less by the late hour and fatigue than by Ali's inability to speak as once he did. His mind, as everyone knows, is clear and sharp as always. It was only his body that shook and stumbled, only his voice that could not sing – still, he sang in a way.

Unable to recite his poems or otherwise float like a butterfly, Ali had taken to magic tricks – literally. Whenever he travels now, he carries an attaché filled with the tools of a magician. In due course, Ali began to pull them on and for Castro. One was particularly enchanting to the Cuban leader – the old trick of the rubber thumb. It is not much of a trick except when performed by the human race's most famous being for one of the world's most famous revolutionary leaders. It consists in nothing more than the illusion of a human digit that serves in fact as a reservoir to hide the disappearing scarves. Children can perform the trick as Ali did for the fascinated Fidel. Whether Castro was in awe of the magic or of the man in his not-to-be-pitied physical condition is hard to tell from the story. But it seems that Fidel was brought into the joy of it all.

Ali's practice is to violate the basic rule of the magician. He always demonstrates how the magic works – this apparently from under the Muslim prohibition of deception. When the time came for him to depart, Ali pressed the rubber thumb to Castro's hand. At first confused, Castro was told that Ali meant for him to have it. The story ends, according to its teller, as the elevator bearing Ali and his entourage away closes to a glimpse of Fidel Castro – smiling, waving, then staring for a moment at the rubber thumb in his hand, before putting it away to turn back to the affairs of the Cuban state.

How does it work that a man – any man, famous or not – can enter the center of some palace of power to defy the realities by enchanting the powerful? What kind of magic is this? In Ali's case, it is a magic the enchantment of which lies beyond the trick. The magic is the surprising power of the silent trickster himself. It is a power that Muhammad Ali has pressed on hands wherever he has gone since the days when he was a kid – Cassius Clay of Grand Avenue in Louisville, Kentucky.

What, or who, then, is this figure the 22-year-old Cassius Clay would become after 1964? And the one he would remain 30 years later, a man in his fifties tricking on Fidel Castro – a trickster spirit trapped in a declining body?

It is all too easy, one supposes, to say that a player of tricks is, by that coincidence alone, a trickster. In fact, the trickster is one of the most common figures in the folklore and culture of so-called premodern societies. Few lack at least one; many have several, or more. More intriguing still is that the trickster is found commonly among those cultures in, but not of, the modern societies – and notably those of the African diaspora living in Europe or North America or in the metropolitan centers of the Caribbean and Africa or Latin America. Not only this, but in the last decades of the twentieth century, as the centers of European diaspora were forced to recognize the truth of their multicultural beings, the trickster had emerged as a ubiquitous figure in and out of all the times and spaces of the global cultures.

What then, more precisely, is a trickster? No one writing today, against a considerable tradition of fascination with the trickster figure, knows more than Lewis Hyde, and knows it with such a grasp of the details across times and cultures. Hyde's *Trickster Makes This World* begins with the following provisional description:

> Trickster is a boundary-crosser. Every group has its edge, its sense of in and out, and the trickster is always there, at the gates of the city and the gates of life, making sure there is commerce. He also attends the internal boundaries by which groups articulate their social life. We constantly distinguish – right and wrong, sacred and profane, clean and dirty, male and female, young and old, living and dead – and in every case trickster will cross the line and confuse the distinction. Trickster is the creative idiot, therefore, the wise fool, the gray-haired baby, the cross dresser, the speaker of sacred profanities. Where someone's sense of honorable behavior has left him unable to act, trickster will appear to suggest an amoral action, something right/wrong that will get life going again. Trickster is the mythic embodiment of ambiguity and ambivalence, doubleness and duplicity, contradiction and paradox.[9]

You can see the trickster at work in any attempt to define him. There is no one characteristic – not even *doubleness*, for he is legion. There is no one literary figure – not even the *creative idiot*, for he is also the *wise fool*. There is no one location – not even the *outside*, because he is also at work in the *inside*. There is no one truth – not even the *mythic*, for he is also very much of *this world*. There is no one method – not even *deceit*, for his tricks tell *truths*. There is no one function – not even *boundary-crosser*, for he also is a *boundary-guard*. The trickster figure goes beyond even the usual terms for such phenomena – *ambivalence, publicity, contradiction, paradox*. Trickster is, in short, trickster – that character who is what he is without qualification, reduction, or emendation.

If you doubt what I say just try to explain to a small child exactly what is going on with all the tricksters in her books – Mickey in the night kitchen, not to mention Asterix, and Maurice Sendak's other monsters and Curious George; or Brer Rabbit and even Beatrix Potter's little rabbits who drive Farmer McGregor nuts; or the West African Ananse, the spider who steals from the jungle giants; or the road runners and coyotes who beset and elude Bugs Bunny and his kind; and even poor little Madeline, the Parisian orphan who so innocently upsets the order of Miss Clavel's house, as she does Paris and Texas and all the places she visits; and on and on.

Mickey hears a loud noise through the sleep. But then he begins to fall – out of bed, out of his clothes, out of his house where his parents are sleeping into an enormous mixing bowl in the night kitchen. Three monster-sized bakers do not notice. They pour their milk and flour and baking soda. They stir and mix. They beat the batter, with Mickey in it. Just as they were putting it in the oven, Mickey breaks out. "I'm not the milk and the milk's not me!" The bakers need milk. Mickey kneads the dough into an airplane and a flight jacket. He jumps in, takes the measuring cup, and flies up and away into the Milky Way and a skyscraper of milk bottle. In he dives. He loses his dough suit and sinks to the bottom, his tiny penis exposed. He sings, "I'm in the milk and the milk's in me. God bless milk, and God bless me." He floats to the top, his cup full. He pours the milk over the lip of the bottle in the Milky Way, down into the batter. The bakers sing, "Milk in the batter! Milk in the batter! We bake cake! And nothing's the matter!" Just then the sun begins to rise. Mickey falls again from the Milky Way bottle down into bed, into his pajamas, back into his fading dream. "And that's why, thanks to Mickey, we have cake every morning."

After Maurice Sendak, Mickey in the Night Kitchen[10]

My three-year-old daughter loves this stuff. She seldom asks what's going on. But when she does, it is almost impossible to explain such stories. They are beyond reasoning with their dream distortions, visible naked sexual organs, devouring monsters (in this story, very gentle ones), appetites, and transformations (here from boy to batter to baker to pilot to fish to boy) – all while falling through night and sky and home. To children, tricksters just are, even when, as Mickey does, they make the world.

This you might not believe, but it happened just as I say:

Just as I finished writing the previous paragraph, Annie herself appeared at the door of my study. She wore a net skirt (last year's Halloween costume), a hippie necklace, dancing shoes and tights, and a field-hand's bandana over her head. I laughed at the sight of her, with the wild mix of genres and colors against her very brown skin. She smiled and smiled, and said: "I'm Cinderella." Children live in these worlds of make-believe, between dreams and realities – worlds they are continuously making and remaking. Two hours earlier – before we made our Saturday morning pancakes – she made a tent of our bed sheets to play, in her words, "Jesus in his castle hiding from the mice who want to put me on a cross and bleed me."

Anna Julia Lemert, Saturday morning, August 25, 2001

Children are part-time tricksters, which is likely why they so love the deceitful beasts and mice, coyotes and spiders that inhabit their world of nighttime stories. Still, one might ask, why are they not terrified? If you are a trickster of a sort yourself, there is nothing to fear in the jungles and night kitchens. Could it be that children have what we've lost? – the enchantment of living with the surprises that come with the neither-this-nor-that of life? Tricksters, much like ghosts, are everywhere and nowhere. Yet, they are hard to see or put in their place. There is a reason for this. Tricksters conjure up the worlds the allegedly mature life requires us to ignore. They drive people out of the ordinary, into the wild thoughts and feelings they must repress if they are to escape the authorities.

Where do tricksters come from? In what is their reality? What exactly are their purposes and their modes of operation? If mythic figures, how can they also be so utterly this-worldly? If child's play, how does it happen that they disturb the adults? And why, most of all, do the most modern of cultures suppress them all the more rigorously? One likely answer is that those cultures, like well-seasoned adults, have much to lose in the tease. Trickster deceives and disturbs. But not wantonly. He upsets the cultural apple cart in order to excite some new commerce. Trickster is a culture transformer.[11]

The first trick of the trickster is that he deceives others by being more and other than the common creature he appears to be. Trickster transforms himself in order to remake the worlds at hand. Thus, in those cultures more accustomed to trickster than ours, the most striking thing is that he is at first appearance so very ordinary – part and parcel of the dull round of days he means to change. His ordinariness is not so much that he appears in the figure of some or another animal creature common to the locale. Nor even, perhaps, that trickster coyote or rabbit or spider takes on the most common of human qualities – greed, desire, seduction, and all the rest with no apparent limit. More even than his mixed animal and human natures, trickster is the one without shame. He usually deceives in some surprising relation to the most basic of bodily functions. Trickster has a voracious appetite for food and sex, from which devolve his alimentary and sexual surprises. He farts, shits, belches, fucks, exposes extraordinary sexual organs, and displaces his penis and other body parts into hollow spaces or atop the trees from which to explore and see and distort the manners of ordinary expectations.

41

Ananse and Akwasi share a meal. Ananse, the spider, sneaks a laxative into Akwasi's food. After dinner, Ananse explains that his name means "Rise-up-and-make-love-to-Aso." (Aso is Akwasi's wife.) He adds that Nyame, his master, requires that he sleep in the same room with Akwasi and Aso. During the night the laxative does its work. Akwasi's bowels groan with pain. In agony, he calls his friend Ananse by name — "Rise-up-and-make-love-to-Aso." While Akwasi is outside shitting, Ananse obeys the deceptive command. Akwasi defecates nine times. Each time Ananse makes love to Aso.

Months later it is plain that Aso is pregnant, which puzzles Akwasi. Aso reminds him that he had told Ananse to rise up and make love to her. In time the child is born. Akwasi decides to give Aso to Ananse. Arriving at Nyame's village, where Ananse lives, he startles the trickster spider, who falls from a ridge pole of his lodge. Ananse, by right, demands a sacrifice from Akwasi. Aso marries Ananse. Their baby is slaughtered, the parts of her body are cast here and there.

Thus was jealously spread among the peoples.

A West African Trickster Story[12]

Ananse, the Ashanti spider, is more overtly a trickster than Mickey in the night kitchen. In Sendak's story Mickey is accidentally the source of the tricks and distortions of the night world. In the West African tale, Ananse pulls the tricks himself. Still, like Mickey, the trickster accounts for a social fact of life — food in the one, jealousy in the other. But in the pure form, the culture explainer/transformer is more overtly sexual. Mickey's penis is tiny. Trickster's penis is often enormous or (as in this Ashanti story) prodigous. Annie and I have encountered cleaned-up versions of the Ananse tale in African-American storybooks. The "pee-nits" (Annie's three-year-old word for penis) may be suppressed, or Ananse may be punished instead of rewarded, but still the spider tricks the higher powers by stealing their food (a condensation of the sexual and hunger appetites into the desire for food alone). Trickster plays with the origins of what some psychoanalysts insist on calling the two basic drives or instincts — to join and incorporate, principally, but also by fucking; to separate people from each other or their things, by shitting and pissing and farting, but also by the trick that steals in order to reinvent the order of social things.

The trickster plays games on others, but his play always serves to break the rules that, once broken, do not easily fall back into place. This is how the culture transformer works – not as the inspiring hero, nor as the creative leader, nor as the inventor of new methods, nor any of the usual ways of imagining the possibility of a better way of life arising from the mundane. Rather, trickster jokes and farts, fucks and shits, pisses and signifies on the objects to which the desire to escape the mundane attaches itself. Even when the reminders are suppressed by the storyteller, as they are with Mickey's innocent penis, and even with Cassius Clay's always somewhat covered sexual energy, they work their tricks on the collective imagination. By associating much-treasured cultural objects with the most common of animal functions, trickster remakes them. In being struck down by a cultural rebel, culture is renewed.

———

After the summer of 1962, and the defeat of Archie Moore that autumn, Cassius Clay gradually transformed himself into the trickster-celebrity he would thereafter be. If his mother was not exactly right to say that God had always meant for him to be as special as to so many he became, she was not far wrong either.

Each of us, with a few exceptions at the fringes of sanity, possesses what the psychoanalysts call a character – that paradox of a theatrical public face laid upon a steady-state of interior traits one might call habits were it not that they are so deeply settled below the surface of conscious choice. In this sense, Cassius Clay, already by the time he met Joe Martin, was a character who revealed his psychological character. Was he thus fated to be a trickster?

Though tricksters enjoy their own correspondence with the gods, it seems improbable that Odessa Clay's god would have chosen a joker of the kind Cassius became. But it does seem possible, at least, that growing up with the interesting provocations of his steady, beyond reproach mother and his dream-disappointed transgressive father could have led to the character

Cassius had and would become. From Odessa he knew and loved the rules of the game. From Cassius, Sr, he must have taken the dangers of artistic temperament as well as some permission to break the rules. In any case, by the time he had grown into the hard disciplined boxer who intended to be the greatest, Cassius was, at the very least, a character who knew the culture about him very, very well – and knew just as well what was in need of repair. No black boy from this river town had to be taught the trouble with white America. Still, somewhere also he learned not only this but also the nuanced moves of his surprising, occasionally delightful, act for responding to it – for transforming it; for at least being among its important transformers.

So where did the transformation that made the transformer occur? To the extent that Cassius Clay was meant – by the gods or his character – to be what he became, then the answer is no one place in particular. But, from another more mundane angle, it is always the case that the class clown who develops a trickster career experiences that one day when, to his astonishment, his classmates laugh out loud to everyone's delight. What may have been inside working its way out all along had to have some or another occasion (one lost to memory forever) when Cassius turned the trick on himself. When that happens, it remains for the trickster to develop the act by which he presents his show. It would be a mistaken social psychology of the human self that claims, as so many do, that the act is unrelated to the actor's true interior nature. As Erving Goffman first explained, better and more strikingly than anyone before,[13] the presentation of our public faces is precisely where we become who we are to ourselves. It remains to find and encourage a series of audiences for the shows we put on, mostly earnest in adolescence. Cassius Clay was but an adolescent of 18 years when he won the gold medal in Rome in 1960. His act as the mayor of the Olympic Village was clearly already well on its way. It was surely both self-consciously a public pitch for attention and also a natural issue of an inherently confident and ebullient personality.

Just about a year before Clay's Los Angeles fight in the summer of 1962, he was in Las Vegas for a ten-round bout with Duke Sabedong on June 26, 1961. He won by decision.

But the more important event of the trip may have been a chance meeting with Gorgeous George, probably the most famous entertainment wrestler of the day. David Remnick describes George: "Gorgeous George (known to his mother as George Raymond Wagner) was the first wrestler of the television era to exploit the possibilities of theatrical narcissism and a flexible sexual identity – a Liberace in tights."[14] Today we think of Madonna and Michael Jackson as the new breed of sexuality tricksters. But they had their precursors in a cast of characters who made their way by an at-the-time shocking display of ambiguous, if not outright gay, sexuality dressed up in sequins that called attention to their usually outrageous claims. Gorgeous George and Liberace, along with Little Richard and in an offbeat way Elvis, were the pioneers. Even when they were not *on* television, their acts were televisual. You had to see to believe. Ali the trickster would soon join the list.

Today televised wrestling, as sexualized entertainment for young boys and childlike men, is once again the fad. This is another time when the wild pretense of violence and sex are everywhere to be found. The days of Gorgeous George were different by far. No one who did not live through the first days of television could fully appreciate the role of televised "professional" wrestling in the dull life of Midwest river towns. The prizefights were one thing. But wrestling was another. My father (a depressingly cautious man) once took my mother (an embarrassingly incautious woman) to the wrestling matches while they were in Chicago attending the meetings of the American Medical Association at the Palmer House. My mother managed somehow (to this day I cannot imagine how) to climb onto the apron of the ring during a break in the action for the sole purpose of waving to my brother and me at home hundreds of miles across the Midwest plains, watching the matches on television. Television in the 1950s in middling America was a strange collage of programs that, in the absence of canned network sit-coms, which were just developing, mixed and confused the wide broadcast with local talents. I don't think Gorgeous George was wrestling that night, but in those days it was not all that strange in the wild mix of activity for a mom to wave from

Chicago to kids back home in Ohio. Wrestling was, in short, very sexy and much else. And George was the one who more than any of the others put wrestling in the living rooms of our towns and, thereby, joined in the fun of getting television started.

Outlandish is the word for Gorgeous George, as it would be for Muhammad Ali. Before the fight in Las Vegas the two appeared on a local radio show, both to hype their upcoming perform- ances. By 1961, Cassius was already well along the road to becoming the trickster character. Still, Clay was amazed by the wrestler's act, from which he borrowed what would become the tricks of his trade. The extreme loudness, the outrageous boasts, the predictions of victories, the promises to kiss his opponent's feet should he lose, and much else – were all borrowed from Gorgeous George.[15] It could well be that Cassius Clay's charac- ter would have become what it became without this vaudeville routine. Still, Ali himself claims that he sharpened the act after that encounter with Gorgeous George.

> I can't say I was humble, but I wasn't too loud. Then they asked Gorgeous George about a wrestling match he was having in the same arena, and he started shouting, "I'll kill him; I'll tear his arm off. If this bum beats me, I'll crawl across the ring and cut off my hair, but it's not gonna happen because I'm the greatest wrestler in the world." And all the time, I was saying to myself, "Man, I want to see this fight. It don't matter if he wins or loses; I want to be there to see what happens." And the whole place was sold out when Gorgeous George wrestled. There was thousands of people including me. And that's when I decided I'd never been shy about talking, but if I talked even more, there was no telling how much money people would pay to see me.[16]

The words are from an interview Ali gave to Thomas Hauser nearly 30 years after the meeting. You could say he was making it up. Or, you could wonder why, so long after he had already become a legend, he would want to give away the trick of his trade. He saw something in the wrestler's act that suited both his character and his ambition. To say that he was acting all those years will do little to heal the wounds Joe Frazier keeps rubbing raw. On balance, it would appear that, right or wrong, Ali knew what he was doing. But was it *merely* a commercial ploy, *simply* an attempt to raise a good gate?

———

Float like a Butterfly, Sting like a Bee. If there is one line, more than any other, that captures Ali's transformation into a trickster, this is it. *I AM the Greatest*, he took from Gorgeous George. But the decision to become boxing's butterfly/bee was his.

The line was not originally Ali's. It came from his own jester-friend in the early years, Drew "Bundini" Brown, who came into Ali's life probably in March of 1963, the year that led up to the championship fight with Sonny Liston. Though Bundini Brown was black, he went with white women and was otherwise an integrationist. Ali had already secretly been attending Nation of Islam meetings, so Brown's differing racial attitudes must have been a problem. But, just as Ali never broke with whites like Angelo Dundee, so he tolerated Brown's different racial practices (at least until they led to a break in 1965, after the championship had been won and Islamic teachings had set in). Brown entered Ali's life just before the fight with Doug Jones, a tough opponent whom Ali beat in a decision but was unable to knock out. In the words of Ferdie Pacheco (Ali's personal doctor and another trusted white):

> Bundini was a poet of the streets; a source of energy that Ali fed off constantly; someone who put words together in a way that connoted exactly what he meant and Ali could understand. "Float like a butterfly; sting like a bee." That was Bundini. He used to say that Ali and the entourage were like a cake, made with flour, eggs, sugar, and that he, Bundini, was the nutmeg which gave it that little extra taste.[17]

Boxers of championship caliber with a promise of income always attract hangers-on. Ali seems to have chosen his reasonably well. Bundini came into the inner circle not long after Howard Bingham. Where Bundini was the one who livened things up and gave Ali words and confidence, Bingham was the one who offered the steady comfort of a friend for keeps. Bundini and Ali broke time and again. Over time there is not enough room close in for another trickster. In the end Bundini died alone.[18] Bingham stayed for life.

Whatever a boxer's public face, the life and work themselves are grueling and lonely. Unlike others, Ali made a show of his training camps. Even his remote Deer Lake camp in the hills of Pennsylvania was open to the public, as is his farmhouse in Michigan today. Still, lonely celebrities on the rise can easily lose themselves to those who crowd around. As did others, Ali gave away a good bit of his considerable life-time earnings to those about him, many of whom were not to be trusted. Still, as these things go, he chose people he could trust – most of all Bingham. Bundini's role was to bolster his ego which, contrary to the public show, was often just as shaken as anyone's would be before a fight. No man strips down before the cameras to fight at such terrible risk without some fear. The act is in the manly face. The feelings are below the surface. Before the Jones fight in 1963 and for two years after, Bundini was the magician who took Ali's fear away on the wings of song.

And what a song it was. Street poets, unlike the cloistered, know their stuff. They sing of what they feel and see. And, in any case, it is impossible to bolster anyone's ego without speaking a plausible truth. Cassius Clay, still a youngster, was indeed possessed of physical gifts well expressed by the butterfly and the bee. So gifted was he that he called the victory round in many of his early fights. His outlandish act turned many against him, including all but a few of the press corps. But his performances demanded respect. His footwork was so beautiful that he seemed to float above the canvas. No heavyweight in living memory had ever moved that way. Writers trained in the old school like Jimmy Cannon of the *New York Post* and A. J. Liebling of the *New Yorker* rebuked Cassius Clay for violating all the rules, notably by floating with his hands lowered and dancing just out of reach of an opponent's jabs. No one had ever done this. Clay did. His defense was in hands so quick that their violence was delayed, much as a bee's sting. You feel it bite. You say, that's not so bad. Then the pain wells up. There have been boxers with good footwork from the miles on the road and hours with the rope; and others with good hands from the endless rounds at the bags. But none before, nor since, with both gifts in such excellent abundance.

So, when Cassius Clay knew in March of 1963 that he had reason to fear Doug Jones, he needed, as we all do at such times, someone to help him sing if he could. So Bundini Brown fed the poet in him, enough at least to nourish what he already knew was within. One of the reasons the Doug Jones fight went badly is that it took place in Madison Square Garden during a newspaper strike in New York City. Without the newspaper publicity and the chatter that newspaper stories can stir among boxing fans, the gate was at risk. So Ali spent the weeks before making the rounds of radio and television shows, talking up the gate. This was the occasion for his one visit as a poet-in-residence at the Bitter End Café in the Village. The outlandish act is hard work. He was spent. Still, the fight was sold out. Clay's inability to put Jones away gave the crowd a thrill. They professed to hate him for his act, when all along they were getting ready to love him more than any fighter since Joe Louis had ever been loved.

As it happened, beyond his feet and hands, Clay had a third physical talent that would serve him well in the short run, despite the ravages it ultimately visited on his nervous system. He could take a punch. Three months after making Doug Jones his eighteenth victim, Clay traveled to London for a bout with the British champion, Henry Cooper. Though Cooper was outmatched, he was a puncher. In the fourth round, he caught Clay unawares and floored him at the end of the round. Clay was hurt. Angelo Dundee famously bought him extra time by opening a small cut in one of his gloves. As the officials tried to figure out the solution (in the end, they had none), Clay had extra time to recover. The next round, refreshed as though nothing had happened, he gave Cooper a lesson. Bleeding profusely, the British champion fell. It was not a brilliant performance, but it let out the secret that, apart from speed and size, Clay was tough and had amazing powers of recovery.

Earlier in 1963, in April, Sonny Liston had humiliated Floyd Patterson for the second time. He had won the heavyweight championship on September 25, 1962, by crushing Patterson in the first round. This was the famous night that Patterson donned a false nose and facial hair to hide his shame. Liston gave Patterson a return. The results were the same. A first-round knockout. There were no other plausible contenders for Liston, the most terrifying of champions. The Liston camp had noted Clay's weak performances against Jones and Cooper. They figured Clay to be a good draw, as indeed he was, and a pushover opponent. So, they offered him the right to challenge for the crown.

The money people agreed with the Liston people. The fight was to take place in February, the next year. By fight night, the odds would be eight-to-one against Clay. The odds could not have been worse. But Cassius Clay proved everyone wrong. On February 25, 1964, the butterfly/bee trickster would come into his own on the contrary wings of a phenomenon that was much more than anyone had bargained on.

––––––

The African-American folktales of Uncle Remus and the trickster Brer Rabbit and the others were passed down orally across the centuries of slavery in the American South. Yet, they are among the more universal of all trickster stories. Traces are said to be found among the North and South American Indians, in Egypt, in West Africa, and even in the far East.[19] Little boys and girls know them from children's books and school lessons. They were surely told to Cassius Clay. How exactly the stories of Brer Rabbit *outfoxing* the powerful and *foxy* Brer Fox may have played in his childhood imagination may never be known. Whatever he may have remembered of these stories, it seems more than merely likely that the trickster was already there in the mind's eye when Cassius Clay met Gorgeous George, or when he came up against terrifying opponents from neighborhood toughs in Louisville to Sonny Liston in Miami, to others still to follow. If there is genius there, it is very probably the bodily genius of one, who like Brer Rabbit, was born and bred in brier-patch and knew exactly how to lure his opponents into the tricks of their defeat.

────── three ──────

TRICKSTER QUEERS THE WORLD

I Don't Have to Be What You Want Me to Be

A Trickster Upsets the World by Stealing Language

I lived in Master Hugh's family about seven years. During this time, I succeeded in learning to read and write. In accomplishing this, I was compelled to resort to various stratagems. I had no regular teacher. My mistress, who had kindly commenced to instruct me, had, in compliance with the advice and direction of her husband, not only ceased to instruct, but had set her face against my being instructed by any one else....

The plan which I adopted, and the one by which I was most successful, was that of making friends of all the little white boys whom I met in the street. As many of these as I could, I converted into teachers. With their kindly aid, obtained at different times and in different places, I finally succeeded in learning to read. When I was sent on errands, I always took my book with me, and by going one part of my errand quickly, I found time to get a lesson before my return. I used also to carry bread with me, enough of which was always in the house, and to which I was always welcome; for I was much better off in this regard than many of the poor white children in our neighborhood. This bread I used to bestow upon the hungry little urchins, who, in return, would give me that more valuable bread of knowledge.

Narrative of the Life of Frederick Douglass, An American Slave (1845)

Almost everybody has something good or bad to say about boxing – aging lovers in New Hampshire, dockworkers in Liverpool, lonely housewives in Ohio, literary stars in Princeton, computer scientists in New Mexico, impoverished villagers along the Congo, Norman Mailer wherever he is, other old men in coffee shops and bars in every town there is – everybody. This is not true of all public spectacles. Boxing is different. Somehow it gets under the most improbable of skins. Even those with scant interest in sports of any kind, not to mention those with a squeamish stomach for violence, are excitable when the subject turns to the fight game, or at least to some or another fighter. This is the uncanny attraction of men, and now women, like Ali.

No other spectacle, no other sport, reaches so widely to embrace the far extremes of the cultural spectrum. If the icon of the boxing *fan* is a cigar-chewing overweight whose reading life is trained on betting slips, then the icon of the boxing *aficionado* is the literary polymath who gains her reputation in the world of high cultural taste only to apply it to boxing. Joyce Carol Oates, for exceptional example, is to boxing as David Halberstam is to rowing and Doris Kearns Goodwin is to baseball.[1] Oates's *On Boxing* is among the more pungent books on the fight game. Her essays are less self-referential than Norman Mailer's *The Fight* and less overwrought than George Plimpton's boxing stories. She is closer in restraint and perspective to the fight commentaries of A. J. Liebling and Murray Kempton. And none, save perhaps Gerald Early, is her rival for framing boxing in human terms.[2] Oates knows the details of the sport, but also its larger possibilities.

> No one whose interest in boxing began as mine did in childhood – as an offshoot of my father's interest – is likely to think of boxing as a symbol for something beyond itself, as if its unique-ness were merely an abbreviation, or iconographic; though I can entertain the idea that life is a metaphor for boxing – for one of those bouts that go on and on, round following round, jabs, missed punches, clinches, nothing determined, again the bell and again and you and your opponent so evenly matched it's impossible not to see that your opponent *is* you: and why this struggle on an elevated platform enclosed by ropes as a pen beneath hot crude pitiless lights in the presence of an impatient crowd? – that sort of hellish-writerly metaphor. Life *is* like boxing in many unsettling respects. But boxing is only like boxing.[3]

As mesmerizing as this may be, something about it is hard to swallow.

Ought boxing be taken with such utter seriousness? Ought anyone, even one so astute as Oates, claim that so unsavory a spectacle is at once both grand and unique? What, in the face of it all, is one to say about unsavories like Don King and the others who, over the years, have made fame and gain out of a game that so often minces ever more grotesquely the social misery of men like Sonny Liston and Mike Tyson?[4] If one is to give Oates her strong idea that life is a metaphor for boxing, then boxing must be the spectacle that inverts the *camera obscura* – the spectacle that puts right side up that which presents itself as head over heels. Looked at this way, she may have a point. Just as celebrity is among the elixirs that dull the ache of the ordinary life, so boxing may be among the antidotes that slow the rush to the false high of the overly meaningful life. Hence the possibility that the boxing celebrity may be unique among the others for joining uppers with downers in a refreshing manner.

When and where life means something, it means it in some very local and particular life. To celebrate Life as such, as though it were something apart from and higher than living, is to bludgeon all those caught in an already again-and-again round of daily life. Those cultures where death and injury are taken for what they are in all their irrevocable intrusions upon the hopeful and wishful are better prepared to accept the ups and downs of life. This may be why women and others of the categorically displaced seem better able to live through the ordinary, even the terrible. In any case, all across Europe and its diaspora much is made of the West's supposed deep respect for human life. For reasons more complicated even than their racist superficies, Americans at least will refer to those who live in the East as lacking their high respect for human life. For Westerners more generally, "the East" is a term of vague moral geography that becomes local only when some physical place is settled for want of markets or enemies – Japan, China, Korea, Vietnam, Iran, Iraq, Afghanistan. The West's East thus functions in its culture much as do white people's black people. Just as the enforced illiteracy of the African slave was required as a sign certain of white superiority and difference in questions of race, so too the East's alleged inhumanity services the West's claim to moral righteousness.[5]

At a family gathering just before the attack on New York's World Trade Center on September 11, 2001, I was present, more or less shamelessly, at a replay of the West's time-weary confidence in its superior humanity. None of the family and friends then gathered could have known of the attacks on America that would come a few days later – nor from where they would come. Just the same, on a blissfully warm September Sunday, two days before the terrible events, a polite conversation of the well-meaning yielded up the line. "Those people have no respect for life." The line came up on a sneaky tangent from local wisdom snatched from some flaccid medium like *Time* magazine. Someone had heard somewhere of a growing number of executions in China. The word as it settled down on that genteel suburban scene was that the latent function of capital crimes in China was to trump up human fresh kill from which to harvest bodily organs for transplanting.

The sun shone brightly. The shade trees covered us all beside the languid pool awaiting its last swimmers of the season. The cool conversation turned ever so slightly to debate. The issue at hand was that of the precise instrument by which unwilling organ donors might be slaughtered. Since the gathering was disproportionately of medical people, talk quickly progressed to technical questions of how to kill the patients so as not to ruin the valued organs. Neither gases nor injections, not to mention electrocution, would do, as they would spoil the organ tissues. Hanging would be way too inefficient. The guillotine was proposed to some enthusiasm. But the final winner was shooting. How exactly a "patient" could be shot efficiently without spoiling the sterile surgical field was never decided as brunch was announced. Only after did it come to me that, had we been overheard by some uninvited skeptic, it would have been impossible to determine where in the world respect for human life was the less feeble.

Then, not two full days later, as if we were the butterflies that caused the storm, some of *those people* destroyed the financial heart of the capitalist empire in New York City. From which, those in authority determined that *we people* should destroy them, dead or alive, by means not immediately announced. Whichever side may be just in this or that instance, the more universal truth is that violence – the ultimate disrespect for human life – is bred without prejudice everywhere a human heart lifts up to meet the limits imposed by death. This may be the wisdom in Joyce Carol Oates's counterintuitive thought on boxing and life. Life may be a metaphor for boxing because living is a continuous succession of rounds in which survival depends on brute-naked strength. Though boxers rarely die in the ring of their sport, humans always die in the circle of their living. Human violence appears so instinctual because so few escape the daily round of body blows by which the wide-awake are reminded, as Floyd Patterson said of his beating at the hands of Ali in Las Vegas on November 22, 1965, that he came to a point where the blows no longer hurt.

> Punches began to land all over my head, and a very, very strange thing began to happen then. A happiness feeling came over me. I knew the end was near. The pain of standing up in the ring, that sharp knife in my back that accompanied every move I made, would soon end. I would soon be out. And as Clay began to land these punches, I was feeling groggy and happy. But then the referee stepped in to break us up . . . You may remember, if you saw the fight in the films, seeing me turn to the referee, shaking my head, "No, *no!*" Many people thought I was protesting his decision to stop the fight. I *really* was protesting his stopping those punches. I wanted to be hit by a really good one. I wanted to go out with a great punch[6]

The mind contorts in the pain to find a bizarre pleasure. To be human is not so much to fear death as to ward off the desire for it – a desire that surges when the daily grinds on too harshly.

In any case, capital-L Life in the West is unbearably fraught with meaning – or, more accurately, with the will to meaning. In any world culture where Life is expected to be meaningful, nothing is more satisfying to the semi-conscious soul than a healthy reminder that life might be anything but – that it might even be a lower-case sort of thing. It is possible thus that the rise to public consciousness of a boxer-trickster at a time in the 1960s when Western culture came under such scrutiny might be events connected in some mysterious way. Could it be that Cassius Clay turned into the trickster-celebrity Muhammad Ali in the days just after his defeat of Sonny Liston on February 25, 1964, *because*, just then, somehow, the world needed just such a character?

Could it be, that in some way a world culture devoted to Life-with-a-capital-L needed Muhammad Ali to set upright its false hope for ultimate meaning?

———

Early in 1964, Cassius Clay was in Miami, Florida, training for the fight with Sonny Liston at the end of February.

Late winters, south Florida is packed with visitors from the North seeking sun. Among the many who had come down from winter-bound New York was Malcolm X. He was on a mission more important than any vacation. Though his relations with Elijah Muhammad, the leader of the Nation of Islam, were already frayed to the breaking point, Malcolm remained the Nation's minister to the bright and promising athlete.

Locals to the Miami boxing world and the few sportswriters and promoters with a stake in the fight had noticed Malcolm regularly at the side of Cassius Clay. Elijah Muhammad knew of course, but he was keeping his distance. He saw the benefits for his Nation of a public association with the heavyweight champion of the world. But everyone thought that Clay was doomed for destruction by the terrifying champion. As fight night drew near, 93 percent of the sportswriters covering the fight believed Liston would win. The very few who bet on Clay were playing hunches. The Nation of Islam had nothing to gain from identification with a loser. Elijah Muhammad was using the deepening friendship between Cassius Clay and Malcolm X to cover his hand should a miracle happen.

Thus, in the most bizarre of all possible conveniences, during the first weeks of 1964, the interests of a fight world that from the first had lived off the white world's culture of aggression converged with those of the insistently black Nation of Islam. The white boxing world feared it would lose its gate if the public found out that Clay was a member of the Nation, while the Nation feared it would lose its long shot at the deep pockets of a world champion. Though there was no collusion, both sides were surely relieved when Clay agreed to ask Malcolm, his guest in Miami, to leave town for the time being.

Malcolm was under censure by the Nation for his open violation of Elijah Muhammad's decree that the Nation's ministers were to keep silent on the assassination of President Kennedy just weeks before. Elijah did not want to bring white wrath down on his movement, which had its own internal problems. Malcolm, the Nation's most brilliant and articulate leader, had become his own man. Though outwardly loyal to Elijah, in the public eye Malcolm was the personification of the Nation of Islam. Jealousy aside, the sacred status of Elijah was original doctrine in the Nation. No one could exceed the anointed leader. Not even in appearances. Elijah had to rein Malcolm in. But this was not easily done. He needed an opening, which Malcolm provided by speaking out on Kennedy's violent death. What he said was not anything new to those who followed the Nation's teachings. Still, for Malcolm at that time, when American nerves were raw, to have said that the murder of the President was nothing more than the chickens of white violence coming home to roost was an utterance that cut two ways at once – against white America and against the Nation itself. Malcolm was nothing if not shrewd. He understood the risks he took.[7] In fact, well before his censure, Malcolm had confronted Elijah Muhammad with the rumors of his sexual improprieties. The declamation on Kennedy's death was, thus, an open challenge to Elijah's authority. As a result, during the days with Cassius Clay in Miami, Malcolm could readily imagine the risks to Clay of a premature acknowledgment of his membership in the Nation. He knew what he had to do. And he did it, it would seem, because, in those days, Cassius Clay and Malcolm loved each other as brothers. Malcolm left Miami, not to return until fight night.

In a certain, but peculiar, sense, the delicate balance of interests between a white-controlled fight game and the Nation of

Islam was just one of the particular and local expressions of what was about to come down on the world at large. Though celebrity cannot arise in the global abstract, its arising tends to diminish the locale from which it took off. Already by early 1964, Louisville was fading into Clay's past. He had come to live and train in Miami with Angelo Dundee, his trainer since the 1960 Olympics. Even more, in spite of his desultory performances the previous year against Henry Cooper and Doug Jones, Cassius Clay was no longer a local boy from Kentucky. He was a figure of acclaim enough to have likely been known to Mrs Helen Trow in faraway rural New England.

Just the same, even as the celebrity gains ground on his fate, he requires a locale – a place to join with friends and supporters like Bundini and Malcolm, a place to play with children or pursue a religious life, or even a place around which to chase beautiful girls as his father had before him. Thus, when a celebrity rises to renown, as Cassius soon would, he rides the waves of the global things that come down to him in his local setting. Malcolm, Dundee, the Nation of Islam, the Miami fight crowd, and Bill MacDonald (the local promoter of the Liston fight) were the local carriers of tensions and prospects that were already straining the layers of global reality.

———

To whites, Charles Sonny Liston was as dark as dark could be. Quite apart from the black of his skin, not many tones darker than Ali's mulatto, Sonny Liston was the very essence of the mythic Black Man whites fear most. Liston's birth, sometime between 1927 and 1934, was clouded by the extreme poverty of rural life somewhere close to Forest City, Arkansas (population ca. 350). His death, sometime during the last week of December 1970, was cloaked in the explicable mystery of shady dealings in Las Vegas, Nevada. He fled the broken-down shack of his impoverished childhood by setting out to find his mother, just a boy with nothing but the clothes on his back and the sack of pecans he poached to raise the bus fare out of town and toward St Louis. He sought his mother, who had already fled the countryside in the same vain hope of a better chance in the city.

But St Louis offered scarcely more hope than the countryside. With no education to speak of, Liston could find no decent work and little to eat. What he found in St Louis was the bare bones of family and plenty of street trouble. Before long the police knew to look out for him. Arrests followed arrests; then petty crimes gave way to violence, then to prison, where he took up boxing – the one available outlet for a ferocity that feeds on the anger of a man unable to be a man by any other means. By the time Sonny Liston had risen through the ranks for his shot at the championship against Floyd Patterson in 1962, he was, to the white eye, darkness itself – angry, physically intimidating, criminal, sexually charged, menacing. He was to the white world – and there is only one other word for it – the Bad Negro himself.

On September 25, 1962, Liston pulverized Floyd Patterson in two minutes and six seconds of the first round. Fight people could not help but remember the last time a championship bout had been won in such a manner – June 22, 1938, when Joe Louis avenged his loss to Max Schmeling in but two fewer seconds. And in the recollection, the fight world drew upon the deeply held racial archetype around which modern prizefighting was organized.

As Liston was ferocity itself, Patterson was preternaturally gentle for a boxer. His abject manner grew from the same ghetto origins as did Liston's anger. Their childhoods were uncannily similar. Both were born into rural poverty in the South. Both migrated to urban poverty in the North. Both found trouble. The early difference was that Liston ended up in prison, where Patterson had the backhanded good fortune to be sent to a reform school, where he gained an education and apparently some relief from the inner fury poverty can breed. Thus, Liston's character was shaped by rage, as Patterson's was by uncertainty. The two were emotional kin by the very economic violence to which Malcolm's chickens coming home referred. This was before the days when much was understood about how the code of the street limited the chances of black men in urban ghettos.[8] Between the few able to attain the good, middle-class life and the many destined for violent crime, there were not many ways to self-respect. To face such stark alternatives with

59

a meager education is to suffer the effects of a well-imposed interior uncertainty. Patterson's emotional honesty was that he fought against it without denying its existence. Though some may find relief in confession, in the fight world, honesty leaves men like Patterson vulnerable – to themselves, most of all; and especially so, when faced with the terror of men like Liston, who cling to violence to deny the uncertainty. Whether boxing is about life, or life about boxing, the fight game is clearly about gender politics, aggravated by the racial terrors that do so much to heighten, while simultaneously frustrating, the black man's hope of becoming a *real* man.

Floyd Patterson, however, was anything but a man suited for so violent a game. The inevitability of boxing is that sooner or later, no matter how good you are, you will meet your match. If nothing else, aging assures it, as the declining body almost always comes up against the sad soul's unrelenting need to assert its manhood, again and again. A fight man who wears self-doubt on his sleeve is sure to lose sooner than later. Hence, the remarkable fact that Patterson became heavyweight champion at all, by defeating Archie Moore in 1956. He lost the crown famously in 1959 to Ingemar Johansson, then just as famously became the first heavyweight to win back the title by crushing Johansson in March 1961. But, even in triumph, Patterson's underlying character slipped out in his regret for the brutality of his win over Johansson.[9] Patterson's problem in the ring was of much more than his own making, however. Against Liston in 1962, Patterson was expected to be the Good Negro who saved the sport and, by implication, America from dishonor, as Joe Louis had against Schmeling 24 years earlier.

The Good Negro/Bad Negro themes were but a byplay of the Great White Hope that no Negro would ever reign as Jack Johnson had done early in the century. And Patterson's impossible situation was made all the worse by the tenor of the racial times. The year 1962 was still the golden age of the liberal Civil Rights Movement, a time when white hope for racial harmony rested on the prospect that a long withheld civil justice would be sop enough to quell the demand for economic justice that stood behind Malcolm's appeal. The civil rights ideal of black and white together would collapse soon enough. But in the summer of 1962, just weeks before Patterson's fight with Liston, the violence to which black and white freedom riders were victim brought home the urgency of a civil right and wrong. The freedom riders were doing nothing more than testing their rights of interracial access to public, interstate bus travel. At stop after stop, white and black riders alike were mercilessly beaten by white racist toughs whose manly prospects in Alabama were nearly as unsettled as were the urban fortunes of men like Liston and Patterson. Barely a year remained before Malcolm's chickens would come home – in the murder of a black civil rights worker Medgar Evers, on June 12, 1963, and, just months later, the assassination of John F. Kennedy in November. That Kennedy had been killed in the South did little to alleviate the initial fear that his growing commitment to civil justice was behind it all. Still today, the idea that an ideologically confused, aimless white man like Lee Harvey Oswald could have been the sole shooter stretches the reasonable mind. But whatever that truth might be, Malcolm was surely speaking a powerful truth. When racial violence bred of economic deprivation comes into the open, the chickens lay their deadly eggs.

Thus, by the time Patterson, the Good Negro, faced the archetypal Bad Negro in late September 1962, he was expected to defend much more than his title, or even his manhood. He was expected, that is, to defend the inner confusion of the American ideal itself. President Kennedy himself had implied as much by inviting Patterson to the White House before the Liston fight to instruct him on the grave national importance of his beating "that guy."[10] By this imperial edict, Kennedy laid down the popular "we." Those were the days when whites of privilege used "we" with impunity. The President of the United States of America hardly needed to explain himself to Floyd Patterson, who knew what was demanded – as surely, he also knew how unlikely he was to deliver.

Imagine the pressure of bearing all the expectations of the white world, along with those of the black. In those days, before Malcolm's message took hold, before even Black Power became the word of the day, before more than a few understood the global implications of the revolt of African and Caribbean colonies against the white colonizers, racial messages came most often in two forms. In the underbelly of the colonized regions they were blunt and vicious insults paid on the threat of public hangings. In the open of the colonizer's society, they were refracted, pronounced often in the most unthinking ways, such as calling the housekeeper by the first name while expecting the formal family name in return. Boxing, however, was one of those places outside the underbelly and apart from polite society, where the truth of it all came into play.

Negro champions were expected, if not to take a stand on the race wars, at least to subject themselves to the impossible expectations of serving as icons of the race. In 1962, that meant being an exemplary Negro – one able to personify the white search for a peaceful solution to the civil rights drama that was playing itself out. The Good Negro/Bad Negro figures came down through the years to settle, in due course, on the backs of Patterson and Liston. And against Liston, Patterson was necessarily the Good Negro. The trope of a Good Negro was of course a figurative expression of white hope masking fear. Its modern origins in the fight game are very well known.

———

Jack Johnson (1878–1946) was the first Negro boxing champion of the modern era. Other blacks had been comparably good, but none was allowed to face-off for the championship. Johnson was so far superior to all comers that the authenticity of the crown would have been compromised had he not been permitted to challenge in due course. He won the championship in 1908 and held it against all comers for eight years. During his defiant reign, Johnson changed the name of the game in more ways than one. If there was a heavyweight who could dance like Cassius Clay, it was Johnson. If there was a black man who could infuriate and terrify whites as Liston would a half-century later, it was Johnson. In the ring, Jack Johnson stuck it to the whites by defeating everyone who challenged him – until 1915, when finally Jesse Willard knocked him out in the twentieth round. Until then, no one, white or black, had touched him.

As a fighter, Papa Jack was so superior that he took apparent pleasure but little risk in toying with his white opponents. Though a brilliant offensive fighter, he would regularly fight on the defensive, simply to tease white opponents – thus to wear them down and demoralize them. On a few occasions, before dressing to fight, he wrapped his penis in towels – this to remind whites gathered about the ring of what they feared most and why they wanted him destroyed. In the days of Jim Crow, most white people still held fast to the notion that blacks were inferior in all ways. Until Johnson came along, it was felt that no black could stand up to a good white fighter. Behind the ideology was, of course, the fear that gave rise to the search for a Great White Hope – a white man who could reaffirm white masculine prowess. The search was a desperate one. When Johnson lost to Willard in Cuba, he was 38 years old, an old 38 at that. Drink, sex, fast driving, nights partying had extracted their price. Still, Johnson was somewhat an exception to the rule that fight men fight on to prove their manhood. In the ring, at least, he fought on not to prove something so much as to earn money for legal bills and the ever-present expenses of his fast life.

It is hard to say to what extent Johnson's fast, very public life and open sexual exploits were his way of proving a point outside the ring that was all too well proven inside. It does seem that in his personal life he was driven to rub salt in the racial wounds he opened inside. Jim Crow racism was like racism wherever it rears its head, but with one difference. White hatred of the Negro was open. While fighting, Jack Johnson heard the nigger-slurs. He met them with cool indifference. In his personal life, defiance took the form of going openly with white women. Whether prostitutes or wives (or both), Johnson traveled with young white women who hungered for what he had to offer.[11] Just as the ringside hecklers tried to do him in emotionally, so the law-and-order cops tried to get him legally for his sexual offenses. After many failures, the government finally won a conviction in 1913, on the false witness of one of Johnson's rejected lovers.

The oddity of the White Slave Traffic Act – better known as the Mann Act – was that, though it seemed aimed at the sexual exploitation of innocent girls, the very use of the remarkable expression "white slave" suggested the deep currents whereby American Puritanism had nearly as much to do with race as with sex. In any case, Johnson may well have been the most notorious of those actually convicted under the Mann Act, and this in spite of the fact that many of the women he was alleged to have dishonored were well-known prostitutes. Before sentencing, Johnson fled the country for Europe, eventually for Cuba, where he lost his title to Willard. In time, as his welcome abroad grew short, Johnson returned to the United States to serve his sentence, then to live out his life on his own terms. He left prison as self-assured as he had always been, and immediately resumed the life of an impeccably well-dressed man of the world.[12] He was killed on June 10, 1946, on the way to see Joe Louis's second fight with Billy Conn, a latter-day Great White Hope. He died as he lived, driving his Lincoln Zephyr too fast for the road. He died, as he had lived – too fast for the racial times.

There is no doubt that Ali had Jack Johnson very much in mind, especially so upon returning in 1970 from a conviction for draft evasion every bit as trumped up as was Johnson's for sexual prowess. But in Ali's first fight after the United States Supreme Court vacated his conviction, Ali vindicated two black men at once.

> That night Ali defeated Jerry Quarry. He cut open the white fighter's eye in the third round. It was an awful mess. Throughout the short fight, Drew "Bundini" Brown, Ali's cornerman and alterego, kept repeating, "Jack Johnson's *heah*!" And, "Ghost in the house! Ghost in the house!" Ali was being vindicated. So was Jack Johnson. Or so it seemed to many.[13]

Jack Johnson was indeed a ghost – and for many more than Ali.

Johnson was the ghost that breathed upon the search for a white man able to gain and keep the crown of masculine prowess. For a good 22 years after Johnson was finally beaten, no black man was given a chance to fight for the heavyweight title – not until Joe Louis (like Johnson, too good to be denied) defeated

James Braddock on June 22, 1937. The ghost of Papa Jack Johnson was upon Louis, even before the championship and certainly after. It was of course behind Louis's second fight with Max Schmeling exactly one year to the day after he became champion. But the ghost was present even more in the demands upon his personal life. Like Johnson, Louis was pursued by women, including white ones. Like Johnson, his sexual life was prodigious. But Joe's backers imposed strict rules. He was never to be seen in public with a white partner; nor was he to say anything in public that was not deferential.[14] But Louis was merely a carrier of Jack Johnson's ghost, which even more terrifyingly haunted Floyd Patterson the night he fought the return of the Bad Negro, Sonny Liston. By 1967, when Ali refused the call to military service in Vietnam, the Bad Negro ghost had lingered on full force in American racial consciousness. With tepid Good Negro ghosts of Joe and Floyd fixed in the white mind, Ali's refusal could only be viewed as BAD. He was pursued and convicted of draft evasion for no other reason than this elemental principle of the American racial code.[15]

The ghost of *the* BAD Black Man has always haunted the modern fight game. A ghost is the lie of a past that will not die. Whites attacked Jack Johnson, whose racial defiance led to the prolonged cycle of pursuit and evasion until, finally, conviction. The truth of white rage is always crooked. So too, Joe Louis's virtuous colored man was a false cover of white liberal sincerity. And when Louis avenged his defeat by Max Schmeling, he was put forth as the personification of American good against Hitler's evil. In turning the two different forms of national racism on their heads, Joe Louis became very probably the first black in America who was adored by whites. But the ghost was present still, in the foolish words of Jimmy Cannon that Louis was "A credit to his race – the human race." This now immortal line says all there is to say about white racial politics. To credit Louis as a member of the human race in this way is precisely to reinforce the prior, deeper conviction that his race did not count. From 1915, when Johnson lost the crown, until 1964, when Cassius Clay won it, the race card was played out by the open rejection of black fighters or, after 1934, when Louis won it, by the insistence that they toe the line of sexual and racial neutrality, which of course is anything but neutral. This was the ghost that haunted Floyd Patterson, and the system Sonny Liston destroyed when he crushed the Good Negro in 1962.

———

Thus it was that Cassius Clay's fight with Sonny Liston in 1964 turned the culture of the fight world upside down. Liston, the bad, was not anyone new. He was by then the eerie shadow of Johnson, different only in that he had dismantled Patterson, a black man required to stand in for the good enough white ones who could not be found. But Cassius Clay, when he entered the ring on February 25, 1964, was already something else – a man neither-good-nor-bad, neither white nor black – beyond understanding to the ways of racially ignorant whites. He was ready to break the mold of America's racial obsession, as he would soon enough overturn the global culture of racial differences.

Most shocking of all to those who had caught Clay's act as he rose through the ranks was his loud mouth. His childlike yelps of greatness put off all but the more astute who saw the connection to show business – to Gorgeous George, even Little Richard. But somehow that sort of self-promotion was not fit for the serious business of the fight game. Wrestling, perhaps. Legitimate theater, surely. But boxing was about life, even if life is not like boxing. And apart from the high-mindedness of it all, in America in 1964 – the ghost of Jack Johnson having been suffocated by the debilitating cultural demands imposed on Joe Louis and Floyd Patterson – there was no public nomenclature for a black man who proclaimed his superiority to whites, then asserted it. Whites at the time, save for the very few who had truly crossed the color line, mostly had Martin Luther King, Jr, in mind when they thought of the new black man, and though King scared them in his own way, they were at least relieved by his call for nonviolence. Men like Malcolm and Cassius – not to mention Stokely Carmichael, the Black Panthers, and others who would soon come on the Black Power scene – were barely thinkable.

The very idea of Black Power, articulated by men and women able to destroy, by word or fist or worse, had been the darkest and most enduring fear of the enforcers of the racial caste system in the United States. This was a fear that made its racism more peculiar, if not worse in effect, than the racisms of the rest of the European diaspora. Even in South Africa, more terrible in its consequences than all the rest, apartheid, being a matter of law, was openly vicious. In the United States, since Lincoln's Emancipation Proclamation in 1863, what the law had forbidden was energized by feelings repressed under the sheets of furtive violence. The Great White Hope was thus very much more than the idle play of gentleman fighters. It was in its way at the heart of the American way of racial injustice.

Ghosts are serious business. They are leakings of the repressed, tremors of the unconscious. They come to life on such living forms as they may find. Jack Johnson was, in the word often used, the shadow of the white man's fears – sex, defiance, violence, and disconcertingly literate. It is seldom mentioned that Johnson, in his way, was literate in the same fashion as Cassius Clay was – unschooled, yet articulate in the ways of the spoken word as of the cultures of the worlds they challenged. One of the reasons why it took the government so long to convict Johnson of any criminal complaint, even a phony one, was that he knew precisely how to handle himself. Randy Roberts, for example, describes Johnson's demeanor at trial when his trouble was most severe:

> As Jack Johnson spoke in his own defense, his hand wandered aimlessly toward his left thigh. He was in trouble – serious trouble – but his face didn't register it. Instead of a worried frown he wore an inscrutable smile. Although on trial for violating the White Slave Traffic Act, he refused to look contrite. His voice registered nothing but scorn for Harry A. Parkin, the United States District Attorney who was questioning him. Yes, Johnson said, he had known many white prostitutes, and he had traveled across America with a few of them. And yes, he knew the government's star witness, Belle Schreiber, particularly well.... Yes, there were a few times when the two spent some nights together, like the time in August 1910 when Belle came to Jack in Atlantic City. She came to him, he emphasized, and why shouldn't she? After all, he had just beaten the great Jim Jeffries for the undisputed heavyweight championship.[16]

What more perfect cultural literacy can there be than for a man on the spot to know exactly what will unsettle his opponent the most – and then openly to speak it? Belle came to Jack for sex precisely because he had defeated the best white man around.

Johnson's literacy was of a different kind from Clay's, if only because Cassius was already living with Jack Johnson's ghost and the havoc it had wreaked. But Clay had the very same ability to face trouble in and out of the ring and to say precisely what he wanted to say. George Plimpton tells the story of being present at a public lecture Ali gave at Saunders Theater at Harvard.[17] The room was packed with several thousand of America's finest young minds. Still, Ali, who was not even a legitimate high school graduate, charmed them all. By the end, the crowd clamored for a poem. Without pause, he said "Me/ We" – in Plimpton's view the shortest poem in the English language and in any case as affecting a way to win a crowd's heart as can be dreamed. The students swooned.

Johnson and Clay both possessed a poetic genius that, though different according to their different times and natures, bespoke the very literacy that inspired the white man's terror of black social competence. It was, in effect, the very sort of cultural literacy that Frederick Douglass stole from the hungry white boys he tricked into teaching him to read and write. When Douglass learned in time to speak, he spoke as none other born to shackles. He became, thereby, in America and much of Europe, one of the first to upset the cautiously settled world of white hopes of black inferiority.[18] When the dispossessed speak, they put the lie to the truth power represses. In being the same, they are capable of being superior.

Still, Cassius Clay was another character, perhaps one of an even more delicate finesse than Jack Johnson. As he did at Harvard one day, he had been doing ever since he came into the public eye at the 1960 Rome Olympics. It is likely there was guile in the theft of the Gorgeous George act, but no one can plan to return "Me/We" on a moment's notice. Charm of the sort Ali has runs deep in the soul. He was an innocent in Rome, where he was the loveable boy-mayor of the Olympic Village, but not so innocent as to be the mere boy that people hoped he would remain. Whites who cared must have thought of his charm as that of the black boy in his place – the one who dances for coins as 12-year-old Cassius had hoped to do the day his bike was stolen and it all began in Joe Martin's gym. But Clay's charm and spontaneous wit gradually won over a good many of those in the know in boxing culture, and even some of those like Jimmy Cannon who were quite convinced that no fighter could win a championship on speed and taunts and hands held low. It just wasn't done.

No one who cared about the sport – and for that matter no one who opened himself to the true nature of black people – had ever seen a fighter, much less a black man, like Clay. He was to them, to us, strange in a way that stretched our racial vocabularies. This elemental fact of his way of being human conspired with the unexamined belief that Sonny Liston was invincible. Liston had, after all, twice slaughtered Floyd Patterson, the black White Man's Hope. The world was thus set up for the fall it took the night of the first Liston–Clay fight. It is entirely likely that Clay knew what he was doing – playing the clown, working the crowd, raising the gate. The act worked, as the trickster knew it would, and never better than in the performance he put on at the ritual weigh-in before the fight.

Long before the day of the fight, before even the fight had been agreed to, Cassius Clay had set out to disturb the imperturbable Liston. In the years before, Clay had several times confronted Liston in public with his act – once at a Las Vegas casino (where Liston may have gotten the upper hand), another time in Denver when Clay drove to Liston's house in the middle of the night, reporters and cameramen in tow. Liston had already gotten the picture of Clay. But what was the image that may have haunted him? Clay continued the public torments in Miami by greeting Liston's arrival at the airport, then pursuing him into the city, each time calling him a chump, an ugly bear – the kind of juice that stings behind the hard visage, just as, a decade later, it stung Joe Frazier to be called an Uncle Tom. Clay had to have known in the 1960s that Liston was sensitive to the public hostility to his reign as champion, just as in the 1970s he surely knew that Joe Frazier's racial pride ran deep. Frazier never forgave Ali, and it would be hard to imagine that Liston could have forgotten Clay's taunts. In Miami, Liston twice tried to intimidate the young man. Twice Clay offered to fight him on the spot, while repeating the insults. Of these face-to-face encounters, David Remnick has shrewdly observed that Liston could not have failed to "notice that Clay, for all his featherweight speed, was a big man, taller than himself."[19] Clay had exactly what Patterson lacked – a confidence to read the situation, to understand his opponent – confidence enough to calm what fears he must have had of Liston.

The two Liston–Clay fights in February 1964 and May 1965 are among the most controversial in boxing history. Even today, almost four decades later, when Ali stills reigns as one of the world's most adored people, there are fight people who refuse to believe what they saw in those fights. It is perfectly understandable why, in early 1964, so many would find it impossible to believe that Clay could beat Liston, or even to imagine that Clay himself could seriously believe he would win. Thus, it was, and still is, hard to figure Clay's act at the weigh-in on fight day.[20]

At the pre-fight weigh-in Cassius Clay's behavior was so certifiably nuts that even his trainer, Angelo Dundee, described him as crazy. Clay and his entourage had mistakenly arrived an hour early for the weigh-in, which probably aggravated whatever he was feeling inside. Unmistakably, his plan was to continue the show of taunts and professions of his own greatness. When, after an hour's wait, the weigh-in took place, Clay was so outrageous as to have been fined by the local boxing authorities, a group generally able to tolerate extremes of all kinds. All this would have been consistent with the Cassius show. One can certainly act out the crazy man routine. But what certified Clay's mania, if not his state of mind, was that his blood pressure was 200 over 100 and his pulse more than twice his normal of 54. It is much more difficult to act out such startling measures of the body's autonomic reflexes.[21] The boxing commission doctor threatened to cancel the fight if his blood pressure did not come down by fight time. According to David Remnick, the word got around so well that there were rumors that Cassius was frightened enough of Liston to have fled town. Yet, whether for show or for real, the only significant person to have been persuaded of Clay's insanity was Liston. Surely Clay was way over the top of even his maniacal personality. But insane? Who is to say? And which one, between Clay and Liston, was the more frightened? Liston's wife Geraldine was quoted as saying just before fight time that Sonny felt Clay was "out of his cotton-picking mind...and you never know what to expect from a madman."[22]

So who was the more frightened? Though Clay admitted later to his fear, the fact is that by fight time his cardiovascular numbers were well within normal. In the afternoon and early evening he had followed routine – ate, rested, amused himself. And, before final preparations, he had actually napped. At the face-off before round 1, as he stood above Liston, Clay resumed his taunts. The show was on. From the opening bell Clay took the offensive. His speed was obvious. His talk continued. The second round was like the first. Clearly the betting odds were wrong, way wrong. At ringside, Joe Louis, by then addled from drugs and the effects of the fight life, called the first one of the greatest rounds he'd seen in a long time. In the third round, Clay's barrage of left hooks opened a cut over Liston's right eye. The upset seemed assured until, late in the fourth round, Clay began to wince. He could not see. Something was burning his eyes.

To this day no one knows what burned Clay's eyes. The astringent used to close wounds like Liston's could well have gotten on his gloves by accident – or something could have been put there intentionally to blind Clay. Cuts are the worst that can happen in the ring. Nothing stirs the cutter and cripples the bleeder like the flow of blood. Quite apart from the injury itself, the blood can blind the fighter, as it can the judges. There are no points for bleeding well. Defeat was in the air, and Liston's was heavy over the ring. The prospect shocked everyone, most of all those with money on Liston. The odds in his favor had been so great that many supposed that sinister forces could have ordered an extreme measure to protect their investment.

Though Clay was backed by the lawful businessmen of Louisville, Liston's mob connections were more the rule of the day. Until Clay changed the rule, the presence of racketeering was another of the more prominent shadows cast over boxing. The huge capital investment necessary to find, prepare, and train a championship fighter was far beyond the resources of any individual fighter, especially so in a day when box office purses and television deals were nothing compared to what they have become today. In his day, Jack Johnson was one of the few to control his finances, which he did by controlling the film rights to his fights. He was the rare exception. In 1964, fixing the outcomes to fix the odds was both a motive for investment and a means for recovering sunk costs. Hence the suspicions, aggravated all the more by the well-known fact of Liston's criminal record and prior association with the underworld. Even if the temporary damage done to Clay's vision was by accident, Liston's innocence was scarcely believable.

Between rounds, the pain and confusion were so great that Clay demanded his gloves be cut off. He wanted out, and for good reason. Apart from the pain itself, to be blind in a small ring against a man of Liston's ferocity – a rage already aggravated by years of taunt and three rounds of inflicted pain and blood – was indeed to face an ugly bear. Who wouldn't want out? But Angelo Dundee, Cassius Clay's brilliant and wise trainer, refused to throw in the towel. He literally pushed his man into the fifth round, seconds before the fight would have been called for Liston. Had he not, there would have been no Muhammad Ali, and the world would have been a different, probably lesser, place. For much of the fifth round, Clay tried to avoid Liston by instinct and cunning. He had no other defense. Liston of course was punishing him. Then, halfway through the round, Cassius's eyes began to clear.

From then on, Liston's fate was sealed. Clay reopened the cut, which by the sixth round exposed the underlying flesh. Liston made it through the round, but as the seventh was about to begin, the fight was called. Clay had won. Muhammad Ali was soon to come.

———

Cassius Clay was defiant in victory. Another of the unforget-table images of him shows the new champion leaning over the ropes – his right hand pumping high, a wide-eyed comic look on his face – yelling at the sportscasters below at ringside, "Eat your words!"[23] Always his own man, Cassius Clay's defiance was, however, worlds apart from Jack Johnson's. Where the original Bad Negro was cool, merciless, and utterly superior, Clay at such moments was, if not quite boyish, at least a little comic, and always one to engage those about him, those whom he had seduced and tricked before the great moment.

The ring itself was chaotic. Liston's men were attending to him. Reporters and officials alike, along with Clay's cornermen, joined the pandemonium. Film clips of the moment show Clay pushed by the crowd, shouting toward the microphone that carried his words, toward the crowd, toward the world beyond. The words are hard to hear, but the message is clear:

> I am the greatest!...I don't have a mark on my face...I upset Sonny Liston...I just turned twenty-two years old...I must be the greatest...I showed the world...Tell the world...I talk to God every day...the real God...I'm the King of the world... I shook up the world...I am the prettiest thing that ever lived.[24]

The whole script is there – the greatest, the prettiest, the youngest, king of the world. The few at ringside who may have actually heard the words might have noticed how out of keeping certain of them were – words that would soon and dramatically shake up the world: "I talk to God everyday...the real God."

Malcolm X returned to Cassius Clay's side after the fight. Clay, still afraid of flying, drove north to New York. He stayed in Harlem's Hotel Theresa. Malcolm openly showed him about town. The days of Cassius Clay were numbered. The Ali to come was no longer in the closet. He was a member of the Nation of Islam. Just days later, on March 6, he would be honored by Elijah Muhammad with the sacred, now familiar name, Muhammad Ali. The price of admission to his new life was the loss of his friend. On orders from the minister of the Nation, Ali broke with Malcolm just before he made his famous pilgrimage to Mecca on a post-fight tour of Africa. Malcolm was hurt, and rightly so, by Ali's rejection. His effort to reach across his own exclusion from the Nation to his one-time brother was treated with disdain – most terribly when Malcolm and Ali met by chance in Accra, Ghana, and Ali refused even to speak to Malcolm. Malcolm had just shy of a year before he would be murdered by agents of the Nation that had largely, if not entirely, taken over the younger man's life. Ali was, in fact, a very young and immature man, who had all of a sudden become an international figure. Whatever Elijah Muhammad was not, he was at least a man able to attract the confidence of his followers, and Ali surely had need of guidance. Though he would remain faithful to Islam for the rest of his days, Ali later regretted his mistreatment of the man he had once loved.

Ali shook up the fight world in Miami. But, even more, he shook up the wider world when he came out as a member of the Nation of Islam. On February 25, after the fight, he had the world in his hands. In the days following, as it became clear that he was truly someone other, and more, than a silly if brilliant little boy, he immediately lost the mostly white half of the world he shook up. If in 2001, few in the European diaspora understood much at all about Islam, imagine how few in 1965 could even begin to fathom the relatively small American movement, the Nation of Islam. All that most could figure was that people like Elijah Muhammad and Malcolm X were strange to their habits of mind. Apart from their threat to the American system of racial things, America's black Muslims *had* to be, as the logic of the times went, agents of a foreign power. This was, remember, just ten years after the end of the worst of the Red Scare in the United States and a good two decades before Ronald Reagan would speak of the Evil Empire. Cold War thinking was nothing if not suspicious of anything it could not understand as unmistakably local, familiar, and loyal to the simple-minded code of the good scout. And, thus, a storm came down on Ali's victory parade.

Muhammad Ali was treated with a contempt that made the pre-fight insult that he was nothing more than a loud-mouthed brat seem mild by contrast. In retrospect, the reasons are plain to see. Where Jack Johnson wrapped his racial defiance in the towel of prodigious sexual potency, Ali turned the racial trick on white America. He took upon himself one of the most American of all cultural traits – what President Dwight Eisenhower had called "faith in faith" – and became more deeply religious than the superficially pious Eisenhower with his American religion. The idea that the Nation of Islam was for some African Americans a uniquely American response to racism was at the time as unthinkable as it would have been for whites to criticize America's one truly indigenous religion, the Church of the Latter-Day Saints, for its overt racism. The Mormons were (and, to some, still are) quite bizarre in many of their ways, but not in their racism.[25] The idea, by contrast, that African Americans could reject white America in the name of a world religion so foreign was as strange as it was for Malcolm to discover on his pilgrimage to Mecca that in Islam white people bowed side by side with colored people. This discovery changed Malcolm's deep racial hatred of whites, thus revealing him to have been the moral superior he was feared to be. Those who hated Malcolm X and now Muhammad Ali because they were American blacks who embraced Islam were truly the moral inferiors. Once again, America's obsession with race reverted to its deep unconscious denominator – and just at the moment when the Civil Rights Movement was educating, at least, the nation on the ways race matters. The turning around of the racial worlds moved on both sides of the color line. Ali was not alone in this. By the end of 1965, and especially in 1966, the slogan and reality of Black Power had begun to force Americans to consider what many Europeans had faced over the preceding two decades of rebellion in their African colonies. The world's colored people were neither children nor obsequious admirers of the colonizer's culture. Ali was very far from being a first mover in all this, any more than were the Panthers and other Black Power proponents. He and they were swept along, as were Malcolm X and Martin Luther King and their followers, by the rising tide of global resistance to white rule. The global movement was finding its way into every nook and cranny of the European diaspora.

Though Ali did not suffer as did the millions left to their own economic misery in Africa, or as did the blacks in the First World who were shot down by local police, he was made to suffer. At the moment of his greatest achievement, he was brutalized by those who thought of his rejection of white largesse as treasonous. He would of course suffer even more famously in the years to follow as his religious principles led him into direct conflict with the American state, including its vast judicial and military machines. But for the two years after his defeat of Liston, the attacks on Ali were verbal for the most part, and muted at that by his own evident brilliance as a showman in and out of the ring. He was hard to deny. Still, the suspicion that rode on the culture's long-denied racial fears entered even the ring.

Ali gave Liston a rematch, as tradition, if not the rule, allowed. There was trouble of all kinds, however, in finding a city that would accept the fight. Local authorities wanted nothing to do with Ali, and especially not with the menacing Fruit of Islam that were now the most visible members of his entourage. After the contract with his Louisville sponsors expired, Ali was managed by the Nation, in particular Herbert Muhammad, Elijah's son. Ali was transformed, as he had begun to transform the racial typecast he refused to accept.

Muhammad Ali's most famous retort to the endless questions and challenges to his new life was, "I don't have to be what you want me to be." All previous boxing champions had been what the culture wanted them to be. Joe Louis and Floyd Patterson had succumbed to the pressure – the one trusting foolishly that it would win him credit in his later years, the other despising himself for doing what his nature made him do. But the damage done to Sonny Liston by the prevailing norms of racial culture was, notwithstanding everything else, a tragic story – and never more so than on the day of his arrival home after winning the championship in 1962. Liston the champion was ready to do and be good; and thus he had every reason to expect an official welcome in Philadelphia, certainly a crowd of some size. When he deplaned, there was no one – not even a third-rate official from the mayor's office, not even a small crowd – but for the ground crews. Sonny Liston was meant to be the Bad Negro, and not even in triumph would he be permitted to forget it. When a culture expects a group, or a representative of that group, to keep to the role for which it has been cast, every effort is made to make sure places are kept.

It is said that culture is a process. And surely it is. But, much like the workings of the unconscious mind, it is devilishly difficult to say how exactly a culture does its work, especially its work of exclusion. On Liston's sad day in Philadelphia, it is plain that the political leaders had decided to keep their distance from the city's bad man, just as early in the century America's legal eagles had set out to punish Jack Johnson, the Bad Negro who haunted Liston. But how did it happen that no one from among the legions of sports-crazed boys and men of that or any other city determined not to go to the airport at least to ogle the man? I once taught at a college when one of its sports teams had won a championship of some kind. The college town was small, with no local media. Yet the word got out that the team was arriving at midnight. I wrapped my boys up and went out to witness the arrival of a team about which I cared very little – and there was a crowd! How does it work, by contrast, that in one of the country's largest cities there weren't at least a few goofballs like me with nothing better to do but look in on some local celebrity's arrival? Such a thing could never be organized. It has to come from the repressing work of some hard-to-define social unconscious. Had it not been America, with its deep confusions about race, the abuse of one of boxing's most brilliantly bad Negroes would make no sense at all. But even if it makes sense, how it works is hard to say. But it does.

Shared hatred that arises from fear works all the more openly when its source comes into the open as someone at once both utterly respectable and sternly at odds with the prevailing norms by which comfort is provided. Muhammad Ali was surely a black man, but not any sort of black whites could figure. They could learn to tolerate the clown, even a clown who could fight and win. But a clown who professed open allegiance to a group at once defiant and inscrutable turns upside down all the norms and manners of a culture. And the effect, like the cause, is at once visible and invisible.

––––––––

Ali's rematch with Sonny Liston was ultimately set for May 25, 1965, after much trouble (including a postponement required by emergency surgery on Ali due to an acute inguinal hernia). The assassination of Malcolm X on February 21, 1965, had sharpened the alarm at Ali's relations with the Nation of Islam. The venue was a boys' club in Lewiston, Maine – a small, industrial town in remote northern New England. At least there, among other reasons, it was thought that black men bent on violence would be easily spotted. Still, the security precautions were extraordinary, and the crowd may have been fewer than the 4,000 some estimated. Only income from the remote broadcast saved the promoters from ruin. But nothing saved those who came to Lewiston from the astonishing way Ali won the fight. Liston, in spite of losing the championship, was still the favorite. Once again Ali defied the odds. It took him but minutes to certify the legitimacy of his win in Miami. The fight was so short that some in the sparse crowd had not even taken their seats. Thomas Hauser's description of the action is one of the more plausible by one of those who believed their eyes.

> What...many...missed was a near-perfect punch that some swore never landed. Ali landed only three blows of consequence in the fight. The first came just after the opening bell, when he rushed across the ring and surprised Liston with a straight right. Then, a minute later, another right stunned the challenger. Liston continued to move forward, trying desperately to cut off the ring. He jabbed. Ali pulled back to make him miss, planted his left foot for leverage, pivoted off his right foot for power, and counterpunched with a straight right that landed flush on Liston's jaw. The force of the blow lifted Liston's left foot, which was balancing most of his weight, and sent the challenger tumbling to the floor.[26]

Ali was himself shocked by the knockdown, worried perhaps that no one would believe it. He stood over Liston, yelling for him to get up and fight. This caused a delay in the count. Ali was finally ushered to a neutral corner. Liston never heard the count until it was too late. The fight was called. Ali had won in no more time than it had taken Liston to establish his own reputation against Patterson. But in this case confusion reigned.

Had Liston taken a dive? To the day of his death, even until now, no one has answered that question, and no one ever will. When a fighter is both bad and a proven criminal, when as well he is in the pocket of the mob, a fixed outcome is always possible – especially as it is likely that the underworld betting interests took a loss on the first fight. Since Liston was nearly a two-to-one favorite, the loss could have been recouped all at once. Liston himself claimed that he wasn't about to get on his feet with a nut like Ali standing over him.[27] The fear that Ali had worked so hard to promote may well have come to improbable fruition that night. Still, today, there are as few who suppose Ali could have lost had Liston gotten up in time as there are those who believe they saw the blow or that it was enough to put down one of boxing's most powerful champions. Even Ali joked about the punch, calling it at first his anchor punch (after one in Jack Johnson's repertoire), then in time his phantom punch.[28]

The fight was investigated, as from time to time the righteous do. There was no evidence of a fix (not even of unusual betting for Ali). As the years passed, there was, however, ample evidence that Ali was perfectly capable of such a crushing victory. Still, there are those who believe Liston took a dive. Once a Bad Negro, always so. How could it be otherwise? Or is the suspicion founded as much on the doubt that any man of Ali's apparent racial politics could be so good as to destroy a man like Liston with such ease? What makes the suspicion surrounding Ali's victories over Liston itself suspect is that so much subsequent history gives Ali the nod, several times over. At least three times in the years remaining to Ali's boxing career, he overcame odds just as daunting as those against him in the first Liston fight or against the probability he was capable of the speed and power of the rematch. His two victories over Joe Frazier, not to mention his stunning upset of George Foreman in 1974, were considered every bit as improbable, against

79

opponents then younger than he and just as terrifying as Liston had been. Yet he won.

There was something about Ali that made his exploits unbelievable, in several ways at once. That something endures to blind the skeptics to the most striking fact of all. No one, not even Sonny Liston himself, knew when he was born. He might have been born in 1927, which would have made him 38 years old, ancient for a fighter – even one in excellent condition, as Liston was.[29] Plus which Liston had never really been challenged before Ali. Thus, what some overlook is that the most remarkable thing about Sonny Liston that night in 1965 was that he was so very well conditioned given his age. The outcomes likely were those of a brilliant, very young man defeating a powerful, very old one. But still, when it comes to the race thing, facts seldom matter as they should.

So Ali shook up the world in several ways at once. In the ring, he was like no one before him. Even more, Ali broke the cultural mold into which black men were forced. Try as the cultural process might, it could not fit him into the Good/Bad Negro scheme, and thus it could not figure his racial nature against white fear of the darkness. And try as it might, neither could the world's tangled culture of racial confusion account for his peculiar new religion with its racial politics of hatred returned on the white devils. It would soon come into play that the only believable theory of his religious affiliation was that he was brainwashed by the Nation, a theory his own father unwittingly advanced: *Black men can't possibly think or believe for themselves – at least not when those who try to think must think outside their long-held mental categories of racial understanding.*

But the facts are quite otherwise. Though the influence of the Nation on Ali was unquestionably powerful enough to force him ruthlessly to abandon his friend Malcolm, it was not powerful enough to cause him to accept the theory of white devils. Though Ali professed, and practiced, the Nation's theory of separation of the races, he never once held rigidly to the white devil dogma. Not only did Angelo Dundee and Ferdie Pacheco, among other whites, remain by his side, but Ali himself enjoyed playful and comfortable relations with white people, most notably the always irritating Howard Cosell. While there was a public convenience for both in the now famous Ali–Cosell friendship, every indication is that it was sincerely felt. You would suppose that had Ali hated whites, he could have found a less obnoxious one to love.

––––––––

But none of the nuances of Ali's athletic prowess and racial trickery, as confounding as they were to the prevailing culture, come close to exhausting the list of ways Ali would shake up the world. Much more would come, such that this trickster-celebrity would become ever more than an icon of his race. Those stories would take on their social force as early as 1967. But for the time of his first several years as champion, the trouble he inspired was already there to be seen.

To speak today, if not in 1965, of someone queering the world, or queering any social arrangement, is to say several things at once. The expression is known to have been used even before the word *queer* served as an epithet for homosexuals.[30] And it continues today, after the epithet was itself turned on its head to serve as a slogan for queer politics – that is, the politics of gay, lesbian, and other-than-heterosexual pride. To queer, simply put, is to set an arrangement into confusion. To queer, thereby, is the work of the trickster who works against a received cultural system under conditions where little can be done to overthrow an oppressive political formation. To queer is to trick the culture, when the political and economic powers are still entrenched enough to limit the hope of fundamental social change.

These were the kinds of times the young Ali played upon in the early years. Even as late as 1965 – with Lyndon Johnson in the White House, the Cold War still the word of the world, the war in Vietnam just getting serious – the liberal system of beliefs and practices was largely unquestioned. In America, at least, the Cold War had undercut left-wing politics. There was no well-institutionalized Left, and hardly any sort of Marxist politics of the kind that flourished in the 1930s. The coming of black radicals like Malcolm was, in a sense, the first truly indigenous radical politics that anyone not raised in or before the Thirties in New York City and a few other locales had experienced. What

Americans of the vast middle knew of politics was limited for the most part to Franklin Roosevelt's patrician progressivism (not well liked), Ike Eisenhower's grandfatherly conservativism (liked very well), and JFK's odd political mix of inspired liberal rhetoric and old-fashioned conservative foreign policy (liked better than you would think). Neither Harry Truman nor Lyndon Johnson mattered. Neither made political sense. Neither was real enough in his own right, and neither inspired a political movement. The student movement was yet to turn radical. Black Power was still months away. And opposition to the war in Vietnam had still three years to go before it joined the other protests to shake the nation. Trouble was coming. This was evident. But, for the years between 1963 and 1965, the old order was still in control. This was the political reality of Ali's youth.

Plus which, Ali himself was never a political man. The politics of his religion were, if anything, deeply conservative, as are all separationist movements. Still, Ali's unusual sort of cultural literacy provoked political consequences, as would be completely evident in 1967 when, even to his own amazement, his refusal of service in Vietnam helped considerably to mobilize national and global opposition to American foreign policy. But, in 1965, for that moment which would soon pass, Ali's politics were hardly politics at all, and certainly not even the politics of counter-consciousness, as the term was used in those days. He was jokingly called the fifth Beatle, but unlike other black tricksters like Little Richard, Ali's effect on those who watched him from afar was of a different order.

It would not be too far wrong to say that already in his youth Ali was a precursor of queer politics in a remarkably sexual way. Though to some, *queering* can have a neutral sound, it cannot be uttered in public without provoking the old fear that those who question the hetero-normal way of life are dangerous to the status quo in more ways than one.

I do not mean to say that Ali's politics were self-consciously sexual. Hardly. He was, like others before him, a hetero man of prodigious capacity and very little ability to keep himself from beautiful women. Unlike Joe Louis, he did nothing in particular to hide his womanizing. It was there to be seen, even if the free spirit of the Sixties made sex a lesser curiosity than it had been in Joe Louis's or Jack Johnson's day. Surely Ali did not flaunt his sex as Johnson had. But he did do one thing with the culture of American sexual norms that may have had as much enduring effect as any other of his tricks.

Ali did not feel the least obligation to the crude sort of masculine ideas that haunt blacks and whites in equal measure. Though the most virile of men, he was not given to machismo. On the contrary, Ali defied the hetero conventions of masculine pride from the very beginning – and nowhere more obviously than his borrowing of the Gorgeous George act. George made himself gorgeous – that is, beautiful – in the culture of wrestling show business, where the play had always been pure machismo. In so doing, he appropriated the worst fears of real men – that they would be called sissies or pussies – and made defiance of the hetero-normal his badge of commercial honor. Ali did much the same, and in so doing he exposed the nether parts of the dominant male.

I can think of no other sport but boxing (possibly wrestling) where well-trained, hefty, and terrible men undress in public in order to do violence (or the appearance of violence) to each other, while much of the time of fighting is given over to the most astonishing of physical embraces. They hold each other in clinches, surely to gain some ounce of strength to face or deliver the next blows. But they also talk to each other. What they whisper in these embraces may not be sweet nothings. But neither are they nothing at all. What Ali is known to have said into the burning ears of Liston, Patterson, Frazier, and Foreman was, in its way, another kind of sweet words. When tough men taunt each other, they deliver harsh truths that are as close as men of this kind ever get to tenderness with each other. They speak the truth that every man who fights on the streets or in the ring must fear, the truth only a few like Floyd Patterson ever admitted to. These terrifying men are afraid, as well they should be. They face opponents whose very prospects of being the men they want to be turn on the slim odds of a remote victory. In many cases their only chance to earn a decent living rests on an ability to destroy the other. Even when a fight is fixed, someone gets hurt. And when it is fair, the loser is hurt as deeply as a macho man of meager odds can be. He finds himself out on his back, or on his feet, defeated in a public test of his essential juice, of his ability to command respect. What today we know as trash talk, and associate with basketball more than any other sport, is in its peculiar manly sort of way a form of false tenderness. Though doing the dozens is a distinctively black thing, it has reached into boys rooms everywhere. Jack Johnson did this in the foxy quietude of his superiority, thereby telling whites that he knew their secret – that they were afraid that the black man was not just equal, but the one who was out to destroy you. Ali did much the same thing, in word and gesture – only he did it with an odd sort of gentleness. When he called Sonny Liston an ugly bear, he told the man what Liston surely felt about himself. The most tragic word ever spoken about the life of Sonny Liston was that "he died the day he was born."[31] Though his life was at the extreme of the tragic, most of the boys and men who enter the boxing life know its truth. They see it all around on their ways to the dirty gyms where they train for their remote chance to break out of the cycle of despair. Before this vain hope became lodged in basketball, or pursued by the nasty means of drug dealing, it was a hope held out by boxing alone. It was Liston's only hope. And when he achieved it, Philadelphia and the world said to him, *Hold on just one minute; you are in fact the worthless scum you know yourself to be*. Ali played on this theme, but not as viciously as it would seem.

With his opponents he played it always with a kind of restraint one recognizes only in the trickster. With the exception of Joe Frazier, most of Ali's opponents understood this. How could they not? They too had stripped naked for the deeply foolish purpose of doing violence in order to prove a masculine ideal that itself is nothing more than the failure of men to be good to the mothers they hold in their hearts. This is why *motherfucker* always comes in, one way or another, when doing the dozens.

Ali in those days was not queer in sexual fact, but he was in his personal presence – in the greatest fighter the world had ever seen, who quoted poetry, danced like a butterfly, and reminded everyone who would listen just how beautiful he was. The truth is that in the days of his youth Muhammad Ali was not just appealing or handsome. He was, as Norman Mailer once said, the kind of beautiful man who could take your breath away. Such a beauty is always sexual, and when it is also manly, it can be terrifying.

The Ali who came to be in those days in late February 1964 was a man who had the self-possession to say that he did not have to be what the world wanted him to be. His way of being who we wanted him to be had the effect, over time, of queering the odd conspiracy of sex and race under the surface of white good intentions.

---

four

THE IRONY OF GLOBAL CULTURES

No Viet Cong Ever Called Me Nigger

Ole Massa's Gun

Ole Massa took uh nigger deer-huntin' an' posted him in uh place an' tole 'im, he says, "Now, you wait right here an' keep yo' gun ready. Ah'm goin' roun' de hill an' skeer up de deer ank' head 'im dis way. When he come past, you shoot 'im."

De nigger said, "Yessir, Ah so will, Massa." He sot dere an' waited wid de gun all cocked an' after while de deer come on past. Pretty soon de white man come on round de hill an' ast 'im did he kill de deer. De nigger says, "Ah ain't seed no deer pass here yit."

"Yes, you doo, too, cause he come right disa way. You couldn't hep but see 'im."

Well Ah sho ain't seed none. All Ah seed wuz uh white man come long by here wid aup pack uh cheers on his head an' Ah tipped mah hat tuh 'im."

Attributed to Larkins White[1]

Word-play: Prison Poem

People who come out of prison can build up the country.

Misfortune is a test of people's fidelity.
Those who protest at injustice are people of true merit.
When the prison-doors are opened, the real dragon will fly out.

Ho Chi Minh[2]

When it comes to tricksters, things are never what they seem. Tricksters deal in reversals. The nigger is told to shoot the white man's prey. Instead he bows to the ole massa' with chairs on his head. The master's nigger exposes the white man's foolishness. The nigger's resistance is offered as obedience. The white man's most vicious insult becomes the nigger's power of deception.[3] And on it goes. The entirely obvious may be anything but, and no more than when the trickster's transformations of self are in question.

The received opinion is that Ali's coming out as a member of the Nation of Islam represented his most dramatic reinvention of self – as, in David Remnick's word, the changeling.[4] In fact, appearances aside, Ali's religious conversion may have been among the *lesser* of his magic acts – when, that is, the magic is the remaking of his emotional being, of his character. For one thing, Ali's interest in the Nation of Islam was anything but occasioned by the exceptional public attention that fell his way after he beat up on Sonny Liston. His religious thinking, like the thinking of most adolescent boys, was an awkward mixture of elementary Sunday School religious ideas and psychologically powerful solutions to the dilemma that stared any American black boy in the face.

Whatever the truth of Ali's claim later in life that he had been deeply affected by the lynching of Emmett Till in 1955[5] (when Cassius was just 13 and beginning his training with Joe Martin), no boy from the West End of Louisville needed so horrendous a story of racial hatred to chasten his sense of the world's unfairness. For country boys from the Deep South, Ella Baker or Martin Luther King may have provided what the Nation of Islam offered many urban boys in the North. One can easily imagine the allure of the Nation's program for a kid from Louisville – urban, but neither North nor South, hence filled with more than the garden variety of America's racial contradictions. Cassius Clay was not by nature anti-white (as his relations with Joe Martin proved from the start). But, his generosity of racial feelings aside, he was still black and male and young, and thus much in need of a way to confirm his interior idea of himself as one who would be the greatest.

The Nation of Islam first came into American life in Detroit, probably in 1930, when Wallace D. Fard began teaching a Gnostic message of global racial history. From the first, the movement offered poor urban blacks an ideology that simultaneously explained the racial oppression they faced every day and set them apart for special purposes that were otherwise hard to come by in the black ghettos. As early as 1933 Fard had ordained Elijah Muhammad to be his successor. Conversely, when Fard disappeared in 1934, Elijah became the Nation's leader and ordained Fard with a divine status.[6] By and large, whites in America knew little or nothing of the Black Muslims before the 1960s. What they learned in time was shocking.

Though Fard's teachings were fraught with odd claims of ancient spaceships and the like, he and, later, Elijah Muhammad had brilliantly organized the Nation so that its appeal to victims of racial oppression went hand in glove with its defiance of white oppression. The stern requirements of sexual purity for women, the ideal of the Muslim household dominated by the man, the dietary restrictions, the strict insistence on personal hygiene and conservative public grooming, not to mention the ever-apparent militant face of the men – all this added particular force to the Nation's doctrines on the racist ways of blue-eyed devils. The practical effect of the whole was to separate followers, not just from whites, but also from others of their own racial kind who were the convenient objects of white disdain. No Jim Crow in this Nation. These Muslims were meant to live in ways that undercut white racial hatred by the fine trick of refusing to be their nigger. This was the Nation within that called out the nation without. The power of the trick was not so much in their threats to respond to white violence, as in their living witness that exposed the social stigmas that were essential to the contradictory American way of racial life. The two elements together – practical instruction and firm ideological orientation – were an exceptionally strong foundation for a social movement that has turned out to be as long in years as it has sometimes been short in numbers.

By contrast to Marcus Garvey's Universal Negro Improvement Association (which had failed early in the 1920s), the

Nation was a model of down-to-earth, this-worldly common sense, however it may have appeared to outsiders. Garvey was given to flamboyance and fantastic ideas about himself as the leader of a mass return migration of American Negroes to Africa. Fard and Elijah Muhammad worked the separatist doctrine in just the opposite direction. Both movements recruited members in the impoverished and socially miserable quarters of the cities. But where Garvey's Association would send them back to Africa, Fard's Nation, in effect, brought Asia and Africa to America. This is why, once the Nation's presence among urban blacks came to white light, it was so strange and terrifying. At the least, and quite apart from the Nation's militancy, Wallace Fard's and Elijah Muhammad's movement was (and, under Louis Farrakhan today, still is) a subtle combination of the sort of other-worldly ideology that often appeals to the most oppressed *and* a vibrant this-worldly ethic that could not help but encourage pride among those who accepted its strict rules of adherence and hard work. From an organizational point of view, there are few religious movements quite like it – other-worldly *and* this-worldly, apocalyptic *and* practical, spiritual in its way *and* insistently tough-minded. In the USA, at least, only the Mormon Church of Jesus Christ of Latter-Day Saints is anything like the Nation of Islam and, in this sense, it too is a uniquely American religion (in Harold Bloom's sense[7]).

What more powerful a social group could there be for a teenage boy of Cassius Clay's circumstances? When Cassius first learned of the Nation, probably in 1958, he was already well along the road toward his personal goal of being the greatest – a mantra he would chant without specific qualification. He was, at the time, a local champion and a rising star in the Golden Gloves competition. The Olympic team was a realistic dream. Still, he boasted beyond the facts. Bemused onlookers took from it little more than the macho strut of a boy good at his sport. But it was very much more than that, and surely young Cassius Clay took encouragement from the teachings of Elijah Muhammad. The following year, 1959 (his junior year in high school), when Ali shocked one of his teachers by proposing the term paper on the Nation of Islam,[8] he was already fascinated by its teachings. It is far from incidental that he first learned of the Nation while in Chicago for a Golden Gloves boxing tournament, which represented a necessary, and successful, venue for asserting his ability to be the greatest. This was a good five years before the Liston fight in 1964 and his friendship with Malcolm X. Five years in the life of a 22-year-old is a very long time.

For a black boy of Clay's ambitions, but of a mere 17 years, the ideology of the Nation was almost perfectly suited to his emotional needs. His talent was just then coming into its own, and the demands that come with athletic success were already presenting themselves. It could hardly be that he had fewer (he probably had more) of the emotional needs that beset boys of that age, usually in ways beyond their ability to understand. Thus, I would say that the only surprise in Clay's attraction to the Nation of Islam is that the faith he attached himself to as an adolescent endured and deepened so very far into adulthood, and long after Elijah Muhammad's death in 1975. Islam (if not exactly the Nation of Islam as it came to be after 1975) helped the boy transform himself into a mature and complicated human being. Whatever his detractors might say, Muhammad Ali has become a man of deep religious faith and genuine compassion for others.

———

Still more telling of Ali's state of mind in 1964 is the way his commitment to the Nation bought him a fortuitous extension of the parental support he had enjoyed in the little world of Grand Avenue in Louisville – and the purchase came at a particularly complicated moment in his emotional development. Though a master in the ring – greater by far at his very masculine sport than any adult man alive – Ali was still an immature 22-year-old, an adolescent who was anything but fully formed as an adult. This may be why Ali granted Elijah Muhammad and his agents a relatively free hand in orchestrating his new Muslim self, at least to the extent that he could tolerate. He was personally promoted among the Nation's faithful, and, for the Nation's wider public, appearances and photo-ops broadcasting his new identity were staged. Internal to the Nation, he was given an extraordinarily sacred name and the status of immediate and close association with Elijah. And these were but the basics. More than ordering Ali to break off relations with Malcolm X, Elijah exerted particular influence over Ali's personal and professional life through the constant presence at Ali's side of Elijah Muhammad's third son, Herbert Muhammad. To the Nation, Ali was a valuable public relations property that the Nation's leader could ill afford not to manage well.

From 1964 until Elijah Muhammad's death in 1975, Ali was more or less obedient to the Minister's directives, even to the improbable degree of accepting a period of excommunication in 1969 for having said, after the banishment over his refusal to fight in the American war in Vietnam, that he wanted to return to boxing for the money.[9] Elijah was apparently willing to take that money when it was pouring in from boxing, but to stand on ceremony when it was far from sure that Ali would ever fight again, much less avoid prison time. That Ali, an independent if not exactly rebellious youth, acquiesced to the Minister's authority suggests just how much he may have needed, or desired, the external control well-protected boys often lack and usually need.

Looking back, if may be difficult to imagine just how sheltered a life Cassius Clay had had up to the time of his worldly fame as heavyweight champion. He came from a stable, if not perfect, home. He enjoyed the benefits of a childhood on the lower, but secure, margins of Louisville's black middle class. He actually owned a new bicycle that could be stolen one fateful day. And, soon after, at the age of 12, when pubescent boys take their leave of even so good a mother as he had, Ali went directly from the protective custody of Odessa to the care of Joe Martin, his first trainer; then, after the 1960 Olympics, to Angelo Dundee. Then, after 1964, Elijah Muhammad stepped into the parental mix. For the duration of his childhood, his youth, and his ill-formed early adulthood, Muhammad Ali was anything but a psychological rebel. His genius in the ring and his fool's game on the public stage left the impression of a maturity that could hardly have been. Elijah Muhammad's biographer, Claude Clegg, saw this clearly:

> Easily enthralled by the Muslim message, Clay proved pliant in the hands of Elijah Muhammad and was amenable to playing

whatever role in the movement that was delegated him. He freely allowed the Muslim leader to use him as a diversion for believers who were dismayed by some of the things that were going on within the Nation. Not unimportantly the fighter seemed to have no qualms about publicly giving homage to his fatherly patron. The Muslim leader, aware of Clay's potential for the movement, quickly bestowed an X upon him, welcomed him into his home, and set aside whole pages of *Muhammad Speaks* to shore up the fighter's reputation among the faithful.[10]

It is possible that Ali was rebelling to a degree against his father, who was enraged by the influence of the Nation on his son's life. But he surely was not rejecting his mother, or other of his caregivers, of whom Angelo Dundee was the most steadfast over his adult lifetime. Clay's transformation into Ali, whatever else it was, had all the earmarks of a coherent attempt to extend the parental benefits of a relatively painless growing up.

The one passing exception to the succession of supportive caregivers in Ali's early life was Archie Moore. After Cassius won the gold medal at the 1960 Olympics, he was ready to pursue a higher, more professional training than (he felt) Joe Martin could provide. Sugar Ray Robinson, his idol, wouldn't give the new kid the time of day. But Archie Moore – a fighter whose cunning was much like Clay's and Robinson's (and whom Clay would defeat in 1962 on the way to his day with Liston) – took Cassius Clay on. Moore named his training camp in the remote hills of Southern California the Salt Mine; and the barn where training was done he called the Bucket of Blood.[11] Moore was a no-nonsense taskmaster. He wanted no one to mistake his ways. The young men in training were expected to live spartan, disciplined lives and to join in the household chores. This was too much for Cassius, who balked: "I ain't gonna wash no dishes like a woman."[12] By Christmas, Ali had been sent home never to return.

Soon after, Angelo Dundee took up where Moore gave up. Dundee was a brilliant trainer for the boy, and eventually the man. His trick on the trickster was never to contradict him, always to hint and tease and suggest – until the champ came around. Cassius Clay, the boy, had to be handled very carefully, precisely because he was so accustomed to supportive, even adoring adults. He was, therefore, an easy mark for Elijah Muhammad, who was cautious like Angelo Dundee, while lavishing attention like Odessa. Whatever went wrong over the years of his relation with the Nation, without Elijah we literally, in more ways than the obvious, would not have had Muhammad Ali, the man.

Elijah Muhammad was an exacting steward of the public image of his Nation. Ali entered into the union with Elijah Muhammad and the Nation at a time when he had good (if not consciously understood) reasons to subject himself to the Minister's guidance. "I AM the greatest," notwithstanding, Ali got what boys need but can't ask for. At the same time, any young man from Louisville, particularly given his race, and even after becoming black champion of the world, who could proclaim himself unqualifiedly the greatest, is going to be a tough ticket to manage. There is no particular reason to think that Elijah possessed any clinical wisdom as to Ali's personal needs. Leaders of that kind of movement are more typically preoccupied with how others understand them. In this respect, the Minister was very good at using Ali for his purposes against the likelihood that such a man-boy could be used by anyone.

Still, on the surface at least, it is easier to divine the benefits of Ali's new Muslim selfhood for the Nation than for Ali himself. Elijah Muhammad, whatever was imperfect about the man, was an adroit steward of his movement's public image. He knew the value of his property, and how to marshal it. A separatist group like the Nation, if it is to give adherents the sense that they are indeed separate and special, must maintain a finely tuned presence in the public eye. Too separate, and the members are denied their sense of superiority. Too aggressive, and they are at risk of being dismissed, if not put down. In 1965, Black Islam in the United States faced the kind of hostility that rains down on those who are at once standoffish and aggressive in a time when the body politic cannot be certain of its ability to contain anymore. There had been, by then, a full decade of growing racial unrest since 1955 in Montgomery, Alabama, when Rosa

Parks, E. D. Nixon, and Martin Luther King, Jr, had disturbed the peace by forcing civil rights onto the national agenda. Though the Nation of Islam would seldom thereafter enjoy relief from public controversy (which of course it required for social energy), the mid-1960s were days of testing, and more difficult even than the years following Elijah's death in 1975, when the splits and dislocations that led to the anointing of Louis Farrakhan as the restorer of Wallace Fard's ideas put the Nation at continual risk of dissolution. In those earlier days when Malcolm X was exiled and Muhammad Ali was brought into the fold, white fear and confusion toward powerful blacks was way out of control.

The nature of white racial psychology (in America, at least) grows from the fear of rebellion by the very black people upon whom white society depended for the labor that built the white world – everything from the economic foundations of its agrarian and then industrial might to the care of its babies and the construction of the illusive "American family." It is said that Abraham Lincoln fought the Civil War not over slavery but over national unity. But in the 1860s these were, in effect, one and the same. National unity, such as it was, turned on the South's economic reliance on the slave system. And in the North, which had already embraced industrial progress, Americans in large numbers had to have realized that the national entity got its global start not from the manufacture of steel, but from the tobacco and cotton trade of the feudal South. What, then, could have been more frightening than the prospect of black power? From the beginning, whatever foolishness had crept into the ideology of the Nation, its famous line about white devils was just the thing to drive whites mad with fear. What white person in those days could have failed to understand, somewhere below conscious life, the extent of the moral contradiction at the heart of American exceptionalism? And this is what any leader like Elijah Muhammad had to deal with, if he could.

The management of what the black feminist Anna Julia Cooper once called (with a very different meaning) "the primal lights and shadows" of the American soul was always a challenge to any who would represent the black world in so white a society.[13] Such a responsibility could well require drastic measures such as the expulsion of Malcolm X for creating a troubling impression before the white gaze. Even more, Malcolm had become a liability because of his own leadership skills. Malcolm was an extraordinarily gifted speaker and a man of superior intelligence, and thereby more terrifying in the public eye. But, because of these qualities, he had become the principal organizer of new mosques as well as the Nation's most visible spokesman. Thus, Malcolm's role in Ali's life was more than personal. Their friendship, though sincerely felt on both sides, was also the issue of Malcolm's vocation to advance the movement. Though we on the outside know little of those on the inside, it is hard to imagine that there could have been anyone better able to focus Cassius Clay's early explorations of the Nation of Islam's ideology. But, having succeeded so brilliantly, Malcolm in effect put his own already uncertain status in the Nation in jeopardy.

When Muhammad Ali came into his own as the world champion, Elijah found the way out of his dilemma. Internally, he had to remove Malcolm, at the risk of exposing himself to the wider following, much less to the white world. This he could only do with a cover, and Muhammad Ali was that cover – one who would absorb the attention that had been focused on Malcolm, thus also one whose adoption would defuse whatever trouble might come down from Malcolm's destruction.

It may seem harsh to say so, and certainly it is not a literal truth, but Ali was, to some serious extent, a reason the Nation could destroy Malcolm. Ali's famous snub of Malcolm in Ghana (with Elijah's son Herbert at Ali's side) was just the sort of confirmation of Malcolm's expulsion that was required. The snub hurt Malcolm deeply, and in time Ali regretted it.[14] But at the moment Ali served his Minister's purposes. When Malcolm was murdered on February 21, 1965, Elijah Muhammad is said to have made his own chickens coming home to roost comment: "Malcolm died according to his preachings. He preached violence, and violence has taken him away."[15] Elijah, it is evident, was willing to have it both ways when it served his interests, as of course it did to denounce Malcolm even in death and in the same terms for which Malcolm had been exiled. Ali said nothing to contradict the Minister, save to insist with all the implausibility of a young man that true members of the Nation of Islam were not violent people.[16]

Though harsh, the interests of the Nation in using Ali to cover its internal struggles are much easier to figure than other moves it made, and none more astonishing than Herbert Muhammad's role in approving, if not quite brokering, Ali's first marriage on June 4, 1964. Sonji Roi, a beautiful cocktail waitress, was anything but a proper Muslim wife. One can far more readily understand why Ali fell so in love with Sonji[17] than why Elijah and Herbert allowed, even encouraged, the union.

In many ways that first marriage typified the state of mind of the young champion who was yet to be toughened by emotional trial. Though Sonji denies it, Ali must have been a sexual naïf, for whom Sonji became instructor. Ali impetuously proposed to her on their first date. Sonji agreed because, as she once said, she had nothing better to do at the time. Ali in his youth very often inspired others to join in the parade of his life. He and Sonji came to have real affection for each other, which made the marriage the more painful, and the breakup after 18 months deeply sad for both of them. Legally, it was Ali who filed for annulment in January 1966. But, in Sonji's mind, the decision was someone else's, "I loved the man."[18] Ali's formal complaint was that she was unwilling to follow the dress code required of Muslim wives – that her public dress was too revealing of her considerable sexual appeal.

What a strange arrangement it was. Surely, Elijah Muhammad, who had his own healthy appetite for sex, knew in the first instance that he was standing by while one of his most valuable cultural properties, who just happened also to be a most virile and immature young man, was joining his life with an unusually sexual woman of whom there was no reason whatsoever to expect conformity to the Nation's puritanical codes. The odds against their forming a perfect Muslim union according to code were much worse than those against Ali in the first Liston fight. The only way the Nation's role in this affair makes any sense is in the realization that Ali's own spiritual marriage to the Nation was built on unsettled ground.

There was trouble soon to come. Though it would not cause Ali to quit his new religion, it did show just how much greater the risks in the alliance were for him than for Elijah. Ali might have been better off in some ways had he not been so devoted to the Nation – but to suggest this is to suggest that history rewrite itself. In any case, on balance, the Nation got from him nothing but good, while the benefits that ran Ali's way turned out to be mixed, to say the least.

———

Late in 1965, after the second Liston fight, events began to overtake Ali. As they did, it was also evident that Ali took – and was granted – a significant berth in the otherwise closely harbored life of the Nation. To some degree, he never fully bought the program – or, perhaps better put, was sufficiently valuable to the Nation as to be permitted a goodly measure of his own personal style, including the Gorgeous George act (which in fact mellowed as the years went by). Certainly, he never took on the defiant blank glare that is familiar to the Fruit of Islam, the Nation's corps of palace guards. If nothing else, you could hardly expect even a more adult version of Cassius Clay to keep the straight face of the black Muslim man. Malcolm X had had that glower, softened only by his intellectual and rhetorical brilliance. But where Malcolm's gifts were a threat, Ali's brilliance, lying elsewhere, was not a leadership threat.

Ali's capital value to the Nation came from the public attention that flooded over the young boxing champion, leaving more than enough celebrity wake to cleanse the Nation's public image. Leaving spiritual matters and personal sincerity aside (and surely time has certified the authenticity of Ali's religious convictions), it is less clear what Ali got out of the original transaction. There were, of course, the personal benefits – and not insignificant financial ones. Though it is evident that Ali's business interests were well enough taken care of by the Nation's handlers – certainly better than they would have been either by the mob that very probably killed Sonny Liston or the greedy consortium that left Joe Louis with the impossible tax burden that would hasten his destruction. In this game, such a benefit is far from nothing at all. If, in addition, Elijah served as still another source of parental love – or the illusion thereof – then surely Ali was anything but deprived by the relationship (especially not if one considers the enduring spiritual benefits Islam has given him in the later years).

Still, on balance, the deeper transformation in Ali's life – the one that led him truly to become adult enough to use his celebrity well – was not due to the Nation's influence directly, except perversely. Not only did Ali's conversion to Islam cause him to be vilified by the old guard in the media (again Jimmy Cannon being among the very worst), but it led him into troubles. Of which, the first was the trouble he made for himself on November 22, 1965, when he mercilessly beat up on Floyd Patterson.

The Patterson fight was just six months after the controversial second fight with Liston in March. Against Liston, Ali's detractors, who were then legion, denied him the possibility that he was good enough to destroy such a man with one punch. Against Patterson, those who hated him denied Ali something much more central to his personal identity. Patterson, always the righteous Good Negro American, refused to call Muhammad Ali by his chosen name. To the champ's ears "Cassius Clay" was an insult. Patterson was far from the only one to stand on such a disrespectful principle. But he was the one who paid the price of one of Ali's most brutal beatings – the kind of brutality that hearkened back to Jack Johnson's slow, merciless destruction of his white opponents. Johnson, at least, had a commercial excuse for the teasings. He usually had film rights to his fights that were more valuable the longer the bout. But Ali was in the midst of a public furor over his religious beliefs, already considered treasonous by the low and shallow with an opinion to express. He would have done himself a public relations favor had he treated Patterson with kid gloves. Before the fight, Ali taunted Patterson, calling him a rabbit, an old Negro, and a Tom. In the fight, he toyed with him, extending the beating for twelve rounds. Patterson himself, in surely one of the more bizarre post-fight reflections, claims that he actually enjoyed the pummeling for the promise it made of a virtuous knockout.[19]

Before the Patterson fight, whatever was said against Ali, it would not have occurred to call him cruel. But to those already provoked by this change of religious heart, Ali's taunts were fuel to fire. In 1965 Ali was still a young 24 years. But he was at the height of an athletic competence rarely matched by anyone in any game. Still, he was a boy – and, like boys everywhere, he was easily riled to rage when a cherished badge of personal respect is questioned. What's in a name? Perhaps, in our culture, more for boys than for girls. But still there is plenty. These, remember, were the days well before what has come to be called, however inadequately, identity politics. In America (at least for African Americans) the beginnings of identity politics are usually traced to the famous Student Non-Violent Coordinating Committee (SNCC) meeting in Waveland, Mississippi, the same month as the first Ali–Patterson fight. Thereafter, Black Power came into play, and people by the thousands began to rethink who they were in relation less to their national allegiances than their ethnic or racial ones. But all this was just coming to pass.

For Ali to have demanded respect for his allegiance to a racial group so terrifying to whites as the Nation was to demand more than mere politeness. It was to ask others to rethink who they were in relation to the now apparent social divisions of American life. Black Power attacks the fundamentals of such bigotries as the Good Negro/Bad Negro racial dichotomy. Patterson could not have played such a hand had it not been dealt him by the prevailing racial caste system. Thus, for Ali to join forces with an important public precursor of Black Power and all the subsequent separatist moves against the myth of national unity was for him to have joined prominently in the unsettling of a foundational principle of American culture. It is one thing for an old man like Elijah to hold forth with such strange ideas, even perhaps for a brilliant radical like Malcolm X, or Louis Farrakhan today, to do the same. It is possible to dismiss them as irrelevant and irreverent. But Ali was never a man who could be said to be irrelevant, however irreverent he may have appeared to be. Ali, thereby, suckered Patterson into the identity politics game, as he did the thousands of unwitting whites who hardly knew what was going on.

Still, Ali was a boy – a rapidly maturing one, but a boy. And boys will defend their fragile sense of personal honor at the least provocation. When that provocation comes from one who ought to know better, the anger can explode. In later years Ali regretted his beating of Patterson. He had grown up. But at the time, he was young. He was, surely, still impressionable, and the boy susceptible to the kind of contradictory influence that Elijah imposed was also emotionally vulnerable. He had, after all, just done a man's work on Liston, which meant he now had to face more than the usual number of adult responsibilities. The wild man act works only up to a point, and one of those points is surely the role expectations of a world champion. With or without the racial burden, the heavyweight championship bore a good many expectations. And none of them could be managed easily – as Patterson realized when he was expected to defend America against the Bad Negro himself, and as Liston realized when he deplaned in Philadelphia to any empty tarmac.

In other sports, there is often a script. Jackie Robinson's role as baseball's first Negro was extraordinarily well scripted, as was Arthur Ashe's in tennis and Tiger Woods' in golf. Politicians and rock stars are very well prepared for the public roles they presume to enter. Even such bizarre public figures as the Miss Americas are very carefully instructed on their duties and personal conduct during the time of their reign. There is no playbook for heavyweight boxing champions. You may say that Joe Louis was an exception to the rule. But Louis had a time of trial before defeating Braddock in 1937 for the championship. He was the one who had to contend directly with the Jack Johnson legend. By contrast, Ali's advance to the championship was a relative breeze. In fact, in Ali's case, the new openness of the racial times, combined with his disconcerting clown act, led to diminished expectations. He got the fight with Liston precisely because, after the poor showing against Henry Cooper in London, he was not taken seriously. Every one believed that Joe Louis was as good as he turned out to be. But Ali was not yet taken seriously, even after the second Liston fight.

Nor did Ali take himself with full seriousness. He was, of course, quite serious about his athletic goals. But no one his age could have anticipated what would be required once he achieved those goals. And none of those burdens would be more onerous than the events that would soon unfold from the first buds of his celebrity – after which, everything would change for him, and require qualities of character no one, not even Ali himself, could have seriously thought possible.

———

On February 17, 1966, not three months after Ali had brutalized Patterson in Las Vegas, he was back in Miami training for another fight. There would soon be a rude knock at the door of this newly settled champion of the world.

The trouble at hand, those first months of 1966, was America's deepening involvement in a war it would never win – a war the loss of which would change everything, even while appearing to change nothing, about the way powerful nations ruled the earth. Just the year before, early in February 1965, when Ali was preparing for the rematch with Liston, President Lyndon Johnson had ordered massive bombing attacks on North Vietnam. To that point, American troops in Southeast Asia were limited to South Vietnam. The war was still, more or less, rightly considered a civil war between the Communist North and the Nationalist South. The American military presence, though slowly increasing in number, was a scant 4 percent of the 605,900 troops that would soon overrun the countryside.[20] They were, technically at least, advisors to the military of a succession of largely corrupt and otherwise inept ally governments.

Perhaps, as much as any other, this was the time when words ceased to have their normal meanings. It was just two short decades after the end of World War II. Until then, and even in the Korean War in the early 1950s, *ally* meant "ally." But sometime during the Vietnam era it came to have its current geopolitical sense, roughly *a lesser partner of little material importance who participates in order to legitimate big power aggression*. In any case, sometime in the short two years of Ali's first reign as heavyweight champion of the world, the American Imperium began to twist and turn world reality – including the normal meanings of words like *ally* and *advisor* – in order to justify its not so soft colonizing adventures. Sometime around then there arose the odd – one might even say ironic – fact of global life that would prevail well into the next century.

Muhammad Ali knew little of this, at least not at the time. Like every young person of draft age, he was worried about being called to fight in the war. This of course is the worry of any young man or woman who has much to live for, and thus good reason to fear not so much death but the disruption of the normal course of daily life. Though Americans proudly sing hymns to our victories on the shores of Tripoli and the halls of Montezuma, our national will to serve in foreign wars has always been feeble, as befitting our isolated island political culture. Not many, even today, could begin to tell you where Tripoli is, just as Ali and other boys his age were clueless about Saigon. All along the twentieth century, as before, Americans fought only when their interests were well threatened. Unlike World War II, when the enemy was visible, vicious, and a direct aggressor to American land and spheres of influence, Vietnam was, and is, a black hole in history. Things would go in there, and never come out. What came out, if anything, was incoherent, if that. Who was the enemy? Why was he, if he was a he, our enemy? What interest of ours was at risk? Mention Hitler or Pearl Harbor, and you get it. Mention Ho Chi Minh, or the Viet Cong, or Hanoi, and nothing in particular came to mind – at least not in 1966. Young people will do extraordinary things for the most unlikely of reasons. Tell them to invade Normandy, or in Korea to hold the 48th parallel, and they can see, in their mind's eye, Hitler's panzers or Mao's millions. The young have always proven themselves ready to die to defend their countries, their homes, their moms, their freedoms, whatever. But you have to give them a reason attached to an enemy or something they can see. For the course of America's decade-long debacle in Vietnam (from 1965, when the war began in earnest, to 1975, when the last American grabbed the last seat on that helicopter), the single most striking thing is that, again and again, the complaint of wounded or frightened ground troops was that they could never see the enemy, never understand their mission, never know exactly where the hell they were going or why.[21]

Visible enemies, however, are not always legitimate ones. Governments at war lie all the time. They are in fact sanctioned to lie in order to gather what they so euphemistically call "intelligence." But the lies and deceits upon which military intelligence and state-sponsored espionage depend are quite another order of deception from those of the trickster. The trickster always brings his trick into the open (which may be why Ali tells people how his magic tricks work). Military power is anything but a trick. Military people can be the most serious people there are. I should add that I know this firsthand. My dear, dear son Matthew, a trickster in daily life, died a marine, and over the most serious of all possible misunderstandings of his military mission. Military action and state power depend, thus, on tragedy to energize their forces. When there is no visible tragedy, power can come to ruin. And when it refuses to admit its defeat, it can turn comedic.

Then, too, there is the irony at the heart of warfare. Those who give themselves over to war at the risk of their lives may come to a tragic end, but their ability to embrace the war is always half-serious, hence ironic – that is, in order to fight, they cannot take the likelihood of their own deaths with complete seriousness. They give themselves to fight for freedom and life itself at the cost of submission to the least free social order there is – one that disciplines them to face the likely unlikelihood of their own deaths. This kind of irony demands, it deserves, a visible opponent, a clear mission, an honest purpose. The propagandists may trump up the tragedies that will inspire the service, but what they trump up must stand the test of time. The tragic story of Vietnam, beginning with the phony 1964 Gulf of Tonkin "attack" on American pride,[22] never once stood the test of time.

Young people are right to fear death. They have so much life ahead of them. And since we all (those of us, that is, who are not yet saints) fear death to some degree or another, we are all cowards. To be brave, as one must be to fight any real fight in life, is to overcome the native cowardice that keeps us alive in the first place. Boxers, therefore, are very brave men because, most of the time, they fall as Floyd Patterson did and must struggle hard to overcome. Muhammad Ali was, thus, a brave man. Liston was probably not wrong to think he was nuts – crazy with fear at least. My son Matthew was a brave man, even when he killed himself one sad day because he feared, among much else, that he'd never get to serve as he dreamed he must. So too, Ali was willing to fight. He had to be told, however, what to fight for, and why. And in February 1966, as throughout the duration of the war in Vietnam, no one could tell him or me or any one else what they were fighting for. Thousands fought anyway, and they were brave. Thousands stood against the war, refusing to serve, and they too were brave.

And, yes, many like Ali just plain did not want to serve, because they could see no reason to lose all that they had worked so hard to gain. Were they cowards? Or were they brave? Either way, this is the question that Ali was soon to put before the American nation.

———

Still, even with rumors of war whirling about, that February afternoon in 1966 Ali was relaxed. He sat idly before his Miami home, visiting with Robert Lipsyte, who, since 1959, had been a sportswriter for the *New York Times*. Lipsyte, important to say, was closer to Ali's generation than to his elders on the boxing beat. He had come into his own as Ali was coming into his, and thus could understand Ali in ways that Jimmy Cannon and the older men never could. Lipsyte himself admitted that he was in Miami as much for a vacation as to cover Ali. So he sat with the man whom he had, in a way, grown up with – and with whom he was friends of a sort – at least friend enough to be welcome in the home that also housed Ali's bodyguards and brothers from the Nation.

They sat there enjoying the sun while Ali did as boys do, calling out to the girls who sauntered by his house not at all by chance. Ali had every reason to enjoy life. He was at the top of the world. He was the greatest in a way that even those who already hated him could not deny. The one threat to it all was held at bay that day. Ali had twice failed the intelligence test for induction into the army. Though he hated being thought of as stupid – "I said I was the greatest, not the smartest"[23] – Ali had had little to worry about until the government revised the lower qualifying score on the military service intelligence test. It is all too easy to conclude that this was done to get Ali, but not even so ponderous a mind as that of the state is likely to have been quite this blunt. What the government could do, and did, was to declare Ali eligible for the draft on this and other grounds. Still, Ali's lawyer was working on this, and Ali had reason to believe he would be spared.

Then, as Lipsyte describes the scene,[24] the champ's sunny afternoon of girl watching was interrupted by the arrival of a television crew at Ali's door. Then and there, without warning, he learned that he had been reclassified and very likely would be drafted. Then began what may be the most compelling of all the legends that grew up around Muhammad Ali – and certainly then began his necessary journey into full adulthood. Robert Lipsyte, to his credit, remains the most reliable witness to what Ali said, because he had every reason to falsify the story. What he describes is a plaintive, confused Ali. "How can they do this to me?," he moaned, with all too apparent anxiety.[25] He did not say then what the revised script of history would have had him say, over and over, from that first moment. In fact, the closest he came to the famous line was an adolescent whine about not knowing anything about Vietnam. He was, according to Lipsyte, selfishly preoccupied with himself – as a victim who would lose his coveted status as the greatest, his newly won wealth, and eventually his championship, perhaps even the girls walking by.

Nothing in those first responses was brave, and, had that been the end of it, those who hated him ever after would have been on firm ground when they called him a draft dodger or, in the words of Red Smith, one of the most respected of the older sportswriters, a squealer: "Cassius makes himself as sorry a spectacle as those unwashed punks who picket and demonstrate against the war."[26] Lipsyte, if not as appalled as his older colleagues in the press, must have thought something similar at first. Yet, he was there to witness the chaos. Ali's brothers in the Nation of Islam teased him about the white man sending him off to get killed. Call after call came in. Ali pissed and moaned, then in frustration at what Lipsyte remembers to have been something like the tenth phone call, he blurted out: "I ain't got no quarrel with them Viet Cong." According to legend, Lipsyte was so caught up in the events of the moment that he thought nothing of it, probably because to him it seemed that the remark was more in keeping with Ali's selfish behavior than any kind of political or religious utterance. Lipsyte had missed the biggest story of the day.

I ain't got no quarrel with them Viet Cong was the next morning's headline, everywhere. Whatever Ali had meant at the moment, once the line took off, so too did a new and vastly more complicated stage in his career as a celebrity. Soon, as happens with legends, the anti-war movement, already slowly gathering force in 1966, appropriated Ali's line. Just as soon, it was transposed into its more dramatic version: *No Viet Cong ever called me Nigger.* And soon enough as well, what Ali said in rage and without the least apparent political purpose, came back to haunt him – to haunt him, that is, in the best way ghosts can do their work. Whatever ontological status ghosts might enjoy, they surely arise from the repressed within – from the feelings we hold loosely in a given moment, from what in a simpler time was called the conscience behind consciousness.

No Viet Cong ever called me Nigger gained a good bit of currency, quite apart from its association with Ali. According to Wayne Smith, an anti-war veteran of Vietnam, "The Viet Cong used to leave propaganda leaflets on the side of the road for us to find saying, BLACK SOLDIERS: NO VIETNAMESE EVER CALLED YOU NIGGER."[27] Whether, if true, the Viet Cong got this from what they thought Ali had said is impossible to say. It is enough that black troops on the ground in Vietnam felt it rang true for them. Surely, as events developed, it could have been said by Ali, who, years later, used a version of it in a famous 1970 interview with *Black Scholar*.[28] Legend making works that way. Once the story has taken on a life of its own, it can spread around the world, and come back to haunt its source, or alleged source.

No one will ever know (especially not, since the principals to the original story, save for Lipsyte, are either off the scene today or left no written record of their impressions). But it is not necessary to know very much more than that the two slogans fused in the popular imagination and became attached forever to Ali. What the popular mind saw in the remark was, we now know, quite remarkable. It was, in fact, a statement that had every bit the force of another of Ali's memorable lines, "I don't have to be what you want me to be."[29] While this one was personal, so to speak, referring of course to his declared religious convictions, "No Viet Cong ever called me Nigger" had a very different and politically more powerful force. The Nigger version came to be fused with what Ali actually said, because even the original statement had a meaning of which at the time Ali himself could not have dreamt. This in fact is the way social theory comes into being. Someone says something. Others pick it up. Then some character comes along and says it as though it were his own – and the folks believe it. Over time they come to think of it as abstract, when all along it was circulating as subterranean gossip. This was how – strange though it may be to suggest it – Muhammad Ali came to be, in effect, a major social theorist of race and globalization.

Soon enough, Ali had to figure out how he felt about this politically and morally potent furor that bounced about the world only to come back to settle on him – a 24-year-old, not yet fully formed young man. And soon enough he did. In coming to terms with that one erratic and unintended episode, Ali's life changed in ways that were, as it turned out, entirely in keeping with the times. America's internal struggle with this war was, in fact, a struggle that merged its deep obsession with race with its just as deep ambivalence about its own global power. From Alexis de Tocqueville in the 1830s to Gunnar Myrdal in the 1940s, observant visitors to America could not help but notice our moral confusion over race. Tocqueville is the source of the idea that we are obsessed by race, as Myrdal is that it is our deepest moral dilemma. That a Frenchman in the 1830s and a Swede in the 1940s both saw immediately how perplexed Americans were (still are) by their race problem is all the more striking because each came during a high watermark of American self-confidence. In the 1830s, during Tocqueville's famous travels, the first post-Revolutionary generation was just then asserting itself. These were the years when the new Americans declared cultural and intellectual independence from Europe, and thus the years when they secularized the older notion that God had ordained America a light to the nations. Soon after, in 1848, the doctrine of manifest destiny came into play. When, a century later, Gunnar Myrdal visited the United States in order to fulfill his commission to write the definitive study of race in America, he clearly saw America at a time when the nation's overblown sense of its global importance was, to the true believers, self-evident witness to the doctrine of American exceptionalism. Myrdal's famous book, *American Dilemma*, appeared in 1944, just as the United States had turned the corner in its wars against the Axis powers, thereafter to stand for a time as the one, truly exceptional world power – utterly unrivaled by any other.

We Americans, whatever good we may do from time to time, have always done good in the name of our overwrought ethic of ourselves. From the first settlers in Massachusetts (who at least had to think they were doing God's work, given that there was little else to recommend their adventures) to all the American adventurers after Vietnam (all from Nixon to Carter to Reagan to the Bushes and who knows whom to follow), we have been taught to expect unusual things of our nation – this, of course, includes a generally unwarranted sense of moral responsibility for the very world we, otherwise, have been reluctant to get involved with. Not all nations think alike, but insofar as they think at all, those that think of themselves as burdened by responsibility for humankind are bound to be aware of their own moral shortcomings. Hence the American dilemma with race. Slavery was bad enough. Jim Crow was even worse, in that it was a legally sanctioned way of covering the sin. But to proclaim national righteousness while exposing such a moral blight is a contradiction not easily gotten around, though God knows we have tried our best.

What, then, does a national culture do (if cultures do anything at all) in order to work through that which it cannot really get around? If, as James Scott says so brilliantly,[30] states see and thus think, then this one throughout most of its history thought long and hard of itself as being more special than it had reason to believe. American exceptionalism is a scholar's doctrine for a clinical problem. Obsessions are to thought as compulsions are to behavior. When one, or the many, is, or are, obsessed, it is because they cannot get the thought out of their heads, because that thought, however recurrently silly, is the one thing that holds emotional (or, better, cultural) life together. When a sinner claims to be virtuous, he asserts his virtue all the more strongly. When a nation no less evil than others claims to be the true incarnation of democratic nationhood, it asserts its privilege all the more aggressively (while saving face with the manners by which such aggressions are permitted). Hence, the impossible moral syllogism: *We are the best. We are evil. We have to be better than others so they won't see our evil.*

Why, then, did so many Americans hail a storm of hatred upon Ali when he asserted his blackness as Islamic virtue? Why did they freeze him out when, to make matters worse, he claimed the privilege of his status as a faithful minister of the Nation of Islam as reason for exemption from the draft and military life? They did so because they are vulnerable to anyone who exposes their own moral contradictions. I am old enough to have not been eligible for military service during Vietnam, but also old enough to have spent a good deal of time counseling those who had a conscientious objection to fighting in that war. None of those young men to whom I listened for hours on end came to their objection easily or clearly. Each was afraid, to be sure. But as each worked through the legal requirements for filing for conscientious objector-status, each came round to an honest understanding of his moral convictions.

This, I know, is hard for those who consider all pacifists phonies. But it is hard because, as I say, those who hate the conscientious are caught up in the dilemma of national self-righteousness – and this must be respected. Had they been brought up in some other place, they would surely have suffered other moral confusions, but not this one, which is quite powerful in its devious way. If your culture teaches such a simple declarative morality as though it were, in the words of our Declaration of Independence, "self-evident," then those brought up in the schools and *Shuler* of that culture will more likely than not believe that ethical thinking is itself a very simple thing. In the stark truth of life itself, moral clarity is anything but – as anyone faced with a true moral dilemma can tell you.

The harshest fact of life is that facts are always different from the feelings that cause individuals to do anything but what might be the right and good. And sometimes it works the other way. People accept a logic in their minds, which logic provokes all kinds of feelings that make no moral sense. Americans, like other peoples, feel quite a lot, and in some areas they do because they have been taught a most peculiar logic, such as: *We are better than all others. This is plain to see. So anyone who does not see this plainly must be against us.* Still today, in New Hampshire, one of the more conservative states in America, automobile license plates are stamped with the phrase "Live free or die." No statement could better illustrate the most primitive element of American morality. Human beings live, at best, more *or less* free. If we were to choose to die when we face the real, unyielding limits on our freedom, most of us would be long dead.

The truth is that moral clarity comes with patient hard work, and even when it comes, it is rarely available as a certainty. This, again, is why the righteous will always have the edge on the ethical. The former think in the clear light of simple primitives, whereas the latter think in the normal mud of uncertainty. Did Muhammad Ali, a 24-year-old, fully understand all of the consequences of his newly announced religious faith? Was, even, that commitment truly and deeply spiritual from the first public declaration? Of course not! – on both counts. Neither is it the case for any 65-year-old man or woman, who remembers life as a 20-something-year old, will tell you. Not even the most uncompromising of adults trust themselves in youth.[31]

Ali certainly did not. His bravado in and around the ring, however much it was supported by the Nation of Islam's official theories of life and race, was more the issue of the act that was necessary to his accomplishments than of some divine spark of moral authority. Even his mother never thought that God expected him to be great in all things. When legend takes over and elevates the level of celebrity, it is all too easy for those in awe to take the heroic figure much too seriously. This, no doubt, is what disturbs those, like Mark Kram, even in a sense Gerald Early, who know very well that Ali is special in some ways but not in all ways. They see the excess that redounds to the unusual, an excess that would make them not just uncommon, but perhaps unique. No human being is unique among others. Some, however, are uncommon – and more times than not the uncommon ones see and do things even they do not fully understand.

In the early years of the new millennium it is relatively easy, for those willing, to look back to the world of the 1960s and to appreciate that *then* global things were turning in a strange way. We, in our time, can see that for centuries the modern world, so called, has been structured such that the better places were those peopled by the self-appointed industrious and the lesser places were filled with people presumed to be less industrious. We can see today that this article of modern faith is a terrible distortion of the facts of global life. Some even recognize that the self-righteously industrious used their entrepreneurial magic to keep the others in their less industrious places, few of them strikingly white. In short, it is easier today to understand the modern world as having been built upon inequalities of power justified by pseudo-scientific dogmas about race. Such an understanding was, surely, perquisite to such moralizing cultures as the American one.

It was never the case that race was uniquely an American problem. Only that it became *the* American dilemma because we tried to have it both ways – to be the most moral, while also being just as racist as all the others. As they are in matters of sexual freedom, Europeans have always struck me as being more relaxed, if not completely comfortable, in their racial ethics. Europeans never denied, as did Americans, that they were once colonizers. Many of their grandparents built their careers on an early record of excellence as colonial administrators. It is not that out-of-the-closet colonizers are any more wide-awake that the closeted American ones, only that there is a refreshing integrity (if that is the word) that comes from taking your turn at beating or hanging or otherwise devastating the people of the colonized territories. Americans, by contrast, found it hard to believe that their brothers to the South were lynching freed black people, much less that they, by their silence, partook of the evil themselves.

Every now and again, there comes along some fool who tells the truth. If Ali understood anything at all about what happened to him in the years after that February afternoon in 1966, he understood quite clearly that it had everything to do with his telling the truth. But he did very much more than tell the truth. Uncertain and confused, even childish at the first, Ali quickly developed a remarkably mature moral attitude toward the American war. As things turned out, Ali's license to box was immediately revoked in all the major boxing cities. Promoters withdrew. Opponents backed away. There was no doubt that Ali would be punished. But, surprisingly, as the government went after him, much as they had gone after Jack Johnson some 50 years before, they painted themselves more and more into a legal, and eventually public relations, corner that could be gotten out of only with very sticky feet.

At each turn, Ali learned more about the truth of his utterances – the one he said and the one attributed to him. In this, he took his own interpretive license with the doctrines of Elijah Muhammad. He became, in a sense (and without knowing exactly what he was doing), a social theorist of race. "No Viet Cong ever called me Nigger" puts together the most telling facts of the modern world – that the powerful are not morally special. And the proof of their not being special is that they are inferior to those they oppress – and in no way more earnestly than in the racisms by which they came to global power in the first place.

In the months following that sunny February day in 1966, Ali already entered into the suffering he feared. Though he found ways to fight, thus to earn some of what he needed to cover the legal and matrimonial debts that grew exponentially, his life was suddenly taken over by a status he did not seek and did not want but had to accept. It is hard to read the record of his life over the years of exile from 1967 to 1971 without appreciating the young man's capacity for moral reasoning. It must have been that uncommon moral force of the man that motivated the government and the money people around him to try to persuade him to take the easy way out, to join the army as a public relations shill for the American war effort. This he would not do. So genuine were his convictions, as they developed, that a judge whom everyone expected to be dead against Ali's petition for conscientious-objector status actually found his claims sincere – though not sincere enough to warrant the exemption. Ali may have been a trickster, and a trickster can be very upsetting to those who have reason to fear their own moral integrity.

On April 28, 1967, Ali was called to Houston for induction into the US Army. When he refused to step forward, even to respond when he was called out as "Cassius Clay," formal legal action against him began. It took the government just days to indict him for draft evasion on May 8. And just weeks later, on June 20, after 20 minutes deliberation, a jury convicted him. He was headed for prison, pending appeal. From then on, for nearly four years, he was exiled from the fight game. He lost millions upon millions of dollars. He made his living (an admittedly expensive one) by lecturing to college students and what theatrical work he could find.

Reality is stranger than fiction, for it seems, in retrospect, that the *relative* deprivations of Ali's years of exile did their work on the popular mind. The college students loved him. Their parents and friends must have heard. And no one could ignore the man's courage of his convictions. It was clear to everyone who bothered to listen that Ali could have avoided the exile and real military service by doing as Joe Louis had done – join the army, fight a few exhibitions, "serve" his country. Had he – had he, that is, been able to – Ali would have had an easy life. He could have kept his cherished crown as truly the greatest. He would have been able to box during the years of his finest athletic skills. Yet, instead, he stood on moral principle, and thus sacrificed the remaining years of his youth when athletes are in their physical prime. He knew, then, that apart from whatever he lost in cash, he would lose the chance to demonstrate the extent to which he was, truly, the greatest boxer – perhaps the greatest athlete – ever.

Not even the most obtuse could miss the point. Call him a draft dodger if you will. But the costs to this proud and complicated man, though not the risk of death in Vietnam, were considerable and *avoidable*. This must have dawned even on those who hated him most. It is as American as apple pie that one's willingness to sacrifice wealth is a sure sign of some kind of moral sincerity – even one that makes no sense. That it made no American sense at all is what turned some heads around.

Surely it cannot be said that Ali's was a cause of the eventual dissolution of public support for the war. Still, by the spring of 1968, the year after Ali was exiled from boxing, Lyndon Johnson realized that he could no longer govern and declined to run for a second term. By late that spring American public opinion turned against the war. Though America's impossible war troubles would continue for many years after, the war in Vietnam was lost in those few months of 1968. Ali's role, such as it was, at the least inspired thousands of African Americans to think again of their allegiances to colored brothers and sisters around the world. And certainly, while hardly a definitive contribution, his stand had some powerful influence on others already inclined to oppose the war.

Whatever Ali lost between June 20, 1967, and April 17, 1971, when the United States Supreme Court vacated his conviction, he gained much more in the esteem in which he was held, not to mention in the esteem with which he held himself. Then is when the boy became the man.

––––––––

Ali the man and Ali the celebrity phenomenon are nothing if they are not ironic – and this poorly used word may well be the key to his role in the scheme of our time.

Many complain without thinking their plaint through that irony is the cultural measure of the present situation. The very idea upsets the superficial calm, in part because those intent upon messing things up seem to use irony as a weapon; hence, there is a deliberate misunderstanding of irony from both sides of the cultural divide. The trouble with irony is that it unsettles a culture like the modern European one because irony is a state of permanent uncertainty. Like the mysteries of the gods,

114

irony passes all understanding, and thus strikes fear in the hearts of those who think everything should and can be understood.

To speak of irony in another way, one may call it the *surd* of our times – as opposed to the *ab*surd, which in its way is little more than a systematic perversion of the reasonable. The paintings of Salvador Dali are absurd. The plays of Samuel Becket go to the surd. One just waits for Godot, who never comes. To speak, thus, of a *surd*, in the strict sense, is to speak of "that which cannot be expressed in finite terms of ordinary numbers or quantities."[32] By contrast, the *absurd* is that which is "plainly opposed to reason, and hence, ridiculous, silly." Thus, to refer to ours as a culture of irony is to describe not the silliness of the times but an irrational element without which nothing makes much sense. In mathematics an irrational is a root term that accounts for a set to which it cannot belong. So, you might say that irony is the irrational of this global culture without which its claims to reason make no sense – an irrational so far beyond reason alone that even to refer to it as "our" culture is to call attention to its most irrational feature – that there is no "ours" at all in a global culture where everything is social differences that skate about under the surface of a superficial harmony. In America especially, but also across the global diaspora of European culture, race as practiced is *absurd*. It makes no sense. But race as a feature of the cultural whole is a *surd* – that which, in making no sense, explains everything about a cultural system that claims to make sense of everything under the sun. Hence, the root of European liberal culture is the irrational claim that all men are created equal – a claim rendered irrational, not by its logic, but by the plain truth that everyone knows it not to be true, or even capable of ever being true. Yet, without the claim, you literally would not have a "West" so called.[33] Hence the irony of modern times, after a certain point, is that the presumed "our" of the culture from which so many had benefited at the expense of others was no longer, thereafter, any kind of "our" at all (even if people went about as though it were).

Prior to the events that in the 1960s, more or less, came somehow into the form they had been seeking for some years before, the modern world enjoyed (or thought it enjoyed) a wide, even global, consensus as to what was good for human-kind. This, of course, turned out rather suddenly to have been a conceit – the conceit of the ones who overpower others all too easily. The modern world was founded, beginning with a ven-geance in the sixteenth century, with global explorations that took the form of conquests of lands the Europeans thought of as open, unsettled, and available – a thought no reasonable person could hold without the conceit that the peoples there encoun-tered – all by definition neither European nor Caucasian – were somehow not truly human. The liberal gloss on the formulation was the idea that they were not truly human *yet*; hence the European idea that the Americans took all too seriously: that the point of colonization was to humanize in the name of eco-nomic progress.

This too is how we, who admit to our descent from those early European adventurers, came to understand ourselves as, in a word, *rational*. There can be no such thing as reason without the prior assumption that the world and the things in it are One. Without the assumption of Unity, there can be no *intelligibility*, as moderns came to understand the word. And, *ipso facto*, if the world is not One, and if thereby it is to be unintelligible, then there can be no reason; hence, too, no universal human good or truth. The logic of it all is beautiful, compelling. If only global things worked this way, in fact.

The difficulty that came into global play – beginning unsus-pectingly around 1950, but coming into the open in the late 1960s or so – was the astonishing experience that world events do *not* work in such a unified, intelligible, and universal manner. Then dawned, for the first time, the possibility that human things are not necessarily rational. Had the colonial peoples rebelled against the colonial powers with more immediate suc-cess, perhaps then the idea of the world as rational might have survived a while longer. But, in fact, beginning with India, then China, then most of the Caribbean and Africa, then Vietnam and Afghanistan, then the client states of the Soviet Union – the colonized subjects of the great European powers rebelled powerfully, successfully in some (usually political) ways, only to embark on post-colonial histories that demonstrated how little value had been the effects of their long tutelage under the reasonable European powers. The history of the post-colonizing world since 1947, when India broke the colonial mold, has been, in a word, uneven. Had it been a powerful reversal of global things such that the colonized took over and ran the world as the former colonizers had, then one could have thought the world reasonable – that is, tragic for the white people, but according to rational plan. Contrariwise, had the post-colonial world, including the newly decolonized nations, gone to hell in a handbasket, then too one might say that the world is intelligible and reasonable – that the problem is that the wrong people are in charge (a global version of the usual liberal explanation of poverty). But as anyone willing to look can readily see, the world really is, again the word, uneven – and uneven in ways that do not encourage the expectation that things will sort themselves out in a reasonable way.

Still, the idea of that world (as distinct but not separate from the people in it) as rational holds a considerable sway. And because it does, the fact that global things might be *ironic*, by nature, strikes the reasonable as perverse. This is why even the *Oxford English Dictionary*, greatest of dictionaries, being faithful to what people *suppose* a term means, gets *irony* only half-right:

Irony, n. A figure of speech in which the intended meaning is the opposite of that expressed by the words used; usually taking the form of sarcasm or ridicule in which laudatory expressions are used to imply condemnation or contempt.

It is true that *irony* is a figure of speech, but then so too is a word like *rational* as a way of describing how the world works. As a matter of fact, even the term *world* is a figure of speech – a trope for referring to the whole of social things as though they were, somehow, one.

Irony, yes, is a figure of speech, a trope that deals in reversals of normal meanings. In this sense irony is a difficult, hence irrational, figure of speech – different in nature from, say, metaphor, which takes the similar or the particular as indicative of the same or the whole, as when people refer to the *world* as if it were some well-known and reasonably organized whole of the social things that transpire in this or that locale. But the *OED*'s illustration of irony plays into the hand dealt it by a rational culture: "usually taking the form of sarcasm or ridicule in which laudatory expressions are used to imply condemnation or contempt." Always circumspect, the dictionary drops the hint that something is not quite right here by beginning with "usually," thus allowing for other possibilities. Still, it is true that irony is "usually" thought of as sarcasm or ridicule, which of course must be the case when the world is thought to be, metaphorically speaking, rational.[34] To suggest that the rational is in some or several particulars, perhaps on the whole, necessarily (as opposed to temporarily) just the opposite of what one can reasonably suppose is in fact to produce the effect, if not the intent, of ridicule.

———

The irony of the global state of affairs upon which Muhammad Ali inadvertently stumbled was that the world, so to speak, was becoming unspeakably irrational. Or, one might say, its ironic nature was becoming more apparent. And in such a state of cultural affairs, things are far worse off than being not exactly what they seem (they are not, that is, simply mysterious in the short run until reasonable heads figure them out). They are, in a word, uneven by their nature and thus, very often and properly so, just the opposite of what they may seem.

Words can be words, and thus vulnerable to historical change, not to mention social confusion. But when words are used to stand for things (itself a far from simple-minded or widely agreed-upon assumption), then they come to mean what the things in question allow them to mean. Real cows cannot do too much to change the noun *cow* by which they are called out by little kids speaking English. By contrast, real (so to speak) social "worlds" can do quite a lot about the words whereby their members speak of them, in whatever language. So, if the world (so to speak) in question is neatly ordered, it may be ordained as "rational" even if this only means that the people who might object are threatened with violence or expulsion (or some such) if they were to speak up.

But the world Muhammad Ali happened upon was one that – in the 20 years or so from when India told the British that their world made no sense to them, to the day Ali slammed down the phone with *I ain't got no quarrel with them Viet Cong* – turned out to be very different from what its inventors had imagined. This is not to say that today there is nothing reasonable or intelligible or rational about social things or human behavior. It is to say that the world (whatever this figure may refer to) has become increasingly an upside-down sort of place – as, more to the point, it may always by nature have been. Who is to say?

But to say anything that might lead to the locution *No Viet Cong ever called me Nigger* is to tell the truth we sons and daughters of Europe do not quite get. It sounds sarcastic to us, when in fact it is merely an expression of the ironic state of global things. If, in still another word, those who are considered the *weakest* do not buy the progressive story of how they are supposed to become stronger – if, far more than repelling colonizing intrusions (as the Viet Cong were doing in Southeast Asia), the weak of the world think they are simply different from the white folks in charge (and, worse yet, if they dare say it), then the world is worlds, then rational becomes irrational, then irony is not so much sarcasm as the surd of global things – that is, the irrational root of the way things are.

Did Ali understand any of this? Did he bring it into being? Was he a closet social philosopher of true meanings? Of course not. But did it happen that his celebrity drew him, against his wits and his will, into a global passion play that nearly everyone alive would, sooner or later, have to attend? Yes, very likely.

No Viet Cong ever called me Nigger, either. But then, ironically, that would not be entirely reasonable – or perhaps it might be.

COMING HOME TO THE HEART OF DARKNESS

When We Were Kings

Once upon a time there was a young king – handsome, brave, brilliant in battle, and endowed with a golden tongue. His super-human qualities were, no doubt, given by descent from the gods.

There came a day, as often there does, when the king was called to war in a far-off land. He left his wife and son with great sadness. He distinguished himself in battle, but wanted nothing more than to return to his kingdom. But the voyage home demanded more of him than the wars. At every turn he was met with the temptation of beautiful young women, the terror of great one-eye monsters or worse, the jealous wrath of the gods. He experienced more than any mortal man can endure, including a visit to the land of the dead where he encountered his dead mother, and other of the heroes and villains of whom he had heard tell since first he sucked at breast.

He suffered greatly at the news from home that those too cow-ardly to challenge him in person connived in his absence to steal his kingdom. They coveted his wife and spoiled his lands. They con-vinced themselves the king would never return home. His son was too weak to defend the kingdom.

But finally the king, having aged in years and wisdom, old over the course of time, returned to his land. He disguised himself as a beggar too frail to be seen for what he was. Even his wife was not quite sure she recognized him. The ruse worked as he sneaked behind the lines of the covetous and cowardly suitors. When finally he revealed himself to those who thought him dead, they begged forgiveness. But the king was merciless in his judgment. His return inspired his son, at last, to stand with his father, to defend his mother and their kingdom.

In the end, the enemies were slaughtered. The king regained his throne. The kingdom was resettled – but nothing was ever quite the same again.

A retelling of the adventures of Odysseus

The problem one faces in telling the story of Muhammad Ali is that there is almost no archive in the usual sense. He does not leave a written legacy from which to divine the deeper meanings. As a result, the tellers of the story inevitably resort to Thomas Hauser's wonderful oral history, *Muhammad Ali: His Life and Times* (which includes a few of the more important statements by the man himself[1]) or to interviews with the declining number of those who knew him in his prime or, of course, to the film archive, of which *When We Were Kings* is the very best.

The reason to mention this most obvious circumstance is that there is a full-length memoir by Ali himself, *The Greatest: My Own Story*.[2] The book is hardly ever referred to, at least not as a serious source of information. You have only to read it to see how little Ali could have had to do with some of the factual details of the book as written. Still, there is a story behind the unreliability of Ali's own story, and one more complicated than might be supposed. The book was in fact well written and wonderfully edited. Its author in deed, Richard Durham, was a professional writer, which accounts for the several literary graces of *The Greatest*. Not only that, but the book's editor was none other than Toni Morrison, who is credited with having repaired and vouchsafed as much of the book as could be rescued. The dilemma is, of course, that the book was written under the influence of the Nation of Islam. Herbert Muhammad, among others, was responsible for vetting the narrative and was not beyond introducing fictions that would bolster the Nation's public program. The most often noted of the inventions is the apocryphal story that Ali threw his Olympic gold medal into the Ohio River out of disgust with the racism he en-countered upon his return from Europe to the American South. Fictions such as this one are so out of character for a man who understood racism from the beginnings, yet wanted all the more to be the world's greatest, as to put the whole of the book into doubt.

Yet, one must question the easy assumption that an ideological influence like that of the Nation of Islam on Ali's memoir destroys a book's value. Among those who have written on Ali's life, Gerald Early goes where no one else dares. He alone among the serious commentators on Ali's life defends *The Greatest*.[3] Early's counterintuitive idea is at once simple and controversial. He reminds that the memoir is a most peculiar literary genre. Since, on the one hand, a memoir is directly from and by the book's subject himself, it is thought to be among the *more* reliable forms of nonfiction writing. On the other hand, since the memoir is directly from, by, and *for* the book's subject, it is suspect for being too much the author's invention of a public self. There is no way to ease the tension here, except perhaps to observe that readers still love the stories, in most cases. They will, for example, take with utter seriousness the self-stories of public figures and other celebrities as if their recollections were, if not gospel, at least more truth than not. Why, however, anyone would trust, say, the memoirs of proven deceivers like Richard Nixon and not trust the self-story of so open a human book as Ali is far from clear. Deceivers trick to hide themselves. Tricksters deceive to expose their truths. Readers, it would seem, trust the shyster more than the trickster.

Though you might suppose it, the problem is not that Ali's story was "as told to" another. *The Autobiography of Malcolm X*, told to and written by Alex Haley, is considered a classic of the genre – and seldom dismissed for the conditions of its authorship. In brief, Gerald Early's point is that *The Greatest* is preposterous in the same way as is every memoir, not to mention autobiography. How does anyone recollect her life without inventing it? How is memory as told to others ever to be anything but a story, thus an account of the purportedly real expressed through the narrative imagination? The very idea that we – any of us, whatever our motives – remember the facts of our pasts to tell them reliably is itself a preposterous idea. The memoir is necessarily a form that lives on the outer limits of truth and fiction. It could not be otherwise.

Early reminds us that we all tell our stories in various ways. The only proper question of the memoir is, simply, What story is being told? – or, more accurately, which of the classic story lines does the teller use to make up the facts of the life? And this is where Early is most persuasive. He observes that *The Greatest* begins and ends with two of Ali's most poignant home stories. The book opens, not with his triumphal return to Louisville after the 1960 Olympics, but with a shameful return after his discrediting loss to Ken Norton in 1973 – the loss that seemed to assure the end of his return from exile, thus the end of his story. *The Greatest* goes on to tell the story of the life to that point, then ends, oddly, with an understated report on the fight in Kinshasa in 1974 when in fact Ali did the impossible. He defeated an opponent more invincible than any he would face. The fight of course was with the very young and powerful George Foreman. Early's comment:

> In the circularity of the autobiography, Ali is, finally, Odysseus returning home from the black male exile: in the opening of the book he comes home to Louisville after the Norton fight, and at the end he has returned to his spiritual home, Africa, to reclaim his birthright – the title – which he has lost through his enforced exile in America.[4]

Could it be that the Odysseus story applies, as Early supposes, to the black man in America who has perhaps the lesser gods on his side, who travels back not to Ithaca, but to the simple darkness of his beginnings in Africa?

Even more poignantly, how could it happen that the retelling of the story of the Greatest takes much the same form as the retold story of his once best friend? Both Ali and Malcolm came home to themselves by way of the Orient – through an Islam that defined the home of the African American for what it ironically was, and is. Each said to his followers that he was not an American, by which he meant not the American white America wanted him to be. Each came out, of course, at a different moment in his life – in his last year in Malcolm's story, at the crucial turning point in adult life in Ali's. Though Ali had visited the Islamic world and

Africa after his public coming out in 1964, this sojourn was more an act of separation from the past. In the retelling of his story, the first visit to Africa, including his snubbing of Malcolm, is barely alluded to. In *The Greatest*, Ali puts the emphasis on his African homecoming for the 1974 fight with Foreman.[5] By contrast, for Malcolm, the return to Africa in 1964 was his coming back to himself as the exile from American Islam and a coming home to the global Islam that rejected racial differences in the name of Allah. One could even say that Ali had less need of this overcoming – that Malcolm, having been his brother for a time, had cleansed the homeward path for Ali. Separated or not, it could not have escaped even a very immature Ali that Malcolm's own African soul had grown gentle toward whites as Ali's had always been. The two men came home by different routes, because they grew up on different borders of black America. Malcolm, once Detroit Red, knew nothing but the darkest of urban ghettos from Detroit to Boston to Chicago to Harlem. He had to travel to Mecca to find whatever peace he made with his black soul in white America. Ali, on the other hand, grew up at close quarters with white Louisville. As a boy of 12, he traveled downtown to trick and fool for small change, a boy's foolishness that led to the stolen bike and the serious business of Joe Martin's training. Ever after, Ali lived with whites and found his home in another direction – the one that led, by a longer journey, to the recovery of the black within that had suffered the uncertainty of his necessary relations with whites.

How exactly does a black man from America come home? The answer must be by any means necessary – and the means chosen from among those available will vary according to the hand dealt him in childhood. Whatever the means, the voyage is just as necessary as for anyone reared on the stories of the Western way. In fact, it may be *more* necessary, in that for him the homecoming odyssey is surely more arduous.

———

Is there a home story that runs deeper than Homer's *Odyssey*? From Homer to Virgil to Paul at Damascus and Augustine of Hippo, to whomever imagined the story of Beowulf and Grendel, to Dante to Milton to Cervantes and Shakespeare, to Goethe to James Fennimore Cooper and Herman Melville, to Joseph Conrad to James Joyce to F. Scott Fitzgerald to Ralph Ellison to Francis Ford Coppola to Maxine Hong Kingston and Toni Morrison, on and on. Before, between, and yet to come – the great artists of the Western imagination have told and retold the story of a brave, young wanderer who travels the world, faces terrible things, and returns to the home for which he was fated.

The young man's odyssey may take him down to the land of the dead or the inferno, into battle with frightful beasts, on fruitless quests after ghosts or whims, into deep spiritual searches for the formative truth or the whale of an obsession, into the dark depths of rivers running down from madness itself, from the far plains to the great city where impossible love leads to death, along the path of his own invisibility to search for a name he never finds. The young man may be a king or a prince, a god or a persecutor of heretics, a fine orator bedeviled by sin, a curiosity seeker or a fool, a sea captain or a warrior, a mimic of uncertain purposes or a jack-of-all-trades from boxing to chauffeuring to revolutionizing. He may even be a she – a Sula or Fa Mu Lan who shuns the town only to come home to haunt it as the woman usurper of the man's uncertain role. His home may be in this world or some other, when he returns, it may be as he left it or much changed; it may be a paradise or a hell; it may be no place at all or some remote castle in tiny Denmark; or it may be some unspeakable horror or death in the pool of discontent; or, more classically, home may turn out to be the one he quit in order to prove himself worthy of his inheritance. The permutations are many, but the story is much the same. One must leave home to find home, the finding of which is the discovery of the meaning of self, of purpose, of life.

If, as it is said, some grand narratives are dead, this one is not – not by any means. More important than its recurrence in the high culture of the West, the same story has come down through the ages in the popular imagination. Versions of it appear, in variant forms, in the folk culture of the West and by migration in many cultures of the world. None are more striking than the

**Cassius Clay, the prince of the world, after the 1960
Olympic Games**
© The Courier-Journal

children's fairy tales that were codified – in nineteenth-century
Europe. Fairy tales tend to come back to a romanticized version
of Homer's first homecoming story. Sleeping Beauty or Cinderella, Snow White or the Frog Prince, the Snow Queen or Thum-
belina – each of these and others among the tales of Charles
Perrault, the Brothers Grimm, and Hans Christian Andersen
turn on a perfect young prince who appears remarkably to
rescue the most beautiful and loyal young woman of the land.
The damsel is commonly at risk of death from the greed of
jealous stepmothers or ugly sisters, a wicked witch or some
other humanoid monster. Yet, the beastly creatures that threaten
the pure and beautiful are always overcome, usually by the
magical intervention of the man who is better than one could
wish any man to be. He is always, by definition, absent – either

126

beside the point of the story itself, or off somewhere taking care of whatever manly business occupies perfect boys.

Why these fairy tales in their variations on the theme of the classics? Bruno Bettelheim's may be the most compelling answer:

> Children, on their own, are often unable to give name, form, or body to either their deepest fears or their most fervent hopes. Without fairy tales, these would remain formless and nameless, the shapeless anxieties which haunt every child in his nightmares, irrespective of whether he experiences them consciously and hence can recall them, or whether they remain repressed or obsess him thereafter all the more. These nameless anxieties are much more intractable than well-defined ones, such as those which are described as being experienced by figures in fairy tales.... Further, the more we can concretize an anxiety, the less ever-present it becomes. If a story giving form to our anxiety takes place in a distant time or place, we can either distance ourselves from it, or sometimes make it our own, as best fits our needs at the moment.[6]

The fairy tale swallows up the terrible things that frighten the child, only to regurgitate them as emotionally safe, thus to tame the terror that makes them interesting.

Between Homer's epic of the hero whose fate is to trump fate and the romantic fairy tale that tames the terrible fears, there is another story of nearly the same longevity in the popular imagination. It is one more true to life than any tragedy or romance can be. In a surprising turn of narrative events, the counternarrative to the Homerian epic turns out to be, if not a fairy tale, then not exactly a tragedy either.

The one young man whose fate is orthogonally correct to his guilt is Oedipus. Sophocles' anti-hero of the human condition recurs usually on some unsettling tangent to Homer's Odysseus. Where Odysseus triumphs over the horrors, Oedipus succumbs unwittingly to the animal lust within that fractures the sacred code of the human without. He in effect returns home too soon. He slays the wrong monster, which turns out to be his father. He loves his mother too much, by the most beastly of violations, for which he punishes himself by becoming the monster who wanders forever – blind, with a grotesque limp. He becomes the veritable heel of Achilles. The one who fought no good battle that could have made him a hero – the one who lives on as the Grendel of our worst nightmares; or, if not that, as the Hamlet who cannot confront the ghost within that denies the ghost of his father. This, then, is the true family romance, the one Freud, piggybacking on Shakespeare, brought into the story culture of the modern world. It is the story of the ordinary *schlemiel* who, in contrast to the Homerian demigod, gets *almost* exactly what he deserves – blind, ugly, animal-like, but wise beyond all wisdom. The Oedipus story is about things not turning out as they should.

Somewhere in this mix come the trickster tales that, oddly, are a mélange of all three. The trickster tale is never pure romance, though there can be romantic elements. Nor is it ever a tragedy pure and simple, though some creatures do suffer unjustly. There are no fates, because the trickster is the unmoved first mover of everything that happens, thus the ubiquitous and devious cause of the world. The trickster is never any one of the three Western story types. Perhaps this is because the trickster is so set upon upsetting the cultural apple cart. Perhaps also because he draws his strength from the dark depths of global resistance to the West, the trickster sneaks his way into all the classic story forms – as the frog who turns out to be the prince, – the fool who turns out to be the savant, – the one who suffers unto his final triumph over death and evil. Though never simply a hero, a fairy, or even a *schlemiel*, the trickster may be the most ironic of all figures – possibly the original popular source of irony itself. He is, that is, the cultural figure who avails himself of whatever is at hand, thus the one (and probably only) real cultural *bricoleur*.[7] In being unlike any other beings – and thus warranted to move outside any standard of truth telling or rule obeying – tricksters are close to being the only figment of the popular imagination that can be all things at once; and, in being all, they are not any. Trickster stories are thus jokes played on the romances associated with the beautiful young people of happy endings. And they are, if not tragedies, stories vastly more primal than any romantic comedy. And, too, they enter into the tragedies for the shocking purpose of setting the fates on edge. The trickster is omnipresent and ever always unpredictable.

If this, then the converse is true. When the trickster enters into the story cultures he finds, he does so trickily, of course. But this deception is not always crass intrusion. It can be beautiful, appealing, compelling. Still, no trick fools the dupe if it bludgeons. The trickster is always the seducer. He appeals to the classic imagination as much as to the popular.[8] Thus, the genius of Homer that he or they or she – whomever may have come to earn that name – was a trickster before the fact. The *Odyssey*, even more than the *Iliad*, is neither romance nor tragedy; and while not straightforwardly a trickster tale, it does draw from the trickster's bag. Odysseus usually, if not always, reverts to the deception in order to win the day. He lies as the trickster does, deceives the one-eyed or blind beasts, seduces the seducing maidens, and connives with Athena to fool the jealous Poseidon whose wrath is the major obstacle to his return. And, most humbly of all, in the epic's dramatic concluding chapters, the returning king dresses up as a beggar to steal behind the lines of those who control his home and kingdom. He is thus the feeble indigent who overcomes, thereby giving hope to the oedipal foolishness with which the rest of us must live. We, so to speak, are those who limp along, blindly looking for the kingdom we once deceived ourselves into thinking was ours, even when in a way it was.

Ours (if there is an *our* of cultural things) is a storied culture. One might even say that the invention of the high-modern world of the late nineteenth century was an attempt to impose the abstract necessities of analytic culture in order to tame the rush of stories that not even the dull sword of Christendom could eliminate. Stories so powerful that even that medieval Christian synthesis, set as it was on bringing back in Aristotle to vulgarize the Greek spirit into its tightly ordered ontology of divine things, was helpless before the popular hunger for stories of all kinds. Thus it happened that cathedrals were built as the ironic tribute to the very human spirit the medieval synthesis tried to crush, but could not. Any of the great Gothic cathedrals of Europe are two things at once – a tribute to the coming scientific age for which the keystone and the vaulted arch were first proofs of man's ability to rise to the skies; but also cartoons for the ordinary with their windows and gargoyles, and decorative statues and tombs designed to inspire spiritual reach while having the contrary effect of whetting the taste of the congregants for stories of wild and weird things, monsters and heroes. The priest droned on in Latin beneath the arches covering God's substance. The people, amid the shit of their goats and chickens, stood around, waiting for the Body, dreaming of the heroes and villains all about. It is not that they lacked faith, but that the grandeur of the Latinate Host was very probably mediated by stories told on the Gothic windows and walls reaching for heaven.

In time's passing away into modern times made possible by the keystone of medieval rationality, the golden age of secular science tried its best to suck the juice out of the narrative soul.[9] But even when modernity achieved its zenith on the short orbit of the twentieth century, unwieldy storytellers queered the modern analytic ideal of cutting all parts into their proper, rational elements. Try as it might, analytic culture fails to keep popular attention focused on its implausible promises of divine or mundane progress. Stories – that is to say, *true* stories as distinct from the distracting blather of commercial culture – are so deeply rooted in the common heart of social things that, in its not quite century-long dominance, analytic culture was never able to do more than smooth the rough edges of the storytelling urge. Try as it might to remove the ghosts and witches by analytic resort to their standard deviation from the formal norms, high-modern culture never really understood the subaltern spaces where people out of line tell each other their rebellious stories.[10] In such places, the stories tell a truth that always exceeds, and disturbs, the analytic cells of rational order. They are true in measure of the brutal honesty as to the most terrible fears. They are the Magic Lantern that threatens the orderly public square.

Is it possible that Muhammad Ali is just such a story? Not, that is, a storyteller so much as a visual figure, like the art in Gothic churches, that reminds people standing in goat shit that the keystone holds the heavens in place by allowing the arches to rise from the common, local soil – to the home of those who have no home on their given land.

————

When one has been around the world – as Ali had been many times before his coming home for solace after the loss to Norton in 1973 – one comes home to Louisville most likely from the North. If by plane, the landing route into Staniford Field cannot avoid the Ohio River that surrounds the city on three sides. The airport is at the near end of a line from the river through downtown toward the deeper South. Most flights cross the river and the northerly interstate highways from Indiana and Ohio and beyond. And, even if that flight takes an exceptional southern approach, no one comes home without looking out for home's most memorable spatial figure – in Ali's case, the Ohio River toward and along whose banks he ran early morning or late evening while preparing himself for the greatest thing. His native place was River City.

A river boy from River City wants to revisit the river in his head. Everything comes down to the river, which is in a way what he knows best – the source of his childhood weather, of the boundary between where he found himself and where he wished to be. For Ali the river in his mind was of course the very river over which he once drove to the Golden Gloves competition in Chicago where it all began. For those from whom he descended, the Ohio was the river over which ancestors from the Clay plantation to the west must have dreamed of escaping or heard tell of the underground escapes of others.

River boy or not, people with Cassius Clay's ancestry cannot help but know rivers – "rivers ancient as the world and older than the flow of human blood," as Langston Hughes put it in his most famous poem.[11] If the rivers are not in the blood of their race, they are in the blood shed in escapes. Those whose people were enslaved sooner or later come to the rivers that so often mark the line between bondage and freedom.

But what happens when the river dreamt of is forever dark with blood, as was the one Ali crossed on his second homecoming to Africa – to Kinshasa on the fabulous and fabled Congo?

————

Not all rivers are dark. Neither the Thames nor the Mississippi is by nature, though the romance of history occasionally makes them so. Some, like the Amazon, may wind their way through the darkest forests, only to settle into the false dream of riches to be found one bright day. And some, like the Danube or the Mekong, may turn dark by one or another pollution – real and environmental in the one case, illusory and political in the other. Still, whatever the fates, rivers are always places remade by their place in the human imagination. In fact, no river, whatever its place in literary geography, is *necessarily* dark – save, perhaps, for one.

The Congo in Africa may well be that exception to the rule of rivers. The Congo River system drains the forests and mountains of the opaque interior of South Central Africa. Since the colonization of the region in the nineteenth century, the Congo has fed the world's appetite for minerals, metal ores, gold, and, most famously, natural rubber. Long after the Congo River basin had ceased to transport the slaves traded to the east and west, the river bore the virtual slaves of Belgium's stake in the region's natural resources. Even today, after years of pillage, the region is the world's leading source of cobalt and industrial diamonds, as well as an important source of petroleum, copper, zinc, tin, uranium, and manganese.

The headwaters of the legendary Congo are deep in the far southeast and Zambia. From remote highlands and swamps the Congo flows, at first, to the north, beginning it sweeping course of nearly 3,000 miles to the sea. Early on its way north, the river passes just 200 miles to the west of Lake Tanganyika, which is part of the westerly water table of Lake Victoria to the east. These two lakes – among the largest inland, freshwater lakes in the world – are separated by a narrow strip of land that uncertainly joins today's Zambia, Burundi, Rwanda, and (to the north) Uganda. In the map-reader's eye, this area of lakes and rivers would appear to be the source of the Nile. But in point of geographic fact, the most southerly tributary of the Nile flows from the highlands below the northernmost lake in the Tanganyika–Victoria system to form a border between Uganda and the Democratic Republic of Congo.

Somewhere between the cartographic imagination and geographic fact one finds the virtual heart of darkness, the center of the Dark Continent of European dread. This was the global place that inspired the explorations of nineteenth-century Europeans, including the famous Dr David Livingstone. This, then, is the heart of Africa – the virtual, if unachieved, spiritual place where darkest Africa flows into the Nile, the world's largest river system, and in religious and cultural cartography a source of European culture. This most fabled of global places is at two degrees north latitude – equatorial Africa!

Deepest Africa, in effect, meets the Nile, out of which Europe composed her culture somewhere just above the equator, not far from Kisangani (once, Stanleyville), where, to the west, the Congo begins to veer to the northwest. Here is one of those rare coordinates where physical, religious, cultural – and in due course, economic – geographies fall into line with each other. Just below Stanleyville are the falls to which Henry Morton Stanley gave his name on his well-publicized searches for Dr Livingstone. Here, more or less, is the geographic center of Africa. In fact, somewhere at this point at which dreams and realities merge, Stanley came upon Dr Livingstone, the lost British explorer, in 1871 – after which the two set off, according to legend, to search Lake Tanganyika for the source of the Nile.

From Kisangani, the Congo continues northerly but to the east before gently curving over a stretch of some 300 miles just above the equator, then turns to the southwest, toward Kinshasa – a descent of 1,000 miles from Kisangani. Before reaching Kinshasa, the river balloons into what the seldom humble explorer permitted to be called Stanleypool. Here the Congo is between four and nine miles wide – the widest section of the river's navigable 1,000 miles from Kisangani to Kinshasa. Just above Kinshasa, the Kasai tributary cuts abruptly into the Congo at the end of its own 1,200-mile course from the southeastern provinces. The Kasai flows directly west from the interior at a point not too far from the headwaters of the Congo proper in the mountains north of Zambia. The Congo and Kasai rivers thus compose a near-complete circle route at the outer limits of the region variously known over the years as the Congo Free State,

the Belgian Congo, Zaire, and the Democratic Republic of Congo
– a state of many names seeking control of a territory of nearly a
million square miles.[12]

Precisely because of its astonishing natural wealth, the rain
forest interior to the surround of the Congo and Kasai rivers
was the epicenter of the very worst crimes of the European
diaspora's world colonial system. Though this river network
was among the early pathways for the movement of slaves to
the New World, its role in the slave trade of the early-modern
world was far from exceptional. What distinguishes the region
of Congo waters is the cruelty with which its peoples were
pressed into labor, to the point of slaughter, in order to feed
the industrial world's hunger for its unique resources. Africa
has suffered terribly at the colonizer's hand, but no worse than
in the lands of the Congo.

From 1886 to 1908, the Congo Free State[13] was the modern
world's only privately owned colony. King Leopold II of
Belgium, a cultural ox amid the boutique finery of Victorian
Europe, was driven to distinguish himself as one of the world's
wealthiest men.[14] Leopold was a master of public relations. In
his day, public relations were managed through the informal
channels of Europe's courtly and political networks, from
which, heavily processed, the official word spilled into the
print media. Leopold had *The Times* of London delivered each
day so that he could track his image abroad. The man knew how
to work the system better perhaps, and surely earlier, than most.
He typified the duplicitous ways of white European colonial
exploitation of darkest Africa. Profit was its purpose. Violence
was its method. Humanitarian blather was its public name. No
one was better than Leopold at disguising his avarice under the
cloak of human charity. All the talk one still on occasion hears of
"civilizing the savages" gained a good bit of its motive force
from the deceptions of Leopold, who, until unrelenting opponents outed him,[15] persuaded the civilized world that he was
bringing the benefits of European life to the people native to
the Congo.

Shrewdly, Leopold saw, as only a man who cares about nothing so much as profit can see, that the region of the Congo River

was a cornucopia of capital gain. Rather than engage the Belgian state on his behalf, he simply declared himself personally the rightful owner of the interior – thus giving a special meaning to the region's first name, Congo *Free* State. From just more than a decade after Henry Morton Stanley first explored the region, Leopold's agents gradually opened to European settlement and control the river pathways of the Congo.

Shrewdness aside, no one wins at the game of exploitation without some luck. Leopold's undeserved good fortune was to have owned what was then the world's most available source of natural rubber just when the new combustion engine and Henry Ford were making the automobile a popular means of transport. Ford would open his first manufacturing plant in Detroit in 1899. By then Leopold had already gained legal control of the Congo's deep rain forests by building a rail link of 215 miles around the falls that make the Congo inefficient for navigation from its estuary until well inland. At the end of the rail line, he built today's Kinshasa, which of course he named Leopoldville. The inland settlement became a base for exploration, trading, and extraction by which Leopold's armies of agents controlled the Congo River and, thereby, the far reaches of the rich interior.

Leopold himself never visited his city or his colony. Rather, by decree and gentle diplomacy among the heads of state in Europe (a kind of royal extended family that also served as a primitive broadcast network), he simply claimed right of ownership to more and more of the region. Like many in the European diaspora, Leopold believed that Africa, and other of the world's colored regions, were in effect free for the asking – or, if not asking, taking. Thus, at the imaginary juncture of white Europe and dark Africa, the whitest of European cultural maneuvers were deployed with unusual aplomb. Under the mythic canopy of the earlier legends of European exploration – for which Stanley's "Dr Livingstone, I presume?" is the epigram – Leopold stealthily transformed this fabled point of cultural imagination into an outpost of the cash nexus of industrial capitalism in the 1890s.

In *King Leopold's Ghost*, Adam Hochschild describes in detail almost too painful to read how Leopold used his strategic genius

to deploy one of the capitalist system's most murderous machines for the extraction of local resources by the subjugation of
native labor power. However much Leopold's cruelty to the
people of the Congo may be attributed to his naive acceptance
of the European myth of white supremacy, the documented
terror of it all was so extreme as to be beyond even the most
forgiving accounts. Many will put the number of West African
people lost in the Middle Passage at two million. By contrast, the
number of lives lost under Belgian rule from 1886 to 1960 in the
Congo may be as great as ten million,[16] more by a good measure
than the number of Jews lost in Europe to the Nazis. Death rides
always on the wings of economic progress. The deaths of black
people native to the darkest continent ride in silence. The very
silence of the millions killed under Leopold's administration of
the Congo speaks to the studied ignorance of white civilization
to its proper guilt for its crimes against humanity. Hitler may
have been an aberration of the European mind, but Leopold and
other of the colonizers of his era were the natural-born killers of
the European system.

Leopold's system was uncanny in its efficiencies. The extraction of natural rubber demanded an unending supply of human
bodies. The naturally occurring substance is the sap of a vine
that grows only in the humidity of the rain forest. In those days,
to gather and prepare it for market, men were forced to climb
trees, often to extreme and dangerous heights, slit open the vine,
capture the oozing sap, then eventually dry it. The drying alone
took its toll in pain. The method was to spread the gooey
substance on the harvester's body, then to tear it away when
dry, which of course tore the skin as well. Payment was in
trinkets and knives (used for the next round of harvest). Men
were enslaved by the simple means of capturing their
wives, who were held, and abused, in bondage until the harvest
quotas were reached. In the end, of course, neither the men nor
the women were assured of their freedom. Those who lived
were pressed deeper and deeper into the forest to find ripe
vines.

Offences as normal as the failure to meet quotas were policed
by the mercenary *Force publique*. Workers were tied to the

ground, face down and whipped across the buttocks by the
chicotte (a rawhide whip of razor-sharp tentacles). All suffered
to the point of death. Many died in fact. Under other circumstances hands were chopped off. Children were not spared.
Resistance was put down by a public display of torture, such
as the one confessed by Raoul de Premorel, a notoriously brutal
rubber station chief in Kasai, who seems to have come to a
degree of remorse postmortem.

> I had two sentries drag him to the front of the store, where his
> wrists were tied together. Then standing him up against a post
> with his arms raised high above his head they tied him securely
> to a cross beam. I now had them raise him by tightening the rope
> until just his toes touched the floor. . . . So I left the poor wretch.
> All night long he hung there, sometimes begging for mercy,
> sometimes in a kind of swoon. All night long his faithful wife
> did what she could to alleviate his suffering. She brought him
> drink and food, she rubbed his aching legs. . . . At last when the
> morning came and my men cut him down, he dropped uncon-
> scious in a heap on the ground. "Take him away," I ordered. . . .
> Whether he lived or not, I do not know.[17]

What kind of man could not know? What kind could endure the
night as his victim begged for mercy? What kind of a man does
this while able to admire, even after the fact, the faithful mercy
of the wife? Only one whose cruelty had somehow passed
beyond pleasure into the order of things. Only a man imbued
by a culture whose professed higher purposes settle as blinding
fog over the system he administers.

Such men were the sort who served as agents for colonizers like
Leopold. Though men like Raoul on the Kasai saw, and in time
may have felt, the grief they caused, they administered a system
directed by a distant command. Leopold, not alone among the
colonizers, was, in effect, like those who ordered pilots to napalm
the villages of Vietnam. Neither they, in the 1960s, nor Leopold
some 60 years before, ever saw their victims. Whether dropping
fire or condoning the *chicotte*, neither came face to face with the
terror they wrought – neither had even to consider the consequences of the killing machines they engineered. The brutality

of the colonial system relied on primitive technologies; still, it was a machine different in degree, but not in kind, from the war that is often said to have been one of the last of the colonizing era.

This incongruous simile of the European diaspora's most tragic flaw may be why the American war along the banks of the Mekong in Vietnam, a nightmare on the edge between fact and fiction, brings to mind the nightmares of Leopold's crimes along the banks of the Congo. The two are forever bound to each other in the artistic imagination by the first unforgettable fictionalized account of European evil in the African interior. Conrad's *Heart of Darkness* – the story of Mr Kurtz lost at river's end to a madness where white and black were indistinguishable – was in turn Francis Ford Coppola's master plot for *Apocalypse Now*, the most chilling story of the horrors at the dark end of the Mekong in Vietnam. Such stories cannot be told and retold under the guise of literary or cinematic art if the fictions are not translucent to the recognition that it is all true.

Conrad's *Heart of Darkness* is a fiction inspired by the strangeness of his own disillusionment before the truth of Europe's noble purposes in Africa. In 1890 he had signed on for six months as a hand on a Congo riverboat, just when Leopold's system was tightening its grip on the region.[18] The trip took Conrad the full 1,000 miles upstream from Leopoldville to Kisangani. He could not have created Mr Kurtz, who by his immersion in the cruelty of the system *became* the heart of darkness, had he not seen firsthand the horrors of men like Raoul, the station chief on the Kasai. The only difference of note between the story told by Conrad and the one told three-quarters of a century later by Coppola in *Apocalypse Now* is that by the time white colonial rule came upon its Vietnam the theme had settled closer to the surface sensibilities of white perception. Coppola filmed his story in the Philippines in 1975–6, soon after the Americans were chased from Vietnam at the end of the long decade of the 1960s when race and violence had entered white consciousness as never before.

This, then, is why the Congo may be the one exception to the rule of rivers. It *is* the heart of darkness in the literary imagination because, in geographic reality, it courses to the actual heart of Africa, where the very worst evils of white rule were perpetrated. No black man in America who comes from slaves of the Middle Passage, however sparse his formal knowledge of the economic history of Africa, can go home spiritually without coming upon the Congo, as Muhammad Ali did in the early autumn of 1974. If trickster does indeed make the world, then the world Ali made, and found, in his homecoming to Africa was the world he found, and to some extent made, in his own search for home in the working through of his Vietnam War morality. To come home, as he did and as who he was, you have to first figure out just how black you are, and in what sense, and only then can you find Africa. He was not the only one for whom a visit to the Congo passed by way of Mekong.

––––––

Just as Cassius Clay the boy trained by running along the Ohio River on the Kentucky side, so Muhammad Ali the man trained for his fight with George Foreman by running along the Congo at Kinshasa.

Among the most compelling scenes in Leon Gast's *When We Were Kings* – the Oscar-winning documentary of Ali's prolonged stay in Congo/Zaire in 1974 – are those of his roadwork beside the river. For a good many Americans and Europeans, the only visual images they have of central Africa, apart from Bogart and Hepburn in *The African Queen*, probably come from Gast's film. It is surely not by chance that, according to Gast, Ali had a hand in staging the scenes beside the Congo.[19] Both before the fight (which was postponed by six weeks because of an injury to Foreman) and after, Ali can be seen along the river, joking with local people, recruiting them to his greatness parade, but also exhibiting his innocent pride in Africa. To the same degree that Ali's memoir *The Greatest* is given short shrift, Leon Gast's *When We Were Kings* documentary is given unqualified respect. I have shown the film numerous times, all over the United States and in Europe, and not once was it new to those in the audience, nor did anyone object to seeing it again, and again. This may be because the story as told by Gast is true to the homecoming epics of the culture, with the exception that it tells a truth that culture generally ignores.

When a black king from America comes home to Africa, it cannot be a homecoming like Ulysses' to Ithaca. The home to which such a man comes is not one etched in memory – at least, not memory in the usual sense. To remember is to come back to something from the past, which suggests that one comes back to something from one's *own* experience. But this kind of primal memory is an illusion. People seldom remember the details of a given day from the previous week. And no one remembers the experiences of years before by calling them up directly from some neurological cellar. When experiences of the long ago are stored for recall, they must be filed according to code, the key to which is this or that story we have been told and the ones we tell ourselves. Even Ulysses of Ithaca must have been surprised, upon his return, by the helpless Penelope of whom he had heard tell from various of the gods and others, living and dead. She, in turn, had heard the whispered lies of her king's death, which is surely one of the reasons she could not recognize him in the guise of an old man.

And we who think of ourselves as more real than a storybook character, are we really all that different? Do we not in fact remember our home experiences mostly through the home stories we file in memory along with other stories told and heard through the course of time? What, then, of a character like Muhammad Ali, who was so self-consciously a character in a story of his own invention? Who is to say that he remembers exactly how the stolen bicycle story went down? Or how much Odessa Clay or Joe Martin, for their own storytelling purposes, helped it along? Whatever he remembers of the Louisville days, all of it must remain as a mélange of fact and fiction, as these memories always are. Then, too, what was the effective and grand counter-narrative that allowed him to become Muhammad Ali – literally, to *recollect*, to collect again, his lived experiences according to fresh meanings? Elijah Muhammad's story of black America was meant to be a counter-narrative – a story by which those who could put themselves into its plot might erase all stranger-than-fictional accounts of the brutalities from which they had descended. And it was most precisely the story Ali used to attempt to erase the tape of his actual origins. But stories taped deeply in shared experience can never be erased.

What, then, does a child of the Middle Passage, like Cassius Clay, remember upon his return, as Muhammad Ali, to a home he never saw? How do the home stories pass down through the ages? Why is it that, for notable example, the signifying monkey story has kept its original African form and force in African-American story traditions?[20] The transmissions could only be by the attenuation of the theme from mouth to ear to mouth to ear, passing only rarely into and out of print. Stories are meant for the ear, and the ear can do wonders for the imagination.

When Muhammad Ali came home to Kinshasa, having renounced the name given his Kentucky fathers by their slave-holders, he came on the wings of stories he heard and told himself. And the wings of this butterfly were anything but silent. For the time of his sojourn in Kinshasa, Ali, the butterfly, was able to stir a storm of African joy. His own pride of self-discovery evoked a pride in those he met, beginning with the flight from New York. One of the more comic scenes in *When We Were Kings* is Ali on that flight to Africa. En route, he is invited in to the cockpit. The pilots are African. He exudes: "I never knew that Africans could fly airplanes. Look at this [he says, pointing to the African pilots of the plane].... They speak both African and English ... and we can't even speak English good." Though Ali's boyishness has yet, even today, to leave him, by 1974 it had been hardened appreciably by the exile and political coming of age after 1967. This trip back home, unlike the one in 1964 after the first Liston fight, was the return of one who had earned his kingly aura in several ways at once. By the time of the fight with Foreman in 1974, Ali was both hardened and chastened – the latter as much by age and the improbable odds against him in the fight to come, as by the harsh exile that cost him his athletic prime. He was still, in his mind's eye, the Greatest, but no longer the solitary figure. Apart from having embraced Islam, as he had been embraced, Ali now could, and did, think of himself as being joined with others. Emotionally, it is one thing to be a global exception, as surely he was (and in different ways still is);

but quite another, more human thing to be a global member of some group that adds tone and perspective to the individual life. In this, it may matter if one is great, but it matters more to heighten the value of the membership – a value that is necessarily compounded by comparison with the memberships left behind.

For an African American to renounce, as few do, his American past is a dramatic step. But it is a step more easily taken when the step forward offers release from so compromised a membership by inclusion in one so pure and simple. When this happens, as it did for Ali, first in the Nation of Islam, then in 1974 in Africa, it surely comes down as an experience more uncomplicated than in fact it is. Men and women who reach adult life without inventing themselves are rare indeed. It would be hard to imagine adult life without some important degree of story-telling. But those men and women to come to adult life out of a storied past such that one must shout "Keep hope alive" against the reality – they must find a story or stories in which the hope is less fragile and the promises more firm. Since no such worlds exist in any known this-worldly reality, one might forgive those, like Ali, who make more of their new stories than may be called for. We forgive them because they have a wisdom that inspires others.

Thus, when Ali came home to Africa in 1974, he was a king without a throne, yet a king nonetheless. Against Liston a decade before, no one in the fight world expected him to win. Most thought it would be the end for him. Yet in 1974 Ali played the character he had himself invented, but played it now according to the script he had been taught by the Nation of Islam. Still he invented the story to suit something inside. The true Nation of Islam story has to do with Asia, with Mecca, with Islam as the vague global resource for black consciousness. Africa was but a part of that story. Its place was more to remind American blacks of their past in bondage to the slave system than to invite a return to Africa. The Nation of Islam was not, in a word, Afrocentric. But on the occasion of Ali's return, *he* was.

That fall of 1974 Ali was on the stale side of 32. Foreman was a very fresh 25. Yet somehow Ali had all the boyish charisma, and

Foreman was the sober, awkward, menacing man. But these were not the most remarkable of differences to the African people who followed Ali wherever he went in and around Kinshasa. Though Ali is several shades lighter than Foreman, everyone knew that Ali was black, but many had assumed that Foreman was white. White is as white does, and the assumption must have been, in the absence of televisual evidence, that anyone who was wearing Ali's proper crown must be white.

The theft of status and its rewards was certainly what people along the Congo knew of whiteness. We make our assumptions based on experience. Facts are something else entirely. Even more important, Ali had won over many of the ordinary people in Zaire. They had heard of his stand against the American War in Vietnam, and heard of his by then famous line about the Viet Cong. Throughout *When We Were Kings*, Leon Gast sets the visiting American kings, Ali and Foreman, against an almost mystical picture of the people of Zaire. The most eerie of the figures is the *feticheuse*, a magic-making woman whose chants were reported (most often by George Plimpton) to be capable of hexing Foreman. The most musical are the images that intersperse BB King and James Brown performing in Kinshasa before African people dancing the dances that go down all across Black Atlantic. The musical extravaganza thus created, if only for the time of the fight, a cultural pan-Africana. But the most modest, easy to overlook, yet compelling image is of an older Zairean man of very slight stature, simple dress, who in excellent English provides the viewer with an African's explanation of the Ali phenomenon in Kinshasa. This one character, totally believable because of his simple manner, has a way of pronouncing "Muhammad Aaah-leee" as though the name itself were magical. This man's most telling aside to the viewer is: "We had never heard anyone speak like that." He is explaining Ali's appeal in Africa and referring to his "got no quarrel with the Viet Cong" line. The man does not say we had never heard any *black* man speak like that. Nor does he remark on the white powers to which Ali's words were addressed. Still, the heft of the impression Ali had made was there to be carried.

143

Ali was coming home as the king – a global figure. In contrast to George Foreman, the reigning king of the fight game, Ali came to Africa with a hard-won but ready-made following – one of the unintended consequences of his boyish search for greatness. Ali had won over the people of Zaire, as he had people around the world, by speaking for the blacks, among others, of the world. What whites of the so-called First World seldom realize is that the centuries of white rule of the colored worlds laid down memories of cruelties nearer in time and harsher in effect than even those experienced by Ali's ancestors in American slavery. The American slaveholder had, we should remember, paid a considerable price for his chattel. However cruel his methods – and they were evil – he had to protect his investment, and thus keep the slave alive.

The Belgian colonizer owned the lands, but not the workers. He paid in worthless junk and had only to keep the killing machine filled with what he considered an endless, and certainly, cheap supply of working bodies. Had the Americans been able to enslave the native peoples, the story there might have been the same. But they had to import their labor, and the Middle Passage had its own heavily vested costs requiring their own financial calculations. It is of course cruel in a way to compare cruelties, but, truth be told, the reasons so many died from Leopold's savagery were economic. The utilitarian capitalist world system grinds away according to the rules of profit, indifferent to its means. The cheaper labor can be treated more cheaply. When unspeakable, calculated violence is the means, as it was in the Congo, the effect endures every bit as much, perhaps even more (though it is not for me to say).

The effect in Zaire was, it turns out, a succession of reincarnations of Leopold's system that, over time, blurred completely the differences between black and white. Africans experience race differently from Americans. Ali's unbridled thrill at the Africa he saw in 1974 may have been a vestige of his own indelible American experience. He knew the stories of the Emmett Tills of America. But did he know of the nameless Africans tortured by the Raouls of Belgian Africa? Probably not. Did he even realize that the stadium where the fight with

Foreman took place was, according to Norman Mailer, stained (literally) with the blood of hundreds executed by Zaire's reigning dictator? There is no reason to believe Ali did, which is not the same as saying he didn't remember in the way such memories pass down through the ages.

___

When Adam Hochschild refers to King Leopold's ghosts, he invokes the terrible effects of the seepage over time of violence into the blood of a people. Leopold was required to give up his ownership of the Congo colony in 1908. The Belgian state took it over, with no appreciable change in the way the people of the Congo were treated. By 1960, when Patrice Lumumba finally liberated the Congo for Africans, the people of the Congo had no memory of anything but white domination for nearly a century. Lumumba had been educated in Europe and was a man of considerable, if tough, intellect. But he was soon overthrown by one of his own men, a regional functionary turned revolutionary, Colonel Joseph Mobutu. Lumumba was assassinated almost immediately, no doubt on Mobutu's order, but certainly too with the authoritative participation of the United States Central Intelligence Agency. Then began Mobutu's reign of terror that would endure until 1997.

Mobutu conducted his reign by installing himself as a messianic figure whose coming to power was foretold from early youth. He changed his name to Mobutu Sese Seko, and the name of the country to Zaire. He concocted a ridiculous costume to accent his messianic view of himself. He deployed the same *Force publique* that Leopold had organized years before. No one dared laugh at the man. In 27 years, Mobutu did nothing more than take over the oppressive apparatus that Leopold had put in place and, again like Leopold, use it for his own selfish purposes. He stole billions of US dollars in Zairean assets. Those not vested in his several fabulous villas and other properties across Europe were kept in Swiss bank accounts for the day when, like most tyrants, he would have to flee his homeland.[21] Because of the West's Cold War stake in African resources, Mobutu easily won the diplomatic support of European and American nations, beginning with his "friend" John F. Kennedy.

Hence, it seems impossible to ask, or answer the question: Though his complexion was black, was not Mobutu as white as could be? Did he not do as white did in Zaire/Congo? And if he did, as surely he did, then what difference does color make in the code of color politics on such a scale as that across equatorial Africa?

The Mobutu who backed the fight on October 30, 1974, was, in a perverse sense, the ghost of King Leopold. His reign wrought such terror on the people of the Congo region that, as time went by, he was required to showcase his administration to the rest of the world. The shows were a veneer on social rot and human suffering. In this he did as Leopold had done. To this end, Mobutu entered into a devil's pact with Don King, the charming but evil American fight promoter.[22] King was able to sign both Foreman and Ali to the fight on the guarantee of a purse of $5 million each. Mobutu guaranteed the $10 million purse, out of Zaire's treasury. It was an enormous sum for the day, thus a measure of the global appeal of the fight. Mobutu himself did not attend the fight, for fear of assassination. He would hold power years more on the force of threats, sharpened by his rape of the local economy, which in time weakened resistance, by destroying what remained of Zaire's economy and Kinshasa's infrastructure.[23] But, by fight night, the people of Kinshasa, and of the world, were preoccupied by nothing more than the thrills promised by what Ali had baptized "the rumble in the jungle."

———

The story of Ali's improbable victory is so well known as to scarcely need retelling. This is the fight of his famous rope-a-dope strategy – still another of Ali's athletic tricks drawn by genius from a body seemingly able to adjust to almost any demand. At 34, Ali was old for a fighter. This was one of the reasons no one expected him to win. He had lost to Frazier in 1971, shortly after coming out of exile. His fights between were undistinguished, save perhaps for the rematches with Ken Norton late in 1973 and Frazier on January 28, 1974. He won both on decision. No knockouts, but clear winners. But then, early in 1973, George Foreman had obliterated Frazier in the second round. Foreman was ferocious. Though the world was yet to hear of Mike Tyson, Foreman struck just that sort of menacing terror in the hearts of any who would try to imagine himself naked in the ring with him. Where Frazer and Ali, different as they were in styles, were boxers, Foreman was in the Liston–Tyson tradition of intimidators. They could fight, but their game was played out from some frightful place where the fear of destruction ruled all who came near. Just as it had been unthinkable that Ali could defeat Liston a decade before, so it was inconceivable that he could win the Foreman fight on October 30, 1974.

But then, earlier, Ali's upset of Liston could be explained after the fact. Liston had been older than it was thought, and Ali possessed all the physical ingenuity of a very young man of exceptional speed and incomparable boxing talent. A decade later, those gifts were gone. Ali had to resort to the deeper genius of the trickster. The trickster only appears to be an outlandish figure. But, whether legendary or a living presence, the trickster does nothing more than play, literally, with the minds and bodies of those about him – and this he does by deception. The trickster, it should be said, deceives honestly. He plays, that is, an authentic trick, usually one that signifies on the expectations at hand. This is exactly what Ali did that night.

Faced with Foreman's superior youth and power, everyone thought Ali would resort to the butterfly/bee routine. If the bee sting was less likely to counter Foreman's punches, the butterfly dance would at least give Ali a chance to wear the champion down. Foreman prepared for the fight by practicing the tactic of cutting off the ring – the method whereby a fighter, in effect, works an opponent into a corner by working the angles of the ring to limit his ability to move freely. As in life itself, "being cornered" is close to the worst that can happen to a boxer – just as "being on the ropes" is thought to be the end of it all. In the first round Ali surprised the experts, including Foreman. He came out, not to dance, but to fight, and he fought with right-hand leads. As Norman Mailer explains in *When We Were Kings*, the right-hand lead is both risking and insulting. Usually, a right-handed boxer will lead with left jabs, holding the right for an opening. A right-hand lead is doubly risky. First, the

147

hand must travel a longer distance to make its mark. Second, in the motion, the body and chin are opened, making then vulnerable to punishment. Yet Ali threw his right hand as if to say, you're not who you think you are. Foreman was amazed and infuriated. The insult was taken. Ali won the round.

Then in subsequent rounds Ali deployed another trick, one that no one, not even his handlers, expected. He had always trained by taking blows from his sparring partners. Many boxers did. The idea is that the body thereby attunes itself to the destructive force and is then able to endure the pain in the fight itself. Still, when early in round 2 he was cornered by Foreman, Ali went to the ropes. Foreman pounded Ali's arms and body mercilessly. Everyone believed it was all over. Ali took blow upon blow. All the while, he was talking to George. "Is that all you got, George? I thought you could hit." Foreman went for the kill. Already infuriated by the insults, of which the right-hand leads were the lesser among Ali's taunts over the six weeks in Africa, Foreman must have thought he had the thing won. But by round 5 he began to fade. If you doubt that this is possible for a world-class athlete, just try any repetitive exercise at full force for, say, 30 seconds. Then, after assessing your exhaustion, multiply that by, say, 30 (that is, five rounds of 3 minutes). And don't forget the heat, the footwork, and the opponent. Even the best-conditioned athlete has his limit. Foreman soon enough came to his. Many years later, after Foreman had become the new man he is today, he himself recalled Ali's taunts that night: "Is that all you got, George? . . . Yep, it sure was, I thought." This time Foreman, a new man, was smiling at the thought of Ali's tricks.

By the eighth round Ali was in charge. He came off the ropes with a fury of punches. One hit Foreman squarely. The slow-motion film shows the sweat spraying from his head. Ali's right hand is cocked ready to finish, but Foreman is stumbling. As he falls, Ali holds his punch, circling Foreman as he goes down for the count. The fight is over. The crowd is ecstatic. The world is amazed. Then, as if the gods had been watching, the rainy season began. Within hours the stadium was flooded. But Ali was back home.

When We Were Kings was not released until 1996, more than 20 years after the fight. In 1997, it was nominated for an Oscar. By then, Ali had long been debilitated by the neurological effects of the 22 fights that came after Kinshasa, including his final great triumph over Frazier in Manila in 1975. They took a heavy toll. Oscar night, George Foreman, transformed in another way into a *Mensch*, was there at Ali's shaking side. Foreman, it is said, was completely devoted to Ali that evening so long after their fight in Africa. He gently steadied Ali as they walked together to receive the Oscar with Gast. They were, it is right to say, still kings in a way that could not have been supposed in 1974, even in Kinshasa. Both were men who, whatever they knew of the evils along the Congo, stood somehow above the world, in a place were race and all the terrible violence done in its name no longer mattered.

What a trick that is!

TRICKSTER BODIES AND CULTURAL DEATH

You'll Die One Day . . . So Better Get Ready

A Trickster Monk Turns Suffering Upside Down

When I was young, I wrote this poem. I penetrated the heart of the Buddha with a heart that was deeply wounded.

> My youth
> an unripe plum.
> Your teeth have left their marks on it.
> The tooth marks still vibrate.
> I remember always,
> remember always. . . .
>
> Fire consumes this century,
> and mountains and forests bear its mark.
> The wind howls across my ears,
> while the whole sky shakes violently in the snowstorm.
>
> Winter's wounds lie still,
> Missing the frozen blade,
> Restless, tossing and turning,
> in agony all night.

I grew up in a time of war. There was destruction all around – children, adults, values, a whole country. As a young person, I suffered a lot. Once the door of awareness has been opened, you cannot close it. The wounds of war in me are still not all healed.

> There are nights I lie awake and embrace my people, my country,
> and the whole planet with my mindful breathing.
>   Without suffering you cannot grow.
>
> **Thich Nhat Hanh**[1]

To be a boxer is to suffer in just about every conceivable way. At the beginning one must turn over one's life to the remote chance that, of all the thousands who have tried before, perhaps you will be a champion. The odds of such an outcome are anything but fair. If you are too good, or too black, or too human, you may never get the chance, because those with the money to pick the contenders rig the game. If you are not considered good enough, then you will suffer the indignity of being led along by some local fight man who wants your fees or your body to spar for the ones he chooses over you. If you get your fights on the way up, you must train in the most miserable of circumstances – smoke-filled walk-up gyms, long runs on hard streets before the sun rises, restless nights when the pain of bruises and aches makes sleep impossible, hangers-on whom you know care nothing really about you, lonely beds missing those you love or those who really might love you. Preliminary fights on the way up, when the house is empty because no one cares about your proud achievements and hard work. The big fights themselves, when no matter what shape you are in, the hands become as cement and sink lower and lower, opening your head to a deadly blow from out of nowhere.

The championship itself, should you be so improbably lucky, carries with it more hangers-on – men who may despise you even while they demand their unearned pay back, others longing for a touch of your wealth or your sex or your fame. And when the championship is well held over time, then comes the aging that always creeps up from the same nowhere of the knockout blows – the wear of years that makes each additional fight more and more a risk of the defeat you have feared from the beginning or of the crippling you denied could ever afflict you as it has the others.

151

And then one night, it is over. Hardly any have named that night so they can go out on top. You, like the vast majority you said you'd never join, leave on your back – disgraced, hurt, foolish. And the worst is yet to come. Well before the end comes, you are no longer able to cover the costs of all the years drawn from faded youth, years of purses ever less flush against the demanding expense of the hangers-on, who hold on ever more tightly as they see the last night coming before you do, but for greed's sake will not tell you, just as you would not listen if they had. And then it is over. And you are left with little but walk-around money at some casino over-lit to keep the low rollers, who remember who you were, maybe. You are left with memories of what once was or might have been, sold now to cover the remains of a life sinking back into the mire from which you were determined to escape. The only difference between the beginning and the end is that there may be some pity – guilt turned over and sealed with plastic to hide the rot. The ever-diminishing few who recognize who you were condescend, saying "Hi, champ" in a falsetto that reveals more than they suppose of the disgust they feel for the color of your skin or the slur in your speech or the shakes vibrating up and down your body puffed up with fat from the grease that makes your slide into the dirt so terrifyingly fast. You die as a child in the playground dirt, where once, before the deadly dream, there had been innocence.

This is the way it is – not just more times than not, but almost always. The fighting man suffers, not so much during his few years in the ring, but in the pain of having come from a place that left no options but to try to be this bizarre exaggerated clown of Masculine Man Himself – only to become a mime, mute before the sad fate of a most terrible impotence. The only way around this story is *through* the suffering, then beyond to some point at which it no longer matters. Nothing in the fight game teaches that such a vanishing point of spiritual freedom might exist. Only a few of the greatest heavyweights have ever achieved it – Jack Johnson (in his way), George Foreman (most purely), Rocky Marciano (perhaps). Others fell by the way. Joe Louis died an addict. Floyd Patterson has lost his memory.

Sonny Liston was murdered in his bed. Joe Frazier lives on with bitterness in his heart.

Of them all, only Muhammad Ali has risen above the wounds that will not heal, there to achieve that vanishing point outside this life where the pain becomes the prize.

———

The body is made for pain. Not just for fighters, but for us all. The pleasures our bodies can give us are capable of lifting the spirit out of whatever misery may be at hand. But bodies are for pain, which is what allows us to take note every once in a while that we are human creatures. Truth is that we seldom allow ourselves to experience the countless minor pains that course through the body. Occasionally they rise acute to the senses. For ordinary folk, these occasions are rare, seldom more than two or three times a day for the young.

But for those who make their lives in the fight game, who train themselves for pain, the experience of pain is part of the daily grind. They are the ones most aware that, if the body is a temple, it is also a prison house of limitations. And this is much the same thing as living with death on a daily basis. Death is not so much a moment when everything comes to some indeterminate end, the beyond of which we cannot know. Rather, it is the ever-present awareness of the one unarguable fact of life – that whatever *this* we enjoy or suffer in the space of our time, it will soon enough pass away. To be human is to know this – and we hardly ever know it in the head (at least, not until those last hours of life). To know that we are dying is to know with the body, just below the level of conscious thought.

In *The Fight*, his book on the Ali–Foreman fight, Norman Mailer describes Ali's body as it was even in 1974 when his physical prime was well past.

> There is always a shock in seeing him again. Not *live* as in television but standing there before you, looking his best. Then the World's Greatest Athlete is in danger of being our most beautiful man, and the vocabulary of Camp is doomed to appear. Women draw an *audible* breath. Men look *down*. They are reminded again of their lack of worth. If Ali never opened his

mouth to quiver the jellies of public opinion, he would still inspire love and hate. For he is the Prince of Heaven – so says the silence around his body when he is luminous.[2]

It was – perhaps still is – a body with such transcendent powers as to touch the hearts of men, like Mailer, who trade on the overwrought show of the male ego. Such men do not often, if ever, describe another man's body as "beautiful." For them to look down in the presence of such masculine beauty is to confess the deeper underlying truth machismo is meant to deny – that the line between the feminine catching of breath in awe and the masculine looking down in shame is a fine one. Ali's body at its most beautiful erased that line.

But Mailer also describes Ali's body when it was depressed. "His pale skin turns the color of coffee with milky water, no cream. There is a sickly green of a depressed morning in the muddy washes of the flesh."[3] This happens to bodies when they are unwell with an awareness of the body's limits, of the presence of death and danger. Mailer's description is of Ali in training for the Foreman fight, when by all honest measures everyone thought the most likely outcome would be for Ali to be seriously hurt, perhaps even killed. (It happens.) Ali had to have known, behind the trickster bravado, that Foreman was more trouble than he had ever seen. This, we can be sure, is trouble a fighter trains himself to know by the daily round of punches from lesser sparring partners, punches taken to the body in preparation for a punishment worse still to come. When you spend your days and weeks thinking of a man who could kill you, it is impossible that the luminous aura around the body not turn sickly green. Such a depression is the weight of life's realities.

Ali's body *was*! Today one wants to say *was*, as if the body he has now – bloated, mumbling, stumbling, and shaking – is a joke of some kind. When, in 1996 in Atlanta, Ali carried the Olympic torch to the caldron of fire, and stood tall before the world, people everywhere cheered lustily, many moved to tears. Did they cheer and weep for what once was? Or for what still is? For those with a sentimental heart, Ali's body today may be an object of pity – not so much a shadow of what it was as an absurd distortion of its former beauty. Yet, if one is to trust what people say, those cheers and tears were not so much regret for what was lost, but love for the soul that outlives the bodily limits. Perhaps people exalted a bodily resurrection of some kind. All of Ali's closest friends today say that no one should feel pity for the man. Far from regretting the state of his body, Ali accepts it and enjoys his life, just as fully as ever.

In the absence of his original body, what is one to do? As it turns out, it is extremely difficult, perhaps impossible, to reproduce the original. The most notable, and probably most successful, attempt to play Ali is Will Smith in Michael Mann's 2001 film *Ali*.[4] Will Smith is in many ways just the right man to be cast in Ali's role. He is himself a trickster of sorts in his musical life, and has credibly played a trickster role in *Six Degrees of Separation*.[5] And Smith does well in getting Ali's voice down. Plus which, the movie itself is really not bad at all. Yet I for one had a very hard time watching it. I refused to see it in first release in the theaters. I waited a long while before watching the video. Even then, I shut it off and sent it back after a few minutes. In fact, the only way I could watch it was to let it run all day long and take in whatever was playing when I came by the screen.

For the longest while, I could not figure out my resistance to Will Smith's *Ali*, until I saw the film *The Greatest*[6] in which Ali plays himself. Quite unlike *Ali*, this is a truly terrible movie, so bad that resistance to viewing it is entirely reasonable. But there was a difference. Ali was totally convincing acting himself. You might say, *of course*! But acting oneself on film is different from the performances of self in daily life. That added degree of self-consciousness can put even a professional actor off stride, as we amateurs all know when some joker calls out our routine for what it is. We are usually left speechless. To act the role one plays by nature is to put too much of what one represses into conscious focus. Yet, in this otherwise forgettable film, Ali played himself memorably, for me at least.

It may be that real-life tricksters like Ali cannot be copied by others. Only they can play themselves. This would stand to reason, because what the trickster does is reshape and distort his body to fit the scene at hand. Trickster work is bodywork before it is anything else. It is not, of course, merely corporeal. But it does begin and end with the body. This was Ali's special gift in all the key moments of his career. Against Liston in 1964, Ali cleverly convinced the man that, in the absence of a sane mind, he also had no body. Then, fight night, Liston came into his presence and saw for the first time that the body was formidable and just as destructive as his own. Against Foreman in 1974, his rope-a-dope was nothing if not a trick of shape shifting. Ali splayed his body out on the ropes inviting the hammer blows in defiance of every article of boxing wisdom. At times he looked foolish, especially when he leaned so far back as to remind George Plimpton of someone leaning out a window to wash it from outside. What Ali did, after tricking Foreman with a right-hand lead and a bit of dancing the first round, was to turn his body into a punching bag – just as inert and absorptive as the real thing. It is the one thing Foreman did not train for, and the one thing capable of sucking all the force out of his blows. By playing a bit of the butterfly, Ali set up Foreman for the bee sting in the eighth round, by the trick of making him believe he had abandoned his butterfly bee routine.

Even so, the most astonishing bodily trick of all was Ali's performance in his last great fight on September 30, 1975 – the "Thrilla in Manila," which was the rubber match with Joe Frazier. There are those who say that the three Ali–Frazier fights were the greatest rivalry in the sport. If so, at least part of the claim is justified by the fact that all three fights went very nearly the scheduled distance – 41 of 42 scheduled rounds, a very rare occurrence in modern boxing.[7] Ali lost the first 15-round match with Frazier on March 8, 1971, just weeks after the United States Supreme Court overturned his draft-evasion conviction. After a long absence from the ring, Ali had had only one tune-up, with Jerry Quarry, and that was a very short fight of three rounds. Ali was out of shape in more ways than one. Yet he endured the full 15 rounds, losing by a decision.

Ali–Frazier II was on January 28, 1974. Though he had been knocked out by Foreman in the second round in January 1973,

Smokin' Joe was, if not at the top of his game, still a considerable force. He was 29, older but not old. Ali won the rematch in a 12-round decision. By the time of Ali–Frazier III, in 1975 in Manila (almost a year after Ali beat Foreman in Zaire, and more than a year and a half after their second fight), both men were clearly on the down side of their careers. Frazier was nearly 33, Ali 35. Yet they both endured all but a few minutes of the full 15 rounds. Ali won the early going. Frazier carried the middle rounds. Then, in the twelfth round, Ali came back and began to hurt Frazier. A cut opened. Blood flowed. A determined punch knocked Frazier's mouthpiece out. By the last minute of the fourteenth round Frazier could not see from the blood and the swelling. His corner threw in the towel. Ali had won. Frazier stumbled to his stool. Ali collapsed. They were, in the full meaning of the word, utterly spent.

Neither would fight as well again. Frazier would retire the following year, only to humiliate himself attempting a comeback in 1981. Ali would fight on with an occasional flourish of the old style, until he was humiliated by being knocked out by Larry Holmes in 1980 (and worse yet losing his last fight to Trevor Berbick in 1981). Two men of nearly the same age. Two men who helped make each other what they were. Two men never able to forget each other, never able to overcome the bitterness that had entered in. And two men who, on October 1, 1975, fought each other as Greek warriors – to the last drop of strength, to the literal end.

Frazier endured the Manila fight by sheer doggedness. He would not let Ali run and hide. He took Ali's jabs head on, always moving in. Frazier was wiser than Foreman had been. He did not give up his arm strength trying to beat Ali into submission. He simply moved in on him. Ali, on the other hand, distorted his body once again. It was not a new trick. In a sense he has used it in the rope-a-dope and in the two previous Frazier bouts. Not new, but this time Ali deployed it to the extreme. He showed the world a body built for suffering, which is the stuff of endurance in such fights.

In a sense, the last Frazier fight was Ali playing the trickster routine to the hilt. Though his life to that point had been one trick after another, the trickster career was built on an ability to make his body into whatever form fit the situation at hand. When, against Liston, he was nothing but a young dancer, he fearlessly stung the bully. When, against Foreman, he was too old for the youngster, he outsmarted him by the plasticity of his body on the ropes. And when, against Frazier, he was fading fast in the years before the neurological damage,[8] he found strength he had no right to have. Ali had lost his legs, always the first part of the body to go. Yet, he made his legs work for him against Frazier. The pain of fatigue, not to mention of the blows Frazier landed, must have been as hard a labor as there is for a man. Yet Ali joined Frazier in suffering through it all, then in the last rounds found his old form enough to bleed his equally worn-down opponent, and to win it all.

When, more than two decades later, Ali stumbled and shook his way with the Olympic torch in Atlanta, all this was long in the past. Still, he stood there as he was, for the entire world to see. Just as, still, he carries about his bag of tricks to play on Fidel Castro and on kids in airports. Some, not Ali, must find the aging, crippled body repulsive. For Ali, this pretty body had always been there for him, as they say today. He had no reason to look down. Once beautiful beyond all male measures, now puffy and slow, it remains the body on which Ali, the trickster-celebrity, plays whatever role he plays in the times he has, and has with us who live in the same world as he does.

Pain is the presence of death in the body. The remarkable thing about the human body is that it is capable of feeling (or concealing) the pain that comes from outside, from the play of mind and emotion with the force of social things as they come upon the individual. Hence, the fourth defining moment in Ali's life in this body – the one entirely outside the ring, but the one that must have caused him more pain than any of the others. In 1981, Jose Torres asked Ali what he considered his biggest mistake. His answer: "The biggest mistake I ever made was when I made the statement that I had no quarrels with the Viet Cong. I made it too early. I was right, but I should have said it later."[9] How could it be that one of his two most memorable statements was badly timed? Note that he defends the commitment, if not the timing. How could he not? His life was shaped by it. That may be why, so many years later, at the very end of his life in the ring, he considered it a mistake.

The 1981 interview took place after he had lost to Larry Holmes, when it was obvious that his career was over. Though he still dismissed the loss to Holmes as a "bad night," Ali surely knew he was on the last rope. He was three weeks shy of his fortieth birthday. He had failed at three marriages and would not marry Lonnie for another five years.[10] He had nine children.[11] He had debts. So many people to care for. But he no longer had the skills, which, among much else, were his only proven means of making money. Though he had done better than most fighters in conserving some of his wealth, he had still been taken advantage of. Of the well more than $30 million made in the ring, only a fraction was left. Other 40-year-old men do the damnedest things. Not Ali. He flailed about for a few years, but ended up (at age 45) making the best of his four marriages and finding a way to live a good life. Still, in 1981, he must have been filled with terror and regret. The Viet Cong remark and all that came with it had cost him a great deal. Among the costs he must have felt most sorely was the nearly four years of his prime in exile – at a time when Larry Holmes wasn't even old enough to be his sparring partner (which, in fact, he was for a while). There were severe financial costs, certainly. But when one loses the body on which one has bet everything, the real cost is the what-could-have-been.

The pain of those years of exile was, probably, not so much the loss of glory. He did more to regain his glory after 1971 than anyone could have dreamt possible. It must have been the cultural death. He had made a very good public show of the years between 1967 and 1971. But these were still the years when, apart from being adored by the ordinary people of color of the world, he was despised by an even greater number, many of whom wanted to put all the blame for the ravages of the 1960s on his shoulders – everything from civil rights to urban turmoil to the counterculture of disrespect to Black Power to the Nation of Islam to the anti-war movement. In point of fact, he had been

implicated in all these events, to varying degrees. While not a
civil rights activist or a building burner, he was one of the first to
popularize (as opposed to originate) a theory of America's racial
injustice. While not a hippie by any means, he was called the
fifth Beatle, and not as a compliment.[12] While anything but a
Black Power purist, he did more even than Malcolm X to give
Black Islam, the most inscrutable of Black Power movements, a
friendly face. And to this day there are those who claim that it
was Muhammad Ali, more even than Walter Cronkite, who
solidified popular opinion against Lyndon Johnson's war in
Vietnam.[13] Ali certainly had all the credentials for a seat in the
pantheon of American hatred, which is why the FBI paid close
attention to his movements. A man like Ali, so utterly lacking in
guile,[14] could not have enjoyed being hated. He was too good at
getting people to give him the love he needed.

Hatred can inflict the worst sort of pain – that of a cultural
death. When a person is cut off, shunned or excommunicated,
whether from a formal group or a casual circle of relations, he
suffers; and men suffer more than women, because they vest so
much in the approval of others. For a man of Ali's character,
being hated had to have been among the most painful of experiences. There is no way, apart from years on the analytic couch,
to train for hatred. Or, if there is, Ali had trained so hard for the
physical pain that he had little room or time for the deeper
preparations for adult life, which in his case would ultimately
be life out of the spotlight.

But then again Ali remade himself. He found a way to find
a woman, Lonnie, who could manage and tolerate him. He
resorted to the deeper benefits of his religious faith, which
taught him to accept everything as the will of Allah, thus as
prize, not punishment. The brash and insistent will probably
think both resorts are weaknesses. For Ali, they became sources
of strength that allowed him to endure the pain of those lost
years when, in addition to being so glamorous, he was also
despicable in more than a few eyes. And surely they were a
refuge in those sad, needless years after Manila when he sub-
jected his central nervous system to crippling punishment. Life
comes as it comes. Would he be the man he is today without the

Parkinson's syndrome that ties him to Lonnie and to his faith? Certainly not. Who among us is what she is without coming to terms with what falls in her way? Ali may be responsible for the neurological damage. But that is different by far from saying he chose it or sought it. But, however the disease came upon him, the important thing is that it provided the means whereby he showed the world how little he deserved the hatred of some, and how much others are right to love him. This, I think, is what drives some people crazy, still. You can't really hate him. So you have to hate those who love him.

But this is only part of the last chapter of the story. The man's raw exposure to pain and death – similar to us all, yet differently managed – does not account fully for the extent of his celebrity. Going back to George Foreman's thought that he became who he is because the world needed such a one, there remains, still open, the question of just what kind of world it is that may need such a character, such a trickster.

Muhammad Ali is still a man of his times. Yet it is very difficult to say what those times might be that they could make this man so much more than any man should be. What is plain is that long after Ali left center stage, he remains a phenomenon hard to define within the terms of ordinary language.

It may well be that the mystery of Ali's unusual longevity in the public imagination is the reason for the outrageous and conflicting feelings he inspires. Mysteries can have that effect on people, because they prompt extremes of feeling that actually aggravate the desire to explain what in fact may be inscrutable. In Ali's case, the excess of adoration that would make him into more than any one man can or ought to be does injustice to the human frailty of the man. Just as much, at the other extreme, there is a twisted bitterness that would bring Ali down a notch or two – so long after his religious faith, ripened on deliquescing flesh, reduced him to a man little ready, much less able, to be more than Allah's unassuming servant. By exciting feelings that can never be reconciled, Ali's celebrity divides his followers into rivals camped on either side of the inscrutable, leaving those who would make sense of it all looking on per-plexed.

Gerald Early is alert to the dangers of misunderstanding by both extremes. The logic here is simple, if the man is in fact a man of his times, then his value as a measure of those times is destroyed if he is not taken seriously.

> This would put him in danger not only of having his consider-able significance misunderstood, but also, ironically, of being diminished as both a public-figure and a black man of some illustrious complexity. Ali, as a result of his touching, or poign-ant, or pathetic, or tragic (take your pick) appearance at the torch-lighting ceremony at the 1996 Olympic Games in Atlanta has become, for new generations that did not grow up with him and for the older generations that did, the Great American Martyr, our new Lincoln, our new Martin Luther King, Oh, Father Abraham, Oh, Father Martin, Oh, Father Muhammad: the man whose hands, once unerring pistons of punishment in the prizefighting ring, tremble from boxing-induced Parkinson's disease [*sic*]; the man whose voice is such a slurred whisper that he, who was once the Louisville Lip because he loved talking so much, does not like to speak in public and rarely does; the once-uncompromising black nationalist now reduced, like Orson Welles at the end, to performing magic tricks for the crowd as if he were parodying his own pop-culture greatness, exposing it as an illusion, just as his nationalism had been, just as his cultist/ religious self had been.[15]

In short, the inscrutability of the Ali celebrity is nothing without the man, and this man endures inexplicably well beyond the expiration of his athletic genius.

Whether this is true of celebrity in general is far from evident. Some, but not many, have survived the decline of their original talent as Ali has. At the end, Frank Sinatra's voice was not the same, but it was still good enough to move a crowd. Michael Jordan played again after aging had done its dirty work, and somehow adjusted his game to his own altered physical state. Ronald Reagan was able to re-script his act just enough to make it to the curtain of his second presidential term before no mask could cover the disease on his mind. Elvis, the king of dead celebrities, was pitiful at the end after drugs had taken his soul – still, he represents the outer limit of the ratio of celebrity to reality. There are others. But only a few, by genius or geniality, outlive the talent that brought them fame.

More commonly, celebrity fades when the persona upon which it rides is still young and beautiful. Surely the reason for the early loss of an emotional gate is that the celebrity is so exposed to the public eye. In the short run the celebrated personality rises above scrutiny. But in the long run the excess of praise erodes the Teflon surface such that no amount of oil can keep the nasty egg of envy from sticking.

Hence, Ali at his most astonishing. Like the trickster, he has been able over time to reshape himself – to overcome the limits of youth, to transcend the ravages of years in exile, to exceed the possibilities of aging, to express himself after the loss of voice and the ruin of his act. But there is no trickster without an audience for his show of deception. Thus, when he changes bodily shape to fit the conditions at hand, he is calling out something in those who enjoy the show, as well as those upon whom the trick is pulled. What could it be that he calls out in others?

Ali's times have been filled with men and women and children who have had to suffer their own cultural deaths. He was a child during the age of the nuclear holocaust and the terrors of Cold War. He was a young man in the 1960s, when the full force of the world's decolonizing movements changed the name of the global game. He entered into retirement early in the 1980s, just when the economic miserliness of the new conservatives was making life more and more miserable for the world's most poor, just as the tiny stratum of the very rich solidified their appalling wealth. He was well settled in Michigan when the Cold War ended, not to the relief of all, but to the tune of terrorisms – many real, many so called – by which people came to understand their world as far from orderly. And he lived through September 11, 2001, with more than a few of his wits about him. At the fund-raising gala in New York City, he was asked what it was like to be a Muslim after such a horrible attack? Without

Muhammad Ali, the aging king of the world, with Hamid Karsai in Afghanistan, 2002
© AP/Wide World Photos

missing a beat, he replied: What was it like to be a Christian during Hitler's holocaust? Ali knew all these things. But, more important, he somehow fit into a world marked by such a concatenation of terrible things, one worse than the other.

What is the current situation? Could it be that it is a situation in which millions of people have good reason to feel despair, and thus good reason to fear that the world is coming to an end? To speak of cultural death in the global sense is to speak of a time when people believe that what they had once known for sure is no more. It is to speak less of the threat of physical destruction with which the nuclear age began than of the fear that one's neighbor, far from being just a little different, may actually be the one who turns you in to the cops, to the Red baiters, to the mullahs – and pulls the trigger that kills everything. Whatever is meant by the term "postmodern" – and there is little accord as to what or if it is – it surely is a slogan, at least, for these times – times in which all that prevailed to varying effect for a good half-millennium is fading away, only to be replaced not by another certitude but by its very absence.[16] Whether such a condition becomes the order of the new days, we shall see. But many, many people the world over fear that it is; and that is what a cultural death is for the many. And it is more than enough to promote the search for whichever saving heroes or celebrities or whomevers there may be who can show the way.

These are also conditions ripe for tricksters, who arise in those places and times when people feel they have no other recourse in this world. This may be why there are so relatively few trickster myths in the so-called modern cultures where historical time invites the continuing hope of social change.[17] Accordingly, this may be why, also, when tricksters do appear in cultures adhering to the dream of progressive time, they appear in periods when the historical prospects for relief are most bleak. Hence, the trickster-fools of carnivals on the liminal eve of long periods of deprivation are most exaggerated in those places where denial is normal to daily life. Behind the masks of Mardi Gras in New Orleans, or Carnival in Rio, all of the sexual and racial exclusions are invited into the open for a time.

In some instances, those in charge of local history desperately stretch the liminal moment in order to ward off the coming deprivation. Like camp counselors at the last night of charades, the ruling class may institutionalize the jokes the lowly play on them. The court jester is nothing if not a way of bringing the fool into the play of power's inevitable limits. There are even historical instances of some duration when the once powerful entertain the trickster in order to hold in place a vestige of what was lost. One such striking case is the Jim Crow era in the American South after the Civil War, when whites extended their rule a full century after the slaves were emancipated in 1863. This they did by entering into the foolishness itself. Though Jim Crow is anything but a joke, there is a trick being turned on the whites who succeeded in legalizing the rule of racial segregation. Mummers and minstrels, who dress up in the black face of

165

those they exclude in the course of social order, reshape their white flesh and dance like crows to mimic not so much the ones portrayed but their very own bondage to social hatred. The trickster is nothing if not plastic to the changing times.

But, important to add, the trickster is not always a celebrity. Occasionally, celebrity may fall to the trickster, only to be wrenched away in time. Perhaps even this happens only rarely, because the trickster is native to cultures without mass media where, usually (not always), the priestly class holds the keys to whatever celebrations are permitted. So, when the trickster becomes a celebrity, it is more often in those modern cultures where tricksters arise less often and then only in some unusual relation to a culture's need to celebrate. This is the case with Muhammad Ali, who is the exception that proves the rule. As he left his youth behind, Ali relied less and less on the trickster game. But he was still quite often taken as the genius deceiver, a status he may well cherish by the bag of tricks he carries about late in life.

———

When it happens that a celebrity manages, for whatever reason or cause, to keep the trickster alive well after its natural time, it happens (and probably only happens) when, as the saying goes, the time is right – when, that is, the social order of things demands it. And when this occurs, things are never what they appear or ought to be. They are not, because, to take the expression seriously, to describe the social opportunity for a certain striking event as "the times being right" is to trade on the often overlooked fact of life that culture, whatever else it may be, is mostly about time.

A time can be right only when times are expected to change. Usually, in timeless cultures, time is overwhelmed by the eternal, such that events in this world are analogies. No one has put this better than Claude Lévi-Strauss in *The Savage Mind*, where he explains that those cultures without a history enjoy an interpretive genius of their own kind. In the case of totemic cultures (with which he, like Émile Durkheim, was preoccupied), the array of animal and vegetable totems constitutes a series of ahistorical events that proscribe the realm of human origins.

Any Australian Wotjobaluk who may belong to the death-adder clan understands his time, so to speak, as a present tied by analogy to the animal from which he gets his identity.[18] Of which Lévi-Strauss has said: "The two series [the natural and the human] exist in time but under an atemporal regime, since being both real, they sail through time together, remaining such as they were at the moment of separation."[19] Such a time is more than simply metaphoric.

When a culture takes seriously its own history, it very often takes on an emblem – for example, a school whose sports teams are called, say, the cardinals, – though no member of the group thinks of herself as actually a bird of this kind. At best, these are pseudo-totems, broken figures of speech that rise briefly to song or shout when the team gains some passing advantage. But when in cultures where, in Lévi-Strauss's alluring phrase, people sail through time with their totemic names, they *are* in some sense cardinals or death-adders, in that the analogy accounts for their origins and their natures. The totem analogue allows them to organize their living and their thinking in a system that may seem strange to the modern mind but makes all the sense in their world. The elegance of the order of their social things is in their way of situating themselves relative to other beings of the *same* sort (other human clans) who live in the same temporal series *and* still other beings of a *different* sort (the emblematic plants or animals) who live in a prior, hence different but just as real, temporal order. The differences between the two – human time and totemic time – are thus swallowed up by the timeless. The nearest ordinary example of such an experience among people, like ourselves, who live in historical time is our recollections of those who died young. I think of President John F. Kennedy as the young man he was when he was murdered, not as either dry bones in a coffin or as the old man he would be in this moment had he lived. His time is frozen, while mine continues. But in the face of separation from a beloved young one, something makes us all savages. We let the time between 1963 and 2003 sail by as though we were still, impossibly, together.

But historical cultures, like the ones that grew up in the Greco-Roman diasporas of late Hebrew and early Christian times, are anything but atemporal. For them time is of the essence, even when it is only the time remaining between the Fall and the Return, the Alpha and the Omega. It may well be that what Walter Russell Mead has called the Abrahamic cultures of Judaism, Christianity, and Islam – and their secular successors, liberalism and Marxism – are cultures of time because (by contrast to all other global civilizations) they were founded on a monotheistic idea. If the source of all time is One, then his or her time must be real in much the same way that ordinary mortal time is. The atemporal of the Abrahamic cultures is, in effect, a much slower time than that of Lévi-Strauss's savage mind. The two temporal series are, in effect, this-worldly and other-worldly, such that what happens in both temporal series is of comparable meaning. If the one deity is the source of all else, then whatever the Calvinists and Unitarians believe, God's time is much more than analogous to our time. It *is* our time, so to speak. Give the savage mind its due. No self-respecting member of the death-adder clan really thinks of himself as a death-adder. He is much more sophisticated than that. He likely thinks (or thought, as the case may be) that, in being somehow *like* the animal totem, his origins – and thus what moderns would call his identity – derive by analogy from the natural history from which he is separated. This may be why we moderns think of allegory as a strong sort of analogy. Since we would impute a meaningful story to everything that happens, we, more even than the savage, take our time all too seriously. How serious can you get about being a death-adder or, better, to cite another Wotjobaluk totem, some flatulent bird like the hot-wind pelican (*Wartwut-Batchangal*)?

Culture, if it is anything important at all, is about how a social group thinks itself in relation to time. Otherwise, the member of a culture has no way to organize in the mind where he belongs. Space can never work as well to this end because, under globalized time (when, curiously, time begins to sail once again), space is generally, if not always, displaced over the seas, the mountain, or just on the other side of the fire pit or latrine. This is why it may be that the trickster is native to those atemporal times in which only the human and the natural sail past each other. The sailing time of the savage mind (unlike that of the globalized cultures) is in fact an illusion. What sails is the human *relative* to the natural order, while in the larger order of things time itself is atemporal; hence, like the light of long-dead stars, nothing really moves in any discernible way.

In fact, scientific discernment is (and here the word can be used) *primitive*. Cultures with histories are not better, but they are more sophisticated if only because their time is vastly more complicated. Once a people introduces something like *meaning* into the story of time, then everything has to mean *something*. Thus, in these cultures the poor and inferior are offered no meaning save for the thin hope of redemption in the other time. When groups and classes in the historical cultures like ours are stuck in place (meaning, that is, *social* place), they may hold out the hope of a better life up to a point. But when history tells them to forget it, the effect is much more powerful. Better to be a farting pelican than a fourth-generation welfare mom after welfare is cut off.

In the West's culture of historical time, this was the case during the so-called Middle Ages, which were an insufferably long stretch of this-worldly time when time itself stood still. From the final collapse of Rome in the first years of the fifth century of the so-called Christian Era to the first dawning of the Renaissance in the thirteenth century – for nearly a millennium, give or take a century or two – time stood still. Hence, the odd figure of speech: the Dark Ages. It was an age when, decidedly after Charlemagne, the Holy Roman Church governed the cultural sphere with a rigid, other-worldly scheme that fixed this world outside of God's time. To speak, therefore, of the *traditional* is to speak, in Max Weber's alluringly apt phrase, of "the eternal yesterday" – of, in effect, the failure of the ancient Greek and Hebrew ideas of continuous or, at least, morally principled social change. Thus it was, as so many from Harvey Cox to Michel Foucault remind us, that the ship of fools celebrated the transcending virtue of those mad enough to enjoy the benefits of life out of ordinary time.[20]

This too is Norman Cohn's famous interpretation of these middle years of Western Christendom as years in which the oppressed poor were drawn in great numbers to millenarian cults of various kinds – to, in effect, countercultures outside the prevailing stasis. Millenarianism looks to another world, to be sure; but in looking outside the world at hand, it looks to a better world than the one offered by the prevailing orthodoxy that lays claim to their earthly souls. In *Pursuit of the Millennium*, Cohn describes, among others, the amoral superman, one of the trickster-like figures of the Free Spirit heresies that spread over much of medieval Europe and endured for nearly five centuries. The Free Spirit cults came in different forms, of which the most striking and enduring were those based on the Catharist, Albigensian, and neo-Manichean heresies. Like most millenarian movements, they thrived among the poorest classes and were at their zenith in the poorest times. Cohn describes them as among the "most perplexing and mysterious phenomena in medieval history,"[21] because the adherents believed so mightily in their own spiritual purity that they considered themselves spirits above the moral order, hence free spirits. "The 'perfect man' could always draw the conclusion that it was permissible for him, even incumbent on him, to do whatever was commonly regard as forbidden." Cohn does not refer to medieval amoral superman as a trickster, but that is what he was – a figure that possessed the essential trickster attributes of life on the margins, between the divine and the lewd, the normal and the devious. With the Renaissance, the amoral superman became less the outsider – the trickster that plays against the exaggerated claims to normalcy. He became the normal itself. What better word is there for the capitalist entrepreneur, the producer of all good, the captain of history, than the amoral superman?

What culture is not vulnerable to the amoral superman when times are very bad? Or, when times are pressingly hard, what culture will not long for, at least a trickster, if not a hero, to inspire some laughter if not quite hope, some understanding if not quite revolutionary zeal? Cultures, it might be said, manage time when the spaces of their confinement are depleted by drought, bound tightly by oppressors, or threatened by nature or human catastrophe. Under these circumstances, of which the millenarian end of all time is the extreme, those so long excluded by the culture that controls the social space with its colonizing calendars may well rise up, setting another culture – which is to say another dimension of time – against the prevailing one.

Cultures are thought to be about what people believe. They are, of course. But they can only be this if they are also about what people fear. Cultures exclude every bit as much as they include. They affirm the good history while denying the bad one. But both histories are the storied cultures of real, once or still existing, peoples gathered against the worst to assert the best they know.

In former times, the trickster was ubiquitous among the poor and the suffering. The rich and powerful understood this, which is why they allowed jesters into their courtly presence to relieve the pressure, to tell the people they understood the unspoken possibility of their own limitations. If tricksters are less evident in modern cultures, or if they are dressed up with their naked parts covered, it may be because the whole purpose of modern time was to assert the eternal progress of human time, a quite improbable idea. Times end, and history stops. So any culture that must affirm the future of the good society must then expunge, or sanitize, its tricksters.

But every now and then, some damn fool sneaks into the open and changes everything. He tricks the true believers into accepting time for the arbitrary, uncertain thing it is. He upsets the cultural apple cart by telling the story of the true meaning of life, which in the end is always the story of death.

———

Somewhere in the last few years Ali repeated for public consumption what he had been saying for years. "You are all going to die one day. . . . So you better get ready."[22] When people like Ali say such a thing calmly, almost as a joke, they say it out of their own deep familiarity with death in their lives. The instinct of some cultures is to say that it is a faith-based wish. For many it may be. But for others it comes from the quietness within. People will judge for themselves whether Ali, like the desert monks, has achieved the quality of enlightened quietude. All I can say is that he sounds like a person who has.

It makes no sense to claim that Ali is *the* man of the present hour, or that these days were made for him. Celebrity does not work that way. But it is true that no trickster, among those practicing their art in a given time, can deceive for the good if his trick does not call out a truth shared by the many who listen to his story and live to tell it. Muhammad Ali, the trickster, is thus neither pure nor purely a trickster, anymore than he is, at the limit of all reason, the embodiment of postmodern man. Ali is a man of pain, hence of death. He is thus a man who has already recognized the deeper nature of his world – its racial evils, its human delights, its physical pleasures, its hard-won battles, its terrible uncertainties, its surprises. The world at hand may differ from previous worlds, if it does, not because it is marked by such things. Worlds have always been filled with injustices, uncertainties, and other dirty surprises. But this one, whatever you call it, may simply be a world in which whatever normals there are, are normally both uncertain and unlikely ever to return to the certitude righteous people once thought they had within reach.

Such a claim is not at all beyond argument. No one knows the answer, though surely everyone has a preference for more of the certain than normally one gets. What is beyond argument (though many will argue it just the same) is that such an uncertain state of affairs is really nothing other than the essential truth of human life. *We are all going to die.* Yet who but a few know how to get ready? The final irony of times like these is not so much that death and violence are everywhere. They are, of course. Rather, it is that such times as these reveal what most human beings spend a lifetime denying – that everything is impermanent, as the Buddhists say; that life can be lived in the present only when one lives for the death held in each breath. One lives by dying. This is the final irony of life. The good news of the present age is that the unavoidable death is now more unavoidable than ever it was before.

In such a time one is inclined to look to a man who knows death. Ali always knew it – as a child of slaves, as a black boy in the American South, as a lapsed son of the Congo, as a man whose art was composed out of pain, as a man who faced three of the most terrifying opponents in boxing history, as a man who lived through the end of it all only to emerge quietly tricking

172

and smilingly scolding – with an authority that comes from having been there before, and more often, than others.

This makes Muhammad Ali more than human. It makes him more *deeply* human. When he stepped into the ring, it undressed him and gave some others the courage to get naked with life themselves. Celebrities can be, and usually are, worshipped. Trickster-celebrities may be, but they do their magic only when they expose the terrible news that all of us shit and piss and fart and want to fuck – the most earthy of human things, the very things by which we spill the remains of our bodies back to the dust from which we came.

Whatever else he once was, Muhammad Ali is in fact a minister, just as he had insisted when the power of his government tried to crush him. Talk about tricks, one last time. What a trick it is to get us to laugh at death, including death in such times as these and the one that awaits us all one fine day.

———

Until that day comes, most of us live on in the big lie that only someone like Ali can deceive us into doubting. People want what in the West we call the good life. Seldom can those who seek such a life say, precisely, what they mean by it. Usually, when called upon to say something, or when a definition spills out inadvertently, these same people will say that the good life has to do with material comfort, perhaps a measure of wealth, a loving family, perhaps with children who might grow up to achieve much the same. The dream is particularly acute in Muhammad Ali's native land, America, where poorly defined high values have so long been the key to success.

Cassius Clay grew up around people who believed that the supreme cultural goal of the American way was achieved through monetary success in a legitimate job, and that when legitimate means were available, then breaking a rule or two may be necessary if not necessarily good.[23] He certainly knew what the ideal was and, in some ways, achieved it. He enjoyed, in his day, a good bit of wealth. He strove, however awkwardly, for the family life his unsettled ways usually disrupted. And, most striking of all, he single-handedly turned prizefighting into a better, more legitimate version of itself.[24]

Still, as Ali nears the end of his life, it is not his success that accounts for his enduring celebrity. Future generations of children will be told stories of Muhammad Ali's athletic brilliance and of his quite admirable human qualities. But among the stories will be, almost certainly, stories of a man who outlived his body – a man revered to the end of his days.

Humans are storytelling creatures. Before they heard their stories, much reduced, on some televisual medium, they read them in books, or heard them at bedtime, or told them around camp fires in caves. Stories always exaggerate. Whether it is the producer seeking audience share, or the bone-weary parent trying to put a child to sleep, or a shaman responsible for comforting the clan, the storyteller is always drawn toward the more dramatic moments and away from the ordinary. This, of course, is how heroes are produced over time.

Muhammad Ali, whatever else he was and is, became a global hero – in many ways he is the first, truly global hero of most, if not all, human beings on the planet. His earlier career as a trickster did not give way so much as melt quietly into the heroic image that gradually took its place in the public view of the man. Near the end of Ali's life, when the trickster is a shadow of his former self, when his body is slow and crippled, the man remains a hero – much to the irritation of some.

It is actually a good thing that people attempt to bring down their heroes. Though the practice may have gotten a bit out of hand today, the thing is that all great heroes must stand up to scrutiny. The better ones do, not always justifiably. Celebrity, in some ways an acute necessity in the electronic age, always puts the hero somewhat out of reach of ordinary life. And this may be why the stories of their dirt are so compelling. People who rely on the celebrity to lift them out of their own soiled lives eventually desire to bring the celebrity-hero down. And so they do. Thomas Jefferson has been proved to have fathered children by his enslaved mistress. Martin Luther King, Jr, has been shown to have had a sex life contrary to his public morality. John F. Kennedy is known to have lied about his health, a scandal that may well outrun the sexual license he took. Yet, celebrity-heroes like these will endure beyond the time of their having been brought down.

Without suggesting that Muhammad Ali's heroic achievements were of the same order as those of Jefferson, King, and Kennedy, one can still enjoy the man in comparison to others of the type. Ali certainly failed to achieve many of the successes he longed for. He was a terrible husband until the last marriage. However much he loved children in general, he was not, for much of his earlier life, a consistent parent. He loved his mother, as she loved him; but he was anything but cute little GG as he lived out his days. Ali has been, and still is, much the ordinary man, even as he has been lifted up into the cloud of celebrity.

The tricksters of earlier times, those whose stories were passed down more often around camp fires than before the television, were in their ways celebrities. But their celebrity could not cover up their private parts. These were the key to the stories told of them. In contrast to Brer Rabbit, Mickey in the night kitchen, Ananse the spider, and all the others, the Ali trickster was a real critter, still alive today. It is entirely possible that no actually existing trickster can be real for long. This is the work of the stories that, in an earlier time, turned trickster into beings outside the realm of human being, and in this day seeks to bring them down to earth.

One might even wonder if there can be anything like a trickster-hero, especially in the case of the old and crippled Muhammad Ali who has become more the hero than the trickster. Perhaps not. Perhaps it is necessary that an aging trickster, if he or she is to remain a celebrity, be transposed into a *mere* hero. If so, in Ali's case his status as one of the elders of the human tribe likely turns on the fact that we already know all the dirt there is to be known about him. He cheated on his wives. He allowed his public relations act to injure men like Joe Frazier. He humiliated Floyd Patterson. He mismanaged his wealth. These and other of his human failings are all very well known. Still he survives.

In the end, Muhammad Ali's appeal to those who admire him in spite of a body that would make them miserable comes from some quality beyond what can be expressed by the trickster, the celebrity, and the hero. He lives quietly. He prays. He receives visitors with love. He comes out into the world to do some good. He earns his living as best he can. He holds to his friends and children and wife. He is, in effect, boring – except for one thing. Ali still excites because he lives today not so much in the past glories, as in the future that awaits us all.

We, for the most part, look away from our deaths. Muhammad Ali looks forward to his. He is not the first religious man to make this claim. But he is on a very short list of public figures who have made their final claim so natural an aspect of their story. In this, he compels human sympathy. The sympathetic hero is always object to the projected wish of the follower. We who wish we were not afraid of our deaths may well find comfort in the belief that we too can live as Ali does. But then, more often than not, we don't. And we don't because it is very hard to live that way – to accept the body's limitations, to pray each day for the dark unknown to come, to bow five times before the Maker of life and death.

Those who live the lie that they will never die cannot help but be drawn to a public man who, it seems, never once lied about anything that matters – a man who has nothing to hide, not even the fact of his distorted body, upon which is written the coming of the end. Still, like Fidel Castro, he makes us laugh and wonder what we are doing here with a rubber thumb in our hands as we return to the affairs of the day.

Death is no joke. If only we could laugh at it, we might come square with it, then laugh at ourselves. What if we actually took death seriously? Then we would be forced to laugh at all of our pretenses – those that cause us to defend egos against the bully of false impression, those that lead great nations to bully weaker ones, and those that inspire the weaker to burn the heels of the warrior nations. What a better world this would be, if only . . .

A trickster is one who pulls off the cloak of human seriousness. Trickster deceives us into facing the irony of this life – that we live to do good in the hope that our good deeds will save us from disappearing from the face of the earth. That is Ali's joke on us – that the good for which we strive is not good enough. Behind his false thumb and his shaking body, Ali laughs, one might suppose, the laughter of the gods. When mortals laugh in this way, they do because they see death in the ordinariness of frail bodies and common lives spent in simple deeds, waiting.

CHRONOLOGY

The Chronology is compiled from various and numerous sources that do not always agree. Unfortunately, some facts are hard to check or reconcile. For some reason, the birthdates (even the spelling of the names) of Ali's ten children are occasionally inscrutable. The facts of this chronology are like all facts – as hard as can be, given the sources. All the controversial ones have been at least double-checked, usually more than that. The leading (but by no means exclusive sources) for Ali are: John Stravinsky, *Muhammad Ali* (New York: Random House, 1997); Thomas Hauser, *Muhammad Ali: His Life and Times* (New York: Simon and Schuster, 1991); Muhammad Ali with Richard Durham, *The Greatest: My Own Story* (New York: Random House, 1975); ESPN Sports web site at espn.com.

Ali and the World: A Chronology

In what follows, d. signifies "defeats" and arabic numbers indicate the round when the fight ended.

1942 January 17: Cassius Marcellus Clay, Jr, born in Louisville, Kentucky.

Duke Ellington composes "American Lullaby"; Eddie Condon and his mixed race jazz band on American television; E. D. Nixon, local black candidate for city council, and civil rights organizer, is defeated in Democratic Primary, Montgomery, Alabama; President Roosevelt signs the Japanese Relocation Order.

1943 Duke Ellington and his orchestra perform "Black, Brown, and Beige" at Carnegie Hall; proceeds are donated to the Russian war-relief fund.

1944 Joe Frazier born in Beaufort, South Carolina; President Roosevelt signs the GI Bill of Rights; Gunnar Myrdal publishes *American Dilemma*.

1945 Germany surrenders to the Allied forces and to the Soviet High Command; Adolf Hitler kills himself in Berlin; Japan surrenders after Hiroshima and Nagasaki are destroyed by atomic bombs; representatives of 50 nations sign the UN charter in San Francisco.

1946 Malcolm Little convicted of grand larceny and breaking and entering, and sent to prison, age 21; Jack Johnson dies in Raleigh, North Carolina.

1947	Dodgers sign Jackie Robinson; India and Pakistan gain independence from Britain.
1948	Gandhi assassinated in New Delhi; State of Israel founded; London hosts first Olympic Games since 1936; Martin Luther King, Jr, ordained as Baptist minister; Universal Declaration of Human Rights adopted and proclaimed by General Assembly, United Nations.
1949	Chinese Communists, led by Mao Tse-tung, defeat the Nationalists and form the People's Republic of China; George Foreman born in Marshall, Texas.
1951	Martin Luther King, Jr, enters Boston University for graduate studies; *The African Queen*, directed by John Huston, premiers.
1952	Malcolm Little paroled from prison, converts to Nation of Islam, and adopts the name Malcolm X.
1953	Malcolm X becomes first minister of Boston temple; Leon Spinks born in St Louis, Missouri.
1954	USA tests hydrogen bomb on Bikini Atoll; French troops sent to Algeria to quell disturbances; Geneva Agreements divide Vietnam into Communist North and pro-Western South; *Brown v. Board of Education* ruling deems segregated schools unconstitutional.
1955	Emmett Till brutally murdered; his assailants are acquitted; first summit conference of Asian and African nations takes place in Bandung, Indonesia; Allen Ginsberg reads "Howl" at Six Gallery in San Francisco; Martin Luther King, Jr, graduates from Boston University with a doctorate in systematic theology; Rosa Parks is arrested and convicted for violating bus segregation laws.

October: Clay's bike stolen; he meets Joe Martin, who introduces him to boxing.

Year		
1956	Clay wins light-heavyweight Golden Gloves title.	Suez Canal crisis; Dizzy Gillespie tours with his big band to the eastern Mediterranean, the Middle East, Pakistan, and South America by invitation of the US State Department; Louis Armstrong visits Africa; Ella Baker, Bayard Rustin, and Stanley Levison form In Friendship, a New York City organization to raise money in support of struggle in the South; Floyd Patterson d. Archie Moore in 5.
1957		President Eisenhower sends federal troops to Little Rock, Arkansas, to enforce desegregation of Central High School.
1959	Clay wins light-heavyweight Golden Gloves title.	Martin Luther King, Jr, visits India to study Mohandas Gandhi's philosophy of nonviolence. After returning to the USA, Martin Luther King, Jr, relocates to Atlanta, Georgia, to direct the activities of the Southern Christian Leadership Conference, where he is joined by Ella Baker and Bayard Rustin; Fidel Castro becomes Prime Minister of Cuba.
1960	Clay wins gold medal at Rome Olympics; hires Angelo Dundee as trainer.	Congo wins independence from Belgium; Patrice Lumumba is named Prime Minister.
1961	June 26: Clay d. Duke Sabedong in 10; meets Gorgeous George, the professional wrestler.	Segregated interstate bus terminals deemed unconstitutional by US Supreme Court; Algeria gains independence from France.
1962	Clay meets Howard Bingham; November 15 d. Archie Moore in 4.	Cuban missile crisis brings world to brink of nuclear war; James Meredith becomes the first African-American student to attend the University of Mississippi; Sonny Liston d. Floyd Patterson in 1.

Year		
1963	Clay meets Drew Bundini Brown; March 22: *Time* magazine features Cassius Marcellus Clay on cover; March 13: win over Doug Jones in 10; June 18: Clay d. Henry Cooper in 5.	South Vietnamese President Diem is killed in a military coup; civil rights leader Medgar Evers is murdered in Alabama; President Kennedy assassinated; Malcolm X suspended from Nation of Islam for "chickens coming home to roost" remark; John Coltrane records "Alabama," inspired by the fate of four black children killed in a church bombing; 250,000 people attend civil rights march on Washington.
1964	February 25: Clay upsets Sonny Liston in 7 to win the heavyweight title. "I shook up the world!" he boasts; Clay confirms association with Nation of Islam and changes name to Muhammad Ali; visits Africa; poses for photos with the Beatles in Miami, Florida; marries Sonji Roi.	Nelson Mandela begins life sentence in South Africa; Martin Luther King, Jr, receives Nobel Peace Prize; Rhodesia and Kenya declare independence; Civil Rights Bill passes 73–27; Malcolm X leaves Nation of Islam and organizes the Muslim Mosque, Inc.; he lectures at rallies across the USA, Africa, and the Middle East.
1965	May 25: Ali d. Liston in 1; November 22: d. Patterson in 12.	Malcolm X is assassinated in New York City; Mobutu Sese Seko becomes President of Republic of Congo, later renamed Zaire; US offensives intensify in Vietnam; 34 people killed in Los Angeles race riots; Martin Luther King, Jr, leads march from Selma to Montgomery, Alabama, and 25,000 people join him; Lyndon Johnson signs the Voting Rights Act; Arthur Ashe wins the NCAA singles crown as a junior at UCLA, becoming the first African American to win that title.

1966 Ali divorces Sonji Roi; February: requests deferment from military service; Howard Cosell broadcasts the name Muhammad Ali; August 23: claims conscientious-objector status at a special draft hearing.

Duke Ellington attends the World Festival of Negro Arts held at Dakar, Senegal; race riots break out in New York, Cleveland, and Chicago; Mike Tyson born in Brooklyn, New York.

1967 April 28: Ali refuses induction into the army; May 8: indicted by federal grand jury; boxing license suspended; convicted for unlawfully resisting military induction; marries Belinda Boyd.

Martin Luther King, Jr, spends four days in a Birmingham jail for demonstrating without a permit; Thurgood Marshall, great-grandson of a slave, is sworn in as Supreme Court Justice, President Johnson attends the ceremony; New York City mayor John Lindsay abolishes the New York cabaret card.

1968 Conviction upheld in appeals court; daughter Maryum born.

North Vietnamese launch Tet Offensive in Vietnam; Walter Cronkite's "We are Mired in Stalemate" broadcast on February 27; Kerner Commission finds USA divided into two societies, one black, one white, separate and unequal; Lyndon B. Johnson declines a second presidential term; Arthur Ashe becomes the first African-American man to win a Grand Slam men's singles title.

1969 Ali visits Africa, again.

1970 Supreme Court decrees conscientious-objector status allowable on religious grounds; conviction overturned; Ali returns to boxing; twin daughters Rasheeda and Jamillah born.

USA invades Cambodia; four students killed by National Guard at Kent State demonstration; two students killed by police at Jackson State in Mississippi; Jimi Hendrix and Janis Joplin die of drug abuse; November 24 is declared Duke Ellington Day in Mexico; South Africa denies Arthur Ashe a spot in their Open tournament, consequently South Africa is excluded from the Davis Cup tennis competition.

Year		
1971	March 8: Ali loses to Joe Frazier in 15; Frazier retains heavyweight title; Frank Sinatra photographs the fight for *Life* magazine; Supreme Court rules all charges against Ali dropped; son Muhammad Jr born.	Louis Armstrong dies; Pentagon Papers detailing US government's faulty disclosure of military involvement in Southeast Asia published in *New York Times*; Attica prison riots in Buffalo, New York, leave 28 inmates and 9 guards dead; George Harrison organizes benefit concert for Bangladesh.
1972	Ali's hajj to Mecca.	Shoot-out at the Munich Olympics leaves 11 Israelis, including 1 athlete, 2 coaches, and 5 Palestinian gunmen dead; President Nixon visits China and Soviet Union, and orders Operation Linebacker II, the "Christmas bombing" of Hanoi.
1973	March 31: Ali loses to Ken Norton in 12; September 10: in rematch Ali d. Norton in 12.	President Allende assassinated in Chile; American Indian Movement protests at Wounded Knee, South Dakota; US Senate Watergate hearings; Foreman d. Joe Frazier in 2; Arthur Ashe competes in the South African Open, and wins the doubles title with Tom Okker.
1974	January 28: Ali d. Joe Frazier in 12; October 30: in Zaire (Congo), Ali d. George Foreman in 8, regains heavyweight title; *Muhammad Ali, The Greatest*, directed by William Klein, premiers.	President Nixon resigns from office due to Watergate scandal; Duke Ellington dies in New York; Ethiopian emperor Haile Selassie ousted in military junta.
1975	Ali dubs his defeat of Joe Frazier in 14 the "Thrilla in Manila"; Ali publishes autobiography (with Richard Durham), *The Greatest*.	Elijah Muhammad dies in Chicago; fall of Saigon; Angola and Mozambique claim independence from Portugal; Vietnam War ends; Arthur Ashe upsets Jimmy Connors and becomes the first African American to win the single's title at Wimbledon.
1976	Daughter Hana born.	

Year		
1977	Ali visits Brazilian soccer great, Pelé, at the NASL Cosmos/Santos exhibition game, where Pelé plays for both teams; "Now there are two greatests," proclaims Ali; divorces Belinda Boyd and marries Veronica Porche; TV premier of *I Am the Greatest: The Adventures of Muhammad Ali*; *The Greatest*, directed by Tom Gries, premiers.	Egyptian president Anwar Sadat visits Jerusalem; Elvis Presley dies in Tennessee.
1978	February 15: Ali loses title to Leon Spinks in 15; September 15: regains title with win over Leon Spinks in 15; daughter Laila born.	President Jimmy Carter hosts jazz event celebrating the achievements of Charles Mingus; band members include Stan Getz, Dizzy Gillespie, Dexter Gordon, and Max Roach; President Carter hosts peace talks between Egypt and Israel at Camp David.
1979	Ali travels to Africa to seek support for an American boycott of the 1980 Olympics.	Margaret Thatcher becomes UK's first female Prime Minister; fall of the Shah of Iran; *Apocalypse Now*, directed by Francis Ford Coppola, premiers.
1980	October 2: TKO loss to Larry Holmes in 11.	John Lennon is shot and killed in New York.
1981	Ali loses to Trevor Berbick in 10.	John Lewis, former chairman of the Student Nonviolent Coordinating Committee in the 1960s, is elected to Atlanta City Council.
1983		US troops invade Granada.
1984	Ali diagnosed with Parkinson's syndrome.	Indira Gandhi assassinated; first black franchise granted in South Africa.

Year		
1986	Divorces Veronica Porche and marries Lonnie Williams.	John Lewis elected to the US House of Representatives; race riots break out in London; President Sadat of Egypt assassinated; US national holiday proclaimed in honor of Martin Luther King, Jr; nuclear disaster in Chernobyl.
1987	Doctors claim Parkinson's syndrome is caused by Ali's 61-event boxing career.	First intifada in Palestine.
1989		Berlin Wall falls; Tiananmen Square massacre in Beijing.
1990	Ali visits Iraq on a peace mission.	Gulf War begins; Nelson Mandela released from prison.
1991	Muhammad Ali: His Life and Times, Ali's authorized oral history by Thomas Hauser, published. Adopts Assad Amin.	Gulf War ends.
1992	Ali's 50th birthday cover story appears in Sports Illustrated.	Race riots escalate in Los Angeles after police officers are acquitted in the beatings of Rodney King.
1993	Howard Bingham publishes book of photographs: Muhammad Ali: A Thirty Year Journey.	Oslo Accords signed by Arafat and Rabin; Nelson Mandela and F. W. de Klerk win Nobel Peace Prize; Arthur Ashe dies in New York at age 49.
1994	Davis Miller nominated for a Pulitzer Prize for his story "The Zen of Muhammad Ali."	Nelson Mandela elected president in South Africa's first all-race elections.

1996	Ali visits Fidel Castro in Cuba; lights Olympic flame in Atlanta; *Muhammad Ali: The Whole Story*, directed by Joseph Consentino and Sandra Consentino, premiers; *When We Were Kings*, directed by Leon Gast and Taylor Hackford, premiers.	Welfare reform in USA repeals the Aid to Families with Dependent Children program and creates Temporary Assistance to Needy Families (TANF).
1997		Duke Ellington Memorial unveiled in NYC's Central Park at 110th Street and 5th Avenue.
1999	Named ''Athlete of the Century'' by *GQ*, chosen *Sports Illustrated's* ''Sportsman of the Century,'' *USA Today's* ''Athlete of the Century,'' the BBC's ''Sports Personality of the Century,'' the State of Kentucky's ''Kentuckian of the Century,'' and the World Sports Award's ''World Sportsman of the Century''; Muhammad Ali publishes *More than a Hero: Muhammad Ali's Life Lessons Presented through his Daughter's Eyes* with daughter Hana Ali.	A district court in North Carolina dissolves a 30-year-old desegregation order.
2000	Ali goes on a humanitarian mission to South Juarez, Mexico; *King of the World*, directed by John Sacret Young, premiers.	The Tulsa Race Riot Commission recommends to the Oklahoma state legislature that reparations be paid to the survivors of the Tulsa race riots of 1921; South Carolina removes the Confederate flag from the capital dome and puts it next to a war memorial; Florida abolishes affirmative action in public schools and public contracts.

2001   Ali honored in Washington, DC, with Service to America Leadership Award by the National Association of Broadcasters Education Foundation (NABEF) in recognition of his lifelong commitment to world peace, tolerance, and human rights, and for his commitment to establishing the Muhammad Ali Center in his hometown; *Nick News Presents: Life Story: Muhammad Ali*, directed by Josh Veselka, premiers; *Ali*, directed by Michael Mann, premiers.

September 11: World Trade Center disaster in New York City; Pentagon attacked; US organizes international anti-terrorist bombing campaign to attack Afghanistan.

2002   *Muhammad Ali through the Eyes of the World*, directed by Phil Grabsky, premiers; architectural plans for the Muhammad Ali Center, Louisville, Kentucky, released; groundbreaking follows; Ali, at 60, visits Kabul.

Controversial Homeland Security Act passed in the USA; new UN weapons inspections team searches Iraq.

NOTES

CHAPTER 1   FROM THE BEGINNINGS

1   The Algonquin story that begins this chapter is a retelling of the version attributed to Lewis Spence in *American Indian Myths and Legends*, ed. Richard Erdoes and Alfonso Ortiz (New York: Pantheon, 1984), 25–6.

2   The Center's website is at www.alicenter.org. Among other plans it announces an agreement with the United Nations to promote a Schools for Global Peace Program which will provide local and international programs teaching children and their teachers how to come to terms with the effects of war and violence in their lives. Just how serious this will turn out to be remains to be seen, but the purpose is obviously much more than glorifying the man himself.

3   By 2003 (according to the Center website), architectural plans for the 93,000 square foot building of six floors of exhibits, a library, café, shops, and event spaces had been released. The final cost is projected at $41 million. Needless to say, the Mayor of Louisville is thrilled at the prospect of such a major attraction at the heart of his usually sleepy town. Once the construction began, it would seem that local interest picked up and contributions advanced apace. Late in 2002 an endowment was established to support operating costs once the Center is open. The website promises construction in 2003 and opening in 2004. One curious note is that once General Colin Powell became US Secretary of State in 2001, he apparently had himself removed from the national Board of endorsers. On a pertinent tangent, the Chamber of Commerce of Berrein Springs, Michigan, where Ali now lives, makes no mention of him, while devoting a full paragraph to its annual Pickle Festival.

4 The story is told in Muhammad Ali with Richard Durham, *The Greatest: My Own Story* (New York: Random House, 1975), 76.
5 Mike Marqusee, *Redemption Song: Muhammad Ali and the Spirit of the Sixties* (London: Verso, 1999), 103.
6 Thomas Hauser, *Muhammad Ali: His Life and Times* (New York: Simon & Schuster, 1991), 15.
7 Ibid., 15–16.
8 The honor was not lost on Ali a quarter-century later. Long after Elijah Muhammad was gone, Ali said: "I was honored that Elijah Muhammad gave me a truly beautiful name. 'Muhammad' means one worthy of praise. 'Ali' was the name of a great general [a cousin of the Prophet Muhammad and the third Caliph after the death of the Prophet]. I've been Muhammad Ali now for twenty-six years. That's four years longer than I was Cassius Clay" (ibid., 102).
9 For details, see Randy Roberts, *Papa Jack: Jack Johnson and the Era of White Hopes* (New York: Free Press, 1983). Also, Al-Tony Gilmore, *Bad Nigger! The National Impact of Jack Johnson* (Port Washington, NY: Kennikat Press, 1975).
10 Holmes, Ali's former sparring partner, crushed Ali, whose body had already begun to decline due to both the years and the illness. Ali's last fight was an even more ignoble defeat in 1981 by Trevor Berbick. Holmes, at least, came to be considered one of the near-great champions. Berbick was at best good, never more.
11 Among the numerous sources: Hauser, *Muhammad Ali*, 18; David Remnick, *King of the World* (New York: Vintage/Random House, 1998), ch. 5. One of the clues to the power of the story is its regular appearance in the many made-for-TV documentaries: for example, Marc Payton, director, *Muhammad Ali* (*Sports Illustrated* video/HBO Sports, Big Fights, Inc., 1989).
12 Hauser, *Muhammad Ali*, 19.
13 Ali's three significant losses were after his long exile from boxing between April 1967 and September 1970 – to Joe Frazier in 1971, to Ken Norton in 1973, and to Leon Spinks in 1978. He avenged all three. His penultimate loss to Larry Holmes in 1980 was long after his skills had eroded with age. Before his refusal of the government's call to military service in Vietnam, he had won 29 professional fights, all but 6 by knockouts. Even after regaining the championship from Foreman in 1974, he fought 22 times, winning all but 5 fight (though not as decisively, to be sure).

14 Quoted by Hunt Helm, "Louisville Remembers the Shy Kid from Central High," *The LouisvilleCourier-Journal.Com* (original story: September 14, 1997), 3–4.
15 The letter is among those collected by David Herbert Donald in *Lincoln at Home* (New York: Simon & Schuster, 2000).
16 The stories of Clay's family history are from John Egerton, "Heritage of a Heavyweight," *New York Times on the Web* (original story: September 28, 1980).
17 Cassius Clay's fascination with the Nation goes back, it would seem, at least to high school days, when he came upon a copy of *Muhammad Speaks* while in Chicago for the Golden Gloves competition. Later he proposed writing a high school term paper on the subject and was refused permission by his horrified teacher. It is noteworthy that the early origins of Ali's interest in the Nation go back to the late 1950s, but so too did the fear of those in authority in the movement itself.
18 It is said, by Justin Kaplan, that in his last years Mark Twain dressed himself in white in order to make himself the most conspicuous man on the planet, which he may well have been even without the cosmetics.
19 "If You Pay Them, They Will Come," *Sports Illustrated* (July 2, 2001), 130–1. George Foreman, by the way, was close behind, in fourth place at $70,000 an appearance. By comparison, retired and very articulate presidents do not make all that much more. In his first year after leaving office, President Bill Clinton took in $125,000 for domestic appearances ($250,000 for international trips). See also Amy Waldman, "Clinton as John Q. Public," *New York Times*, August 11, 2001.
20 *American Legends – Our Nation's Most Fascinating Heroes, Icons, and Leaders* (New York: Time Inc., 2001).
21 Mark Kram, *Ghosts of Manila: The Fateful Blood Feud between Muhammad Ali and Joe Frazier* (New York: Harper/Collins, 2001), 2. Tragically, Kram died shortly after returning from the Mike Tyson–Lennox Lewis championship fight in January 2002.
22 Hauser, *Muhammad Ali*, 105. For a wonderful capsule account of Cannon's role in the scheme of old-line sportswriters, see Remnick, *King of the World*, 150–5.
23 Kram, *Ghosts of Manila*, 159. The gorilla taunt is famously in Ali's poem for Frazier/Ali III: "It will be a killer / And a chiller / And a thrilla / When I get the gorilla / In Manila" (Hauser, *Muhammad Ali*, 313). Considering how the pre-fight taunt has deteriorated

into something less than an art form, it is a little surprising that Frazier, not at all an ignorant man, holds on to the anger. One wonders what he might have thought about Mike Tyson's 2002 taunt before the Lennox Lewis fight: "I'm going to eat your babies." Tyson, by the way, earned $17.5 million for the fight (three times what Ali and Frazier earned in Manila). Tyson was handily defeated for his gate-raising efforts.

24 Norman Mailer is the source of the aesthetic taste line. See Leon Gast's film *When We Were Kings* (New York: Polygram Film Productions USA Video, 1996). For another of Mailer's descriptions of the scene, see Norman Mailer, *The Fight* (Boston: Little, Brown, 1975), 208, where he says, referring to Foreman: "He went over like a six-foot sixty-year-old butler who has just heard tragic news, yes, fell over all of a long collapsing two seconds, down came the Champion in sections and Ali revolved with him in a close circle, hand primed to hit him one more time, and never the need, a wholly intimate escort to the floor."

25 Hauser, *Muhammad Ali*, 494.

26 Quoted in Marqusee, *Redemption Song*, 80–1. Marqusee prefaces the quote by pointing out, no doubt aptly, that Foreman made the statement after he had become a born-again Christian.

CHAPTER 2 CELEBRITY, TRICKS, AND CULTURE

1 Joel Chandler Harris, *Uncle Remus: His Songs and His Sayings. Folklore of the Old Plantation* (New York: D. Appleton and Company, 1881), 23–5, 29–31. Harris is often credited with introducing the standard method for writing the dialect of the slave Negro. More importantly, his collection is unquestionably the source of many plantation Negro folktales, most famously the Uncle Remus and Brer Rabbit cycle.

2 After his seventh professional fight in June 1961, Ali's fights were televised – which was another first for him. Prior to Ali, new professionals did not appear on television. But then television had not been around all that long either. Thomas Hauser, *Muhammad Ali: His Life and Times* (New York: Simon & Schuster, 1991), 42.

3 Conn's status as the one white fighter who could take the crown back from the Brown Bomber was based on his surprising showing in their first bout in 1941, when he extended Louis to 13 rounds before being knocked out. In the rematch he went down

in 8. In the interim, Louis had served his tour in the military during World War II.

4   Four of his first five fights yielded purses of less than $600. The July 1962 bout was the largest by far at $15,000, followed by his first serious payday against Archie Moore in November, $45,000. The numbers are from Muhammad Ali with Richard Durham, *The Greatest: My Own Story* (New York: Random House, 1975), 12, which may not be the most accurate of sources. The book was written under the influence of the Nation, and the purpose of the table of Ali's winnings was largely to demonstrate that of his nearly $30 million of prize money up to 1975, $27 million had been earned under the management of Herbert Muhammad, as opposed to just under a tenth of that amount with the Louisville sponsors. Still, for the early years the meager money is normal for an unknown, as Clay was then.

5   The date is offered by Mike Marqusee, *Redemption Song: Muhammad Ali and the Spirit of the Sixties* (London: Verso, 1999), 19, who also traces boxing back to the Greeks.

6   Lewis Hyde opens his brilliant book on the trickster with a wonderful account of the coyote, in nature and in the natural imagination (Lewis Hyde, *Trickster Makes This World* (New York: Farrar, Strauss, and Giroux, 1998), part I). No current book considers the trickster so comprehensively as Hyde's. The classic work on the subject is Paul Radin, *The Trickster: A Study of American Indian Mythology* (New York: Shocken Books, 1956), in which the coyote figures in the Winnebago trickster stories.

7   See Lewis Hyde, "Trickster and Gender," in *Trickster Makes This World*, 335–43. Hyde makes a somewhat convincing attempt to explain that, among other reasons, in patriarchies, as most premodern societies were, the trickster must be male to upset the male system. One of the reasons why this is not a very convincing claim is that in modern ones, which are to a large extent male-dominated, there are plenty of female tricksters stories, of which Toni Morrison's *Sula* and Maxine Hong Kingston's *The Woman Warrior* are the obvious cases. For a brilliantly inventive account of the tricksters and related themes with respect to sex, see Wendy Doninger, *The Bedtrick: Tales of Sex and Masquerade* (Chicago: University of Chicago Press, 2000). Relatedly, Sharon Thompson draws on Radin's phrase "drastic entertainments" in her powerful essay " 'Drastic Entertainments': Teenage Mothers' Signifying Narratives," in *Uncertain Terms: Negotiating Gender in American*

Culture, ed. Faye Ginsburg and Anna Lowenhaupt Tsing (Boston: Beacon Press, 1990), ch. 16.

8 Gay Talese, "Boxing Fidel," in *The Muhammad Ali Reader*, ed. Gerald Early (New York: William Morrow, 1998), 266–86.

9 Hyde, *Trickster Makes this World*, 7.

10 Maurice Sendak, *In the Night Kitchen* (New York: Harper Collins, 1970). This is a retelling of Sendak's story. Lines quoted appear at various places in the book.

11 See William J. Hynes, "Mapping the Characteristics of Mythic Tricksters: A Heuristic Guide," in *Mythical Trickster Figures*, ed. William J. Hynes and William G. Doty (Tuscaloosa: University of Alabama Press, 1993), 33–45. Hynes's essay offers an excellent summary of trickster characteristics, suggesting why the figure is a cultural transformer.

12 Robert D. Pelton, *The Trickster in West Africa* (Berkeley: University of California Press, 1980), 42.

13 Erving Goffman, *The Presentation of Self in Everyday Life* (Garden City, NY: Doubleday, 1959).

14 David Remnick, *King of the World* (New York: Vintage/Random House, 1998), 119.

15 Hauser, *Muhammad Ali*, 39; compare Remnick, *King of the World*, 119.

16 Hauser, *Muhammad Ali*, 39.

17 Pacheco, in ibid., 136.

18 Mark Kram uses Ali's abandonment of Bundini as one of the subsidiary illustrations of his complaint about Ali's cruelty. In this case, Kram may have a point.

19 Chandler Harris, *Uncle Remus*, 5–8. Harris may be the first to make this claim, which has since been made with force by Lewis Hyde among others. Relatedly, see Henry Louis Gates, *The Signifying Monkey* (New York: Oxford University Press, 1988), upon which Hyde draws.

CHAPTER 3 TRICKSTER QUEERS THE WORLD

1 David Halberstam, *The Amateurs* (New York: Fawcett Books, 1996). Doris Kearns Goodwin, *Wait till Next Year: A Memoir* (New York: Touchstone Books, 1998).

2 Joyce Carol Oates, *On Boxing* (Garden City, NY: Doubleday, 1987). Among others of comparable insight, see Gerald Early,

"Introduction: Tales of the Wonderboy," in *The Muhammad Ali Reader*, ed. Gerald Early (New York: William Morrow, 1998), pp. vi–xx; and Gerald Early, "Battling Siki: The Boxer as Natural Man," among other boxing essays in Early, *The Culture of Bruising* (Hopewell, NJ, and New York: Ecco Press, 1992). Among many *New Yorker* essays on boxing by A. J. Liebling, see the collection *A Neutral Corner* (San Francisco: North Point Press, 1990); James Baldwin, "The Fight: Patterson vs. Liston," in *The Fights*, ed. Charles Itoff and Richard Ford (San Francisco: Chronicle Books, 1996); also the various commentaries and essays of Norman Mailer and George Plimpton on fighting and Ali's career, especially the 1974 Ali–Foreman fight in Zaire (about which more later): Norman Mailer, *The Fight* (Boston: Little, Brown, 1975), and George Plimpton, *Shadow Box* (New York: Putnam, 1977).

3   Oates, *On Boxing*, 4.
4   On Liston, the best, and most sympathetic, book is Nick Tosches, *The Devil and Sonny Liston* (Boston: Little, Brown, 2000). On Don King, see Jack Newfield, *Only in America: The Life and Times of Don King* (New York: William Morrow, 1995). Both Tosches and Newfield are respected old school writers with a new school understanding of the fight game. It is sad, I think, that Mike Tyson – easily as fascinating a character as Liston (though one without his Ali) – has not yet been given a full-length study by a major writer. Sadder still is the fact that Mark Kram, a much-respected *Sports Illustrated* boxing writer, died before he could write his book on Tyson. Kram died just days after returning from Tyson's crushing defeat by Lennox Lewis in Memphis on June 8, 2002.
5   The classic work, on what is now a long list, is Edward Said, *Orientalism* (New York: Vintage, 1979). But see also the emergence of the idea's corollary in the wake of September 11, 2001: "Occidentalism," by Avishai Margalit and Ian Buruma, *New York Review of Books*, January 17, 2002.
6   Floyd Patterson with Gay Talese, "In Defense of Clay," in *Muhammad Ali Reader*, ed. Early, 68.
7   Though, somewhat surprisingly, he was a little surprised that his chickens coming home to roost made headlines when whites were saying much the same thing. See Alex Haley, *Autobiography of Malcolm X* (New York: Ballantine, 1964), ch. 16, especially pp. 328–42 on the censure.
8   Elijah Anderson, *The Code of the Street: Decency, Violence, and the Moral Life of the Inner City* (New York: W. W. Norton, 1999).

9   David Remnick, *King of the World* (New York: Vintage/Random House, 1998), 21.

10 Ibid., 14.

11 See especially Randy Roberts, "White Hopes and White Women," in *Papa Jack: Jack Johnson and the Era of White Hopes* (New York: Free Press, 1983), ch. 5.

12 A Library of Congress photograph of Johnson the year following his release from prison in 1921 shows him dressed to the nines, with felt hat and walking stick, with a smile so alluring as to convey just how seductive the man was. The photo is set apparently at a horse-racing venue, as if to accent the life he had lived and would continue to live. Reproduced in Roberts, *Papa Jack*.

13 Roberts, *Papa Jack*, 228. Roberts attributes the story to Plimpton, *Shadow Box*, 152–4.

14 See Richard Bak, "The Long Shadow of Papa Jack," in *Joe Louis: The Great Black Hope* (Dallas Texas: Taylor Publishing, 1996), ch. 3.

15 Richard Bak, "Cruel Twilight," in *Joe Louis*, ch. 10. In the minds of the white establishment, Louis was never more perfectly the Good Negro than when he welcomed induction into the army during World War II – and gladly lent his name to the patriotic cause (for which he was repaid by being hounded by the tax authorities when, late in life, his blind trust of a white handler who in effect robbed him blind and left him with a tax debt that ruined the clean reputation he had so naively agreed to assume).

16 Roberts, *Papa Jack*, pp. xi–xii.

17 Plimpton's Harvard poem story is told near the end of Leon Gast's award-winning film, *When We Were Kings* (Polygram Film Productions/USA Video, 1996).

18 Lewis Hyde, *Trickster Makes This World* (New York: Farrar, Strauss and Giroux, 1999), ch. 10. But see also William McFeeley's excellent biography of Douglass, *Frederick Douglass* (New York: Touchstone Books, 1991).

19 Remnick, *King of the World*, 173.

20 The best description of these events is by Remnick, *King of the World*, 177–90. The following description of events is based on Remnick.

21 Remnick, *King of the World*, 181. Even Clay's closest handlers could not decide whether it was an act or not. While Dundee thought he was nuts, Clay's personal physician, Ferdie Pacheco, considered it a brilliant act. See Thomas Hauser, *Muhammad Ali: His Life and Times* (New York: Simon & Schuster, 1991), 70. For

what it may be worth, the highest my blood pressure has ever been when measured under stress was no more than 20 percent over an already high normal.

22 Remnick, *King of the World*, 182.

23 Photo by Tony Triolo, *Sports Illustrated*; reproduced in Remnick, *King of the World*, 184.

24 Transcribed from Marc Payton, director, *Muhammad Ali*, (*Sports Illustrated* video HBO Sports, 1989). Another version of the moment is Thomas Hauser's (*Muhammad Ali*, 78), which is longer and presumably from another recorded source. "I am the prettiest thing that ever lived" is from Hauser.

25 See Harold Bloom, *American Religion: The Emergence of a Post-Christian Nation* (New York: Touchstone Books, 1993).

26 Hauser, *Muhammad Ali*, 126. At the extreme of skepticism that Ali threw anything remotely resembling a blow capable of knocking down a man like Liston is Tosches, *Devil and Sonny Liston*, 220–4.

27 Hauser, *Muhammad Ali*, 128.

28 Tosches claims that Ali himself had doubts about the blow (*Devil and Sonny Liston*, 224). In Gast's *When We Were Kings* there is a sequence of Ali, apparently at his Pennsylvania training camp, joking about the phantom punch, which is both hilarious and a surprisingly good explanation of its speed as the reason so few thought it actually landed. One never knows what a trickster's jokes may mean – whether in this case Ali is tricking in the story, or whether the punch was the deception. I've seen slow motion of the event many times and, while I can see the room for doubt, I don't have trouble seeing the blow as the cause of Liston's fall. But, again, like his magic tricks in later life, who knows what Ali knows?

29 Liston himself, according to Tosches (*Devil and Sonny Liston*, 220) felt that he had over-trained, which is plausible given the postponement. Still, just as Jack Johnson's 38 years were years of hard living, so were Liston's.

30 The *locus classicus* of this view of queering is, among her many writings, Judith Butler, *Gender Trouble* (New York: Routledge, 1990). For a discussion, see Charles Lemert, *Dark Thoughts: Race and the Eclipse of Society* (New York: Routledge, 2002), ch. 7, on Butler and the Harlem Renaissance writer Nella Larsen.

31 Tosches, *Devil and Sonny Liston*, 7.

CHAPTER 4   THE IRONY OF GLOBAL CULTURES

1   Zora Neale Hurston, *Every Tongue Got to Confess: Negro Folk-tales from the Gulf States*, ed. by Carla Kaplan (New York: Harper Collins Publishers, 2001), 109–10.

2   Ho Chi Minh, *Prison Diary* (Hanoi: Foreign Languages Publishing House, 1972), 10; reprinted in *The Sixties Papers*, ed. Judith Clavir Albert and Stewart Edward Albert (New York: Praeger, 1984), 314.

3   One of the most striking things about these folktales is just how easily the word *nigger* enters duplicitously – as neither simply an obliging report of the master's customary word or, even, as black-on-black signifying, but as both-at-once. The tales were, of course, told and passed down in the folk community, and thus one would expect the story language to be as important as the story told, both being a kind of doubled or tripled code of sorts. On the question of who gets to say "Nigger" (the title from the talks from which the book emerged), see Randall Kennedy, *Nigger: The Strange Career of a Troublesome Word* (New York: Pantheon Books, 2002), especially ch. 1.

4   David Remnick, *The King of the World* (New York: Vintage Books/ Random House, 1998), ch. 12.

5   The principal source for the claim is probably Ali's memoir, *The Greatest: My Own Story* (New York: Random House, 1975), 35. Years later, Ali reported a short version of the importance of Emmett's death to Thomas Hauser, *Muhammad Ali: this Life and Times* (New York: Simon & Schuster, 1991), 89. David Remnick takes Ali at his word on this in *King of the World*, 87–8. Though much that is reported in *The Greatest* as fact may not be, this is one instance where it may be, since it is likely that Cassius Clay, like all other black children, was deeply affected by the story of the lynching of a boy his own age. In brief, Till was in Money, Mississippi, the summer of 1955 to visit relatives. He was from Chicago, where race relations were somewhat easier. He had made a passing remark to a white woman, a boyish kind of flirtation, much as his friends did in the North. For this he was shot and thrown in the river. When Ali reports the story in *The Greatest*, the emphasis is on the decision of Till's mother to have an open casket at her son's funeral so that the evidence of brutality would be plain to see.

6   Eric Bennett succinctly describes Elijah's use of Fard in the following way: "In 1934 Fard disappeared as mysteriously as he

arrived, and every speculation about his disappearance remains unsubstantiated. Elijah Muhammad capitalized on this mystery, transforming Fard's disappearance into a serviceable mythology upon which he based the Nation's religious authority. By 1942 the Nation had assigned Fard divine status as an embodiment of Allah; through the end of the twentieth century Fard provided the spiritual foundation of the Nation's life." See Eric Bennett, "Fard, Wallace D." in *Africana: The Encyclopedia of the African and African American Experience*, ed. Kwame Anthony Appiah and Henry Louis Gates, Jr (New York: Civitas/Perseus Books, 1999), 732.

7 Harold Bloom makes the most extraordinary and persuasive claim as to the special American qualities of the Mormon religion. See Bloom, *American Religion* (New York: Simon & Schuster, 1992).

8 Remnick (*King of the World*, 125–7) refers to Ali's high school explorations of the Nation's ideas as the big secret of his youth. If his 1975 memoir is to be trusted, his spiritual commitment to the Nation was one made long before the coming out. When the gate was at risk for the first Liston fight in 1964 and Ali was confronted over both his open friendship with Malcolm X and his evident practice of a Muslim way of life, he claims to have said to the promoter: "I know I can beat Liston, and I don't want to call the fight off, but if you have to call it off because of my faith, then the fight's off." I know something about religious commitment, and such a statement, if he made it, by a 22-year-old who had such an agenda for himself is certainly proof of a long-term attachment to the ideas (an attachment that, whatever he said then, obviously endured for the rest of his life). See *The Greatest*, 103.

9 Hauser, *Muhammad Ali*, 193–4.

10 Claude Andrew Clegg, III, *An Original Man: The Life and Times of Elijah Muhammad* (New York: St Martin's Press, 1991), 211. The diversions were, of course, the removal of Malcolm and the Minister's own sexual misconduct.

11 Hauser, *Muhammad Ali*, 32.

12 Ibid., 34.

13 *The Voice of Anna Julia Cooper*, ed. Charles Lemert and Esme Bahn (Boulder, CO: Rowman and Littlefield, 1997), 117.

14 Alex Haley, Malcolm's biographer and friend, said: "that hurt Malcolm more than any other person turning from him that I know of. Malcolm was very hurt by it all" (Hauser, *Muhammad Ali*, 110).

15 Remnick, *King of the World*, 240.
16 Remnick attributes the remark to Ali, but the source is not exactly clear. The implication is that it comes from his interview with Gordon Parks (Remnick, *King of the World*, 239–40). I could not find it in Hauser, where one does find several of Ali's regrets over Malcolm's death (Hauser, *Muhammad Ali*, 111–12, e.g.). These of course were remarks made long after the event.
17 Ibid., 113–16.
18 Ibid., 131.
19 Floyd Patterson with Gay Talese, "In Defense of Cassius Clay," in *The Muhammad Ali Reader*, ed. Gerald Early (New York: Weisbach/William Morrow, 1998), 68.
20 The high watermark for troops on the American side was 1968, when there were 539,000 Americans and some 66,000 from other nations (mostly South Koreans). See Spencer C. Tucker, *Encyclopedia of the Vietnam War: A Political, Social and Military History* (Santa Barbara, CA: ABC-Clio, Inc., 1998).
21 One among the many examples of firsthand accounts of the hopeless frustration on the ground is the report of Captain Joseph B. Anderson, Jr: "There were only a very few incidents of sustained fighting during my tours. Mostly you walked and walked, and searched and searched. If you made contact, it would be over in 30–40 minutes. One burst and they're gone" (in Wallace Terry, *Bloods: An Oral History of the Vietnam War by Black Veterans* (New York: Ballantine, 1984), 222–3).
22 The episode occurred in August 1964, when a North Vietnamese torpedo boat was claimed to have attacked two US destroyers. President Johnson used the incident to push through the United States Congress the Gulf of Tonkin Resolution, which served thereafter in lieu of a formal declaration of war. The facts of the incident were never clear.
23 Hauser, *Muhammad Ali*, 143. Hauser attributes the quote to Jose Torres, *Sting Like a Bee* (New York: Abelard-Schuman, 1971), 148.
24 Hauser, *Muhammad Ali*, 144–45. Also, see the long quote attributed to Lipsyte in Howard L. Bingham and Max Wallace, *Muhammad Ali's Greatest Fight: Cassius Clay vs The United States of America* (New York: M. Evans and Company, Inc., 2000), 113–15.
25 Lipsyte, in Hauser, *Muhammad Ali*, 144.
26 Ibid., 145. Originally in the *New York Herald Tribune*, February 23, 1966. Red Smith eventually became one of Ali's strongest supporters.

27 Quoted by Bingham and Wallace, *Muhammad Ali's Greatest Fight*, 168.
28 "The *Black Scholar* Interviews Muhammad Ali," in *Muhammad Ali Reader*, ed. Early, 83.
29 For background, see Robert Lipsyte, " 'I Don't Have to Be What You Want Me to Be,' says Muhammad Ali," in *Muhammad Ali Reader*, ed. Early, 90–100. Also, Robert Lipsyte, *Free to be Muhammad Ali* (New York: Harper & Row, 1978).
30 James Scott, *Seeing Like a State: How Certain Schemes to Improve the Human Condition have Failed* (New Haven: Yale University Press, 1998).
31 It is entirely possible that one of the most courageous and uncompromising women in contemporary American life is Andrea Dworkin, who writes openly about her lack of self-assurance in adolescence in *Heartbreak: The Political Memoir of a Feminist Militant* (New York: Basic Books, 2002).
32 All dictionary definitions, here and elsewhere, are from the *Oxford English Dictionary*, 2nd edn, unless otherwise noted. Curiously, the definition of *surd* is found only in the 1st edn of the *OED*, where it is limited to its meaning in mathematics as "an irrational."
33 For a more detailed account of this see Charles Lemert, *Dark Thoughts: Race and the Eclipse of Society* (New York: Routledge, 2002).
34 One of the most charming extended essays based on this misunderstanding of irony as sarcasm is Jedediah Purdy, *For Common Things: Irony, Trust, and Commitment in America Today* (New York: Vintage/Random House, 1999). The *locus classicus*, in English at least, for the idea that irony is now the normal state of worldly affairs is Richard Rorty, *Irony, Contingency, Solidarity* (New York: Cambridge University Press, 1989).

CHAPTER 5   COMING HOME TO THE HEART OF DARKNESS

1 Thomas Hauser, *Muhammad Ali: His Life and Times* (New York: Simon & Schuster, 1991). See also the *Black Scholar, Playboy*, and *Sport* interviews with Ali in *The Muhammad Ali Reader*, ed. Gerald Early (New York: William Morrow, 1998).
2 Muhammad Ali with Richard Durham, *The Greatest: My Own Story* (New York: Random House, 1975).

3   Gerald Early, "Some Preposterous Propositions from the Heroic Life of Muhammad Ali: A Reading of *The Greatest: My Own Story*," in *Muhammad Ali: The People's Champ*, ed. Elliott J. Gorn (Urbana: University of Illinois Press, 1995), 70–87.

4   Early, in *Muhammad Ali Reader*, 83.

5   Three of 22 chapters are devoted to the 1974 fight in Zaire/Congo; see *The Greatest*, 366–413. The book also devotes the better part of another chapter (pp. 202–13) to Ali's 1969 visit to Africa. In effect, about 15 percent of the book, including its dramatic conclusion, refers directly to Ali and Africa, with barely a word of his African encounter with Malcolm in 1964. The story is told, thus, with Malcolm and his death as a distant event in his past. Apart from the constructions imposed by Herbert Muhammad, the story line of *The Greatest* required not only that the snub of Malcolm be downplayed, but that the dramatic 1974 return to Africa be given the central place. When interviewed by Thomas Hauser sometime after *The Greatest*, in 1975, Ali expressed regret and sadness for Malcolm (Hauser, *Muhammad Ali*, 111–12).

6   Bruno Bettelheim, Introduction to *The Random House Book of Fairy Tales* (New York: Random House, 1985), pp. x–xi.

7   Ever since Claude Lévi-Strauss first used the French *bricoleur* as a model for the concrete thinking of the premodern mind, the expression has haunted social scientists. Lévi-Strauss's explanation is that the *"bricoleur* is adept at performing a large number of diverse tasks; but, unlike the engineer, he does not subordinate each of them to the availability of raw materials and tools conceived and procured for the purpose of the project. . . . The rules of his game are always 'make do' with whatever is at hand" (Lévi-Strauss, *The Savage Mind* (Chicago: University of Chicago Press, 1966), 17). Among American sociologists of culture, the most famous application of the expression is Ann Swidler's definition of culture as "a bag of tricks or an oddly assorted tool kit." See Swidler, *Talk of Love: How Culture Matters* (Chicago: University of Chicago Press, 2001), 23, where the definition is based on an earlier 1986 article. One of the curious slippages between the source and this particular use of the expression is between the questions of whether the *bricoleur* is a way of thinking or a way of thinking *about* culture – whether, that is, the applicable tool kit is thinking itself or the thing thought. Swidler's view seems to incline toward the latter, though she clearly says that we must not assume that culture is a thing over against the individual from which she picks and chooses what tools

there are. Curiously, Lévi-Strauss's view is likely to owe to Emile Durkheim, who would have said that culture, especially, is over against the individual. Whatever one thinks about these technical questions, the trickster is a true *bricoleur*, in that he is both the culture itself and the bag of tricks that deceives it by deceiving himself. The trickster, then, is neither concrete nor abstract, but both-at-once in a way that renders such ideas as either the concrete (as opposed to the general) or the individual (as opposed to her culture) useless, at least for the time of his power over the game at hand.

8   The most strikingly clear and thorough explanation of the difference between popular culture and mass culture is Michael Kammen, *American Culture/American Tastes: Social Change and the Twentieth Century* (New York: Knopf, 1999), ch. 1.

9   Charles Lemert, *Dark Thoughts: Race and the Eclipse of Society* (New York: Routledge, 2002), especially ch. 1.

10 Still the most impressive discussion of the subject is James Scott, *Domination and the Arts of Resistance: Hidden Transcripts* (New Haven: Yale University Press, 1990).

11 Langston Hughes, "The Negro Speaks of Rivers," quoted from *The Columbia Anthology of American Poetry*, ed. Jay Pirini (New York: Columbia University Press, 1995), 477.

12 The Democratic Republic of Congo, once Zaire, and before that a Belgian colony is to be distinguished from the Republic of Congo, a former French colony. The Republic of Congo's capital city is Brazzaville, just across the Congo from Kinshasa. Though the Republic is resource-rich, it is smaller and sparsely populated. The Democratic Republic of Congo has a population of more than 50 million.

13 The name Congo Free State applies from the first explorations of the region by the English in 1874 through the end of Leopold's ownership in 1908. Thereafter, Belgian Congo is generally used until Mobutu Sese Seko's rule, after independence, from 1906 to 1997, when Mobutu had it renamed Zaire. Since 1997, when forces led by Laurent-Desire Kabila won the internal struggle for control, the name Democratic Republic of Congo applies – hence, the difference from the French Republic of Congo on the eastern banks of the river.

14 My source for most of what I say about Leopold is Adam Hochschild, *King Leopold's Ghost: A Story of Greed, Terror, and Heroism in Colonial Africa* (Boston: Mariner Books/Houghton Mifflin, 1999),

than which it would be hard to imagine a better book on the subject.

15 The first to expose Leopold's system was an American, George Washington Williams. But the most persistent and effective over time was a Belgian journalist, E. D. Morel, who gave a good bit of his life to attacking Leopold. Hochschild's *King Leopold's Ghost* is of course about the haunting effects Leopold had on the region, but it is nearly as much a tale of the ghosts of Morel and others who haunted the man until he gave up in 1998.

16 Ibid., ch. 15.

17 Quoted by Hochschild, *King Leopold's Ghost*, 295.

18 Ibid., 140–6. Hochschild's account of Conrad's time in the Congo is the most thorough and, from what I can tell, reliable of those I have read. But it is important to say that it is virtually impossible to write about the Congo without reference to Conrad. Others who have done so include Michela Wrong, *In the Footsteps of Mr Kurtz: Living on the Brink of Disaster in Mobutu's Congo* (New York: Harper Collins, 2001), 8–12, and *passim*; Bill Berkeley, *The Graves are Not Yet Full: Race, Tribe and Power in the Heart of Africa* (New York: Basic Books, 2001), 115. On the tragic beauty of Africa, see Ryszard Kapuscínski, *The Shadow of the Sun* (New York: Random House, 2001), and Basil Davidson, *The Black Man's Burden: Africa and the Curse of the Nation-State* (New York: Three Rivers Press, 1992).

19 Leon Gast, in the postscript on Ali in *When We Were Kings* (New York: Polygram Film Productions/USA Video, 1996).

20 See, again, Lewis Hyde, *Trickster Makes This World* (New York: Farrar, Strauss, and Giroux, 1998), ch. 10, where, among other sources, he discusses Henry Louis Gates, *The Signifying Monkey* (New York: Oxford University Press, 1988).

21 A chilling, recent account of Mobutu's reign, and theft, is Wrong, *In the Footsteps of Mr Kurtz*.

22 Only a man of great charm could pull together such an extravaganza as the fight in Kinshasa. In *When We Were Kings*, George Plimpton speaks eloquently of King's welcoming embrace of others, but always of the lives he ruined by his ruthless preoccupation with his own fame and fortune.

23 Again Wrong, *In the Footsteps of Mr Kurtz*, who reports, among other astonishments, the fact that Kinshasa's once modern telephone system collapsed at the end, leaving cell phones as the only means of modern communication.

CHAPTER 6   TRICKSTER BODIES AND CULTURAL DEATH

Extracts from Thich Nhat Hanh on pp. 150–1 (see note 1 below) reprinted by kind permission of Parallax Press, Berkeley, California.

1   Thich Nhat Hanh, *Call Me by my True Names: The Collected Poems of Thich Nhat Hanh* (Berkeley: Parallax Press, 1999) and *Heart of the Buddha's Teaching* (Berkeley: Parallax Press, 1998).
2   Norman Mailer, *The Fight* (Boston: Little, Brown, 1975), 3.
3   Ibid.
4   Michael Mann, director, *Ali* (distributed by Columbia Pictures for Overbrook Films, 2001).
5   The idea that Ali was the first rapper is linked to the fact that hip-hop is very much trickster music – music that takes the variant stuff of street life and replays it on a heavy, unrelenting rhyme. Will Smith began as a hip-hop musician and still performs and records. The 1993 film *Six Degrees of Separation* is about a beautiful young black man who queers the marriage of a rich white Manhattan couple – by coming into their home deceptively, exposing them to his queer sex, then refusing to leave them until he has eaten the heart of the wife, played by Stockard Channing, who in the end leaves her husband, played by Donald Sutherland.
6   *The Greatest*, staring Ali as himself, appeared in 1977, directed by Tom Gries.
7   By contrast, by the time Mike Tyson faced Lennox Lewis in June 2002, he had fought fewer than 200 rounds in 16 years and was totally spent by the third round of eight with Lewis. In 2002, Tyson was still 36, just about the age Ali was in 1974–5 when he and Frazier went 26 rounds.
8   Ferdie Pacheco, Ali's personal physician and one who loved Ali to the fullest, quit eventually because he wanted no part in the damage Ali did to himself by continuing to fight after 1975. Pacheco believed that the third Frazier fight was Ali's last chance to avoid the damage that was already coming his way. (See Pacheco, in Thomas Hauser, *Muhammad Ali: His Life and Times* (New York: Simon & Schuster, 1991), 349.) Conclusive diagnosis was made in 1984.
9   Jose Torres, *Sport* interview with Muhammad Ali (1981), in *The Muhammad Ali Reader*, ed. Gerald Early (New York: William Morrow, 1998). 214.

10 Ali was married to Sonji Roi from 1964 to 1966; to Belinda Boyd (from 1967 to 1977), when the marriage broke up over his infatuation with Veronica Porche, who was his wife from 1977 to 1986. His relationship with Aaisha Ali was during the marriage to Belinda Boyd. He married Lonnie Williams in 1986.

11 Ali's nine children (and their birth dates) are Maryum (1968), Jamillah and Rasheeda (1970), Muhammad, Jr (1971) – all born of the marriage with Belinda Boyd. Veronica Porche was the mother of Hana (1976) and Laila (1978). There were no children of the marriage with Sonji. With Lonnie, Ali adopted Assad Amin (1991).

12 By Jimmy Canonn, in Hauser, *Muhammad Ali*, 145.

13 Walter Cronkite first visited Vietnam in 1965, but it is his telecast after the Tet Offensive in 1968 that is said to have shifted American public opinion to the attitude that the war could not be won. Shortly after, President Lyndon B. Johnson lost the New Hampshire Democratic primary to Eugene McCarthy, and in March declined to run for a second full term.

14 In the 1981 interview the very next question after "biggest mistake" was: "What is your most serious character flaw?" His answer: gullibility.

15 Gerald Early, "Introduction: Tales of the Wonderboy," in *Muhammad Ali Reader*, ed. Early, p. vii. Note that Ali suffers from Parkinson's syndrome, not the disease itself. Also, I take it that the locution "cultist/religious" is an attempt to distinguish Ali's allegiance to the Nation of Islam from his unquestionably genuine Islamic faith. Otherwise, Early is way off here.

16 Charles Lemert, *Postmodernism is Not What You Think* (Oxford: Blackwell, 1997).

17 In this, as in much else concerning the trickster, the debt is to Lewis Hyde, especially part 4 on "The Trap of Culture," in *Trickster Makes This World* (New York: Farrar, Strauss, and Giroux, 1998).

18 The example is from Emile Durkheim and Marcel Mauss, *Primitive Classifications* (Chicago: Phoenix Books/University of Chicago Press, 1967), 61.

19 Claude Lévi-Strauss, *The Savage Mind* (Chicago: University of Chicago Press, 1966), 233.

20 Harvey Cox, *The Feast of Fools* (Cambridge, MA: Harvard University Press, 1969). The Foucault reference is to his long chapter on the ship of fools in *Madness and Civilization: A History of Insanity in*

the Age of Reason (New York: Random House, 1965). See also Mikhail Bakhtin's many writings on the subject of reversal and carnival, especially *Rabelais and his World* (Bloomington, IN: Indiana University Press, 1984).

21 Norman Cohn, *Pursuit of the Millennium*, 3rd edn (New York: Oxford University Press, 1970), 150. Quote following, ibid.

22 I took these words from a televised interview with Ali, but cannot now find the exact source. He often said such things, in his CBS *60 Minutes* special segment of Ed Bradley, for one instance, and in one of his interviews with Thomas Hauser, where he said: "We're all gonna die. I don't care who you are, you're gonna die" (*Muhammad Ali*, 503).

23 The classic statement of the American formula was written during the Great Depression in 1938. Since then there have been numerous others. Still Robert K. Merton's is the most succinct: "Social Structure and Anomie," reprinted in *idem, Social Theory and Social Structure* (New York: Free Press, 1957), 131–60. This was not, of course, the first. Criticisms of the success ethic of modern life were, in a way, at the foundation of the industrial wealth in the West, notably Thorstein Veblen's *The Theory of the Leisure Class* (1899) and even Marx's sneering critique of Mr Moneybags in *Capital I* (1867), not to mention literary examples like William Dean Howells, *The Rise of Silas Lapham* (1885).

24 Ali came into a game that had always been a back-room affair – a smoky spectacle where those with wealth could find release for their repressed desires by betting on which man would suffer unto injury in the ring. Since Ali came upon the scene in 1964, boxing has not been purified, but it has become less notably entangled with the underworld and crime. Today there are calls for reform or abolition, to be sure; but these come from the inherent violence of the sport which every now and then takes an ugly turn when a gladiator dies in the ring or another bites off an ear. Still, as much as Mike Tyson is vilified for his various crimes against men and women, one does not suppose that his behavior is controlled by the mob. Ali was largely responsible for this change.

ACKNOWLEDGMENTS

Victoria Stahl helped with research on all aspects of the book and is the first author of (but not the one finally responsible for) the Chronology, which was compiled from sources too numerous to mention. Still, I should mention with gratitude Thomas Hauser's oral history, *Muhammad Ali: His Life and Times*, which is the indispensable guide to facts and opinions on Ali's life through the 1980s. From first to last, Victoria joined in the spirit and the details of the work.

Anthony Elliott proposed the idea in the first place, and then joined John Thompson in supporting it from beginning to end. Anthony, Rand Valentine, and one other (a reader of evident but unnamed identity) went through the entire manuscript, with generous care, offering numerous corrections and questions that demanded attention. Jean van Altena many times saved me from myself – I am not sure how anyone could be a better editor. Ann Bone, among others at Polity, oversaw the production with patience. I learned a great deal from seminars on or about Ali at schools where I was privileged to visit for a week's time or more, notably at the universities of Kentucky, of the West of England (Bristol), of Alberta (Edmonton). Also, Wesleyan students in Sociology 399 in the fall term, 2002, helped me think through the trickster theme in American culture. In the end, I did as I saw fit, following the advice of others where I could, my own head where I had to.

Anna Julia Lemert, then in the early years of life, was my constant companion in watching all the Ali videos. We sat before Leon Gast's *When We Were Kings* for hours at a time. I harbor the idea that, if she pursues her talent for dance, she will have been inspired first by the Ali shuffle.

The book is dedicated to the memory of my first-born, Matthew, who was a trickster who wanted so to be a hero. This he was for me and for those who loved him closely – but not, sadly, for himself. Brian Fay invoked the Achilles allusion for Matt in his introduction of Immanuel Wallerstein, the first Matthew Lemert Memorial Lecturer in Sociology at Wesleyan. Brian knew Matthew and could not have gotten the point of his heroic strivings more perfectly.

How in the end does one acknowledge the man himself, Muhammad Ali? Perhaps simply by remembering the men and women, living and dead, in remote global places who suffered the consequences of their refusals to let things stand as, for all too long, they so unjustly had been. I think, in particular, of the men, women, and children who died in the rain forests of the Congo laboring to produce a good portion of the wealth of modern Europe, and those of the Ohio and Mississippi valleys who suffered similarly in North America. Their descendants, whether black or white or other, are the global citizens who made Muhammad Ali the king of the world. To tell the story of the Louisville boy Cassius who became Ali the king is to tell a story of the nameless people who admire the celebrity-hero because, in their name, he tricked two generations of colonizers out of a good many of their easy manners.

Charles Lemert, Killingworth, CT

INDEX

Index